NO PITY

The cold-blooded murder which enthralled Edwardian Britain

Colin Evans

Etive Independent Publishing

Best Wished

Colin

ISBN-13: 9798387800009
ISBN-10: 1477123456

Cover design by: Art Painter
Library of Congress Control Number: 2018675309
Printed in the United States of America

PREFACE

WHY do we love murder dramas? Many of us fear death, particularly our own or that of a loved one. We are sickened by the harrowing details of war and terrorist atrocities. We despair over victims of knifings, and weep for young women borne away by sex attackers. But, when it comes to wanting some light relief after watching The Great British Bake-Off we turn without a thought to Killer In My Village or Midsomer Murders. Why? Some psychologists believe an element of fantasy is involved, and is only subdued by the experience of reality. Perhaps we do not think deeply enough about violent death. You can splash all the tomato ketchup in the world onto a stage or a TV set and it will never come close to what it is really, really like. How in a split-second vital life becomes the sad blackness of nothing.

The irrepressible historian Lucy Worsley presented a TV series 'A Very British Murder' which examined how murder first became a public entertainment in the early Victorian age with the melodrama – stage productions based on true stories, watched by packed audiences who hissed and shouted abuse at the villain, and groaned and simpered over the fate of the victim. One-sheet newspapers called Broadsides dwelt on the grisly details of such tragedies, often using cartoons to depict the dastardly act, and sold hundreds of thousands of copies. Later in the 19th century, as the Press industry boomed, sensationalist newspapers ensured that everyone in the country knew about the latest ghastly killing and *wanted* to know about it. Murder literature boomed.

As Professor Worsley demonstrated, this fascination has continued to grow so that, on any day of the week, murder programmes, fact and fiction, dominate the TV schedule. It suggests there is something in the human psyche which craves the vicarious extreme. How else can we sip a cup of tea while watching someone cutting another person's throat, or shooting them full of holes? When it happens in gory real life, society retreats into a brief introspection but it is not long before we are in front of that bloodstained screen again, lapping up the horror.

This book is about a 'true crime' murder and because of its unusual circumstances (and the way I have approached it) could fall into the category of melodrama. But I hope that it is also viewed as a pursuit of justice and as a reminder that the act of murder is human kind's gross finality as well as a potential entertainment.

Colin Evans, 2023

In loving memory of Joan Alexander (1922-2020),
a connoisseur of the murder drama

CONTENTS

Murder most foul, allegedly committed by the most innocent looking of killers, James Crossley Parrott (artist's sketch). © Reach PLC

SCENE OF CRIME

Knutsford

2023: population 14000, voted in several surveys as one of the best places in England to live - a growing, affluent and historic town, noted for its architecture, literary associations, and restaurants.

1901: population 5000, a deeply conservative seat of patriotism and Imperial authority, famous for its links with the Victorian author Elizabeth Gaskell, its annual Royal May Day Festival, its executions by hanging at Knutsford Prison, and a tragedy which might well have been included in the TV series 'A Very British Murder'.

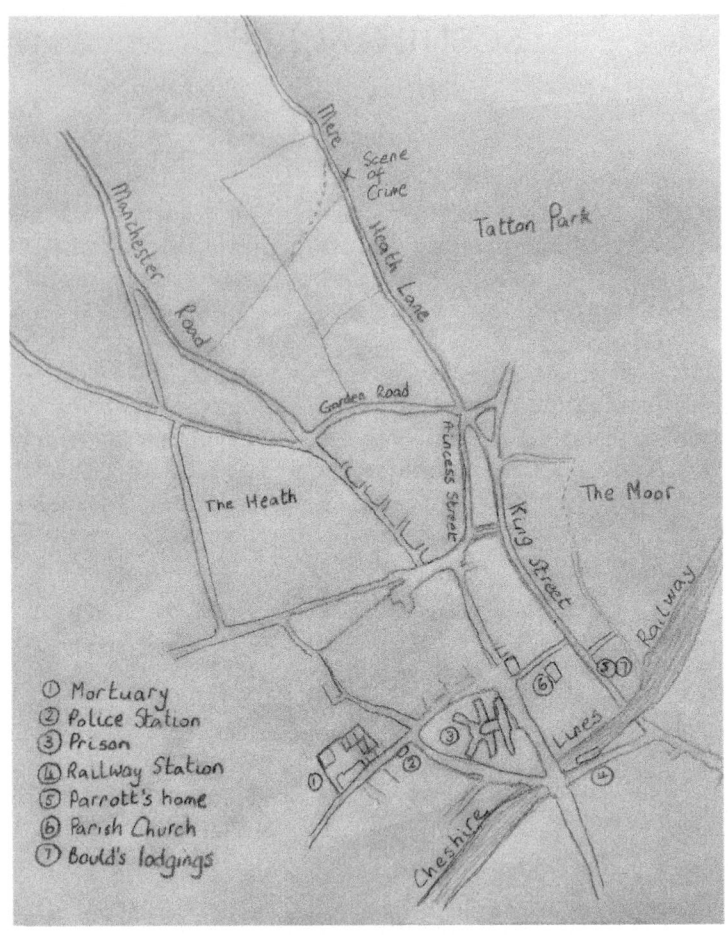

Sketch of murder site and places of interest

MAIN CHARACTERS

JOHN BOULD - the victim
JAMES CROSSLEY PARROTT - the suspect

Family

Mary Ann Parrott – Parrott's mother
Thomas Parrott - his father
James Parrott snr - his grandfather
John Parrott and Thomas Holland Parrott - his brothers
Mary and Edith Parrott - his sisters
Alfred and Annie Islip - his uncle and aunt
Teresa Neagle - Bould's half sister

The Police

Sergeant William Pierce - led the investigation
Colonel John Hammersley - Chief Constable of Cheshire
Superintendents John Okell and William Leah

The Courtrooms

H C Yates - coroner of Cheshire
Mr Justice Grantham - Assizes judge
Lance Bentley and Ellis Griffith - defence barristers
Abel Thomas - prosecution barrister
Edwin Ashworth - defence solicitor
Tom Jackson - solicitor's clerk
Leicester Caldecutt - Clerk to Justices

Chief Witnesses

Mary Jane Francis - domestic servant
Dorothy Jackson - schoolgirl
George Rowe - boot polish manufacturer
Dr Harry Pritchard - surgeon
Harry Yarwood - wheelwright
Thompson Flood – joiner
Mary Flood – wife of Thompson Flood
John Parkes - gardener
Hugh Daniel – gardener
Charlotte and Bernard Engberson – Bould's landlady and her husband
Dr George Smith - workhouse medical officer
James Goodbody – firearms expert

Significant others

Major James Osmonde Nelson - prison governor
Doctor Theodore Fennell - prison medical officer
PCs Fred Davies and John Turner - Pierce's constables
Emily and Murray Speakman – employers of Mary Jane Francis
Gertrude Rowe – wife of George Rowe
Edward Bowker – bookshop owner
Our Knutsford Correspondent - reporter on local newspaper

NOTE

Certain amounts of money are mentioned in this book. It is difficult to give them modern values as comparative tables vary greatly. However, the reader might estimate the real worth of money in that era by referring to the following pointers when UK currency was in pounds, shillings and pence (12 pennies to the shilling, 20 shillings to the pound).

Wages – the annual earnings of three of the characters involved:Mary Jane Francis, a domestic servant (£12 plus full board); John Bould, a journeyman tailor (£60-65) and Police Sergeant William Pierce (£75-£80 plus accommodation in a police house).

Living costs – John Bould lodged with a family at 7s 6d a week with full board; rentals for small cottages in the area were about 10s a week.

Purchasing power - a Raleigh cycle cost £10; a self adjusting truss 3s 6d; a bottle of Glenlivet whisky 3s 6d; anti-bilious tablets 1s per box.

INTRODUCTION

F or many years we lived in a delightful rural spot, an oasis amid the clamour of modern life. But every Sunday morning I heard the sound of violence. It resonated from behind a hillock, 400 yards away from our front door. Sharp *cracks*, dull *thuds*, heavy *whacks* of pistols and revolvers being discharged, disturbing the otherwise quiet lanes and fields around us. You could not see the gunmen and, somehow, that made the noise even more threatening. The fact that this was a fully licensed shooting club made little difference. Guns are guns. They fire bullets which can rip a human target to shreds. I wished they would find somewhere else to practise.

The gun which triggered a sensational murder case in 1901 was small and light. I guess the last sound the victim heard was a *crack* rather than a *thud* or a *whack*. Although, if he survived for just a few seconds after being felled, he might have registered a man's voice murmuring into his ear: 'That's done for you, John Bould.'

It was a ruthless and rare crime.

Britain's murder rate was low at the turn of the 19th/20th centuries, and death by pre-meditated shooting was way down the table of 'who dunnits?' When a judge wore the black cap it was usually to sentence a man for killing his wife, or some other unfortunate member of his family, after a drunken row.

But it was not simply that John Bould was gunned down, like a scene from one of the cheap yellowback thrillers sold at Victorian railway stations all over the country – there were also the appalling facts that it happened on Easter Sunday and in a town famous for its literature, architecture, romance and, most significantly, for the upkeep of law and order. The author's home town.

Indeed, the murder scene was just 800 yards from where my ancestors lived through the late Victorian and Edwardian eras, and a similar distance from the office of the local newspaper where, in 1964, I launched my career as a reporter. Later I worked in Manchester, covering many murder cases, and I find it strangely amusing that now, long retired, I have only just come across the most baffling and bizarre of all. Damn, it was right under my nose all the time. While gainfully employed on the Knutsford Guardian, I could have strolled up the short hill from the office, turned left into the square and then right onto the main road and knocked on Mrs Lee's front door to ask: "What can you tell me about the Bould shooting? After all, you were one of the chief witnesses." Or, during tea, I might have turned to Mum, saying: "Come on, give me the gen. Your family were on the spot. It will make a great scoop."

The 'scoop' was to discover what exactly happened on that cool, damp Easter Sunday evening when Mary Jane Francis, a cheerful servant at one of the town's big houses, lied to her mistress that she was going to church. When she returned two hours later, pale-faced and in some distress, she blurted out: "I'm sorry I'm late – a man took liberties with me. Oh, and there's been a murder."

I can imagine her employer Mrs Speakman responding acidly: "Don't be silly. We don't have murders in Knutsford."

Knutsford. How many times have I seen that word followed by *'quaint, picturesque, immortalised by the Victorian author Elizabeth Gaskell in her novel Cranford'* or similar tourist poster type blurbs? Who am I to argue? After all, as a young 'hack', I wrote that kind of stuff all the time, while, occasionally, muttering to myself: 'But don't go to our house 'cos you'll be hit by the stink of the sewage works and the open rubbish tip.' Every quaint town has a mucky side.

I wonder what John Bould made of it. A delightful place to be shot dead, perhaps, although the way he died, riddled with bullets from a revolver, and for no apparent reason, was more American Wild West than Cheshire heartland.

This journeyman tailor, poor and little known in life, achieved fame as the victim in a killing which shocked the nation. Senseless, it seemed. But unless the perpetrator is insane, permanently or temporarily, few murders are truly senseless. Usually a motive, however paltry, lurks in the background. Finding it, ah! now that's the trick. Surely, I thought, my knowledge of Knutsford, indeed, my own family history, would be a big advantage.

Born and raised in Knutsford, I started work at the Guardian as a 16 years-old 'rookie' reporter. The office and the newspaper had changed little in the 63 years since the shooting. Victorian dust danced through the air when you lifted the old, hide-bound files in the back room. Much of the attitude to newspaper work was also hide-bound, but it gave me a solid grounding in journalism. The basics were hammered home. Accuracy was essential. The Editor, squeaking about the lino-covered floor in his stained Hush Puppy shoes, handed me a fold-up Corona typewriter once used by a WW1 correspondent. It had chipped keys, possibly from shrapnel, and a worn-out ribbon. "Be careful with that – they don't make 'em anymore," he warned.

The office was at 113 King Street (phone Knutsford 4114) with the hill of Minshull Street opposite, and the White Lion and The Angel on each corner of the junction. Up Minshull Street, turn right into Tatton Street and there, within sniffing distance of the Lord Eldon pub, was the Flatters family's red brick terraced house with a yard at the rear from where they ran a removals company. In 1901, one of the Flatters' clan was a skinny nine years-old girl, Daisy. She became my grandmother.

Continuing along Tatton Street and into Mere Heath Lane, you came to the cricket club ground and then to the boys' club's sports fields where, from the age of nine, I enjoyed many happy hours playing football and cricket without realising that, on the other side of the hawthorn hedge, an innocent, law-abiding man had once been blasted to death.

When I set out to trace the episode, I tried hard to stick to the facts, as Charles Dickens' character Mr Gradgrind had advised, only to come badly unstuck. The obstacles which plagued the police in their enquiries in 1901 had, over the years, developed into solid walls, and my experience of the town and its history sometimes proved more hindrance than help, leading me into dusty cul-de-sacs and up blind alleys.

And so I have filled in some of the gaps with 'educated' guesswork and with the dramatisation so beloved by TV historians.

The reader might ask how I can justify using devices of imagination while investigating a true life event. All I can say is that while adding a spade or two of fictional mortar, I have slapped a Grade 1 preservation order on the factual foundations and evidential brickwork of the Knutsford Murder Mystery.

CHAPTER 1

'But to be sure, what a town Cranford is for kindness'
-Elizabeth Gaskell (Cranford, 1853)

'It is my belief that the lowest and vilest alleys of London
do not present a more dreadful record of sin than the
smiling, beautiful countryside' – Sherlock Holmes
(The Adventure Of The Copper Beeches, 1892)

MARY Jane Francis felt decidedly unwell. And that would not do, not with Mrs Speakman frowning at her and demanding an explanation. Mistresses did not like 'delicate' servants. But, while she knew she was in trouble, Mary Jane did not have the strength to get up. She slumped back into the chair, took the hankie kindly proffered by Jane Pickstock, the cook, and clamped it to her forehead. In her coat pocket was a bottle of medicine that she had picked up earlier from the surgery, but what she needed now was something stronger. If not alcohol, then a little sympathy might help. After all, it was not every Sunday that you got manhandled by a pervert before almost tripping over a man's body. And all in the space of 10 minutes! In Knutsford, of all places. But neither strong drink nor consoling words were on offer in Mrs Speakman's kitchen.

"Let me understand this correctly, Mary Jane Francis," she said sternly using her maid's full name for salutary effect. "Are you telling me that a man, hmm, assaulted you in some way and then died?"

It did not often happen but Mary Jane was momentarily lost for words. Accepted, she was all hot and bothered and had probably garbled her story but her employer had it all wrong. "No m'am. There were two men. One did terrible things to me. And I was on my way back here because I didn't want to be late and then I saw the other man, lying in the hedge."

"I see, but you said he was dead. How do you know?" Mrs Speakman paused for thought. "I mean, he might have been drunk or something. There's too much of it happening nowadays. Only last week there was a fracas in the Market Place…"

Mary Jane had had enough. She had been in service all her life, knew about 'keeping her place', appreciated that her employment with Mrs Speakman was precariously balanced, but, for the second time that evening, she screamed. Mrs Speakman stepped back, astonished. "Haven't I told you already," her maid shouted. "He's dead. They think he was murdered. I was there!"

"Good heavens," murmured Mrs Speakman. She gripped the edge of the kitchen table for support, realising that they had a scandal on their hands. "Good heavens."

Jane, the cook said: "I'll make a pot of tea."

Reports of a body being discovered in Knutsford quickly appeared in regional newspapers, such as Manchester's Courier and Evening News, but police refused to immediately release full details and while reporters gorged on rumours of a shooting, editors initially trod warily with vague headlines like 'The Knutsford Tragedy' and 'The Knutsford Mystery'. No doubt Mrs Speakman and others hoped it would stay that way, just a fleeting blemish on the town's reputation which eventually could be brushed over. But it was only a matter of time before the storm broke. On April 11, four days after the incident, and with the post-mortem findings at hand, the 'Tragedy' officially turned into the 'Murder', although the 'Mystery' remained and deepened.

The Manchester Guardian, for one, gave it big licks with the stark headline:

'THE KNUTSFORD MURDER'

'There seems to be no doubt now that the man John Bould who was found dead on Sunday evening was murdered. The post-mortem examination by Dr Smith revealed the fact that five shots had been fired and that all of them struck the unfortunate man….'

The article ran on for a full column. This was a major story. Similar reports flooded the country from Cork in the south of Ireland to East Anglia; from Thurso in the north east of Scotland to Truro in Cornwall. Whether informed by the national and regional dailies or the smallest weekly journal, you knew about John Bould. And you also knew that Knutsford's soft marshmallow image, the setting for Mrs Gaskell's Cranford, was now spiked with a barbed wire notoriety – and fear. Police had yet to make an arrest. An armed killer was on the loose.

Instead of wanting to view Mrs Gaskell's grave at the town's Unitarian Chapel, or to wander along the twisting architectural time-line of King Street, tourists poured in from all over the North-West demanding directions to the murder scene or to the imposing Sessions Court where the early judicial hearings into the case were held. The delicacy of Victorian drawing-room conversation and manners, so subtly exploited by Gaskell, was submerged by the hubbub of real-life drama and scandal. Lawyers, police chiefs, prominent townsfolk and reporters gathered in The Royal George and The Angel hotels. Pubs like Fred Lee's White Lion and Annie Jackson's The Feathers did a roaring trade. The Cheshire Lines railway, linking Manchester and Chester with Knutsford midway, put on special trains.

Then, another shock. Almost a fortnight after the murder, police announced they had taken a suspect into custody. A young local man. Crowds gathered around his home and the gaol where he was held.

On everyone's lips were two questions:

"Why?" and "How could a such an innocent looking lad do a thing like that?"

The police were already under fire for taking so long to make an arrest and many locals refused to accept that they had the right man. 'A bit peculiar but no more than a boy,' was the opinion of some who knew him. Others proclaimed their sympathy for his family, who had already suffered hard times and now had to contend with a devastating blow.

Meanwhile, James Crossley Parrott, aged 21, of King Street, Knutsford, sat quietly in his cell, wondering whether he might soon be hanged. Funny, he thought, to be 'dropped' only spitting distance from his home and the parish church where he was baptised. Mother wouldn't like that.

As he pondered his fate, Parrott smiled the thin smile which some people found disquieting. Supercilious, arrogant even, they reckoned. Not a real smile at all. More a smirk.

He recalled that strange and dark winter's morning when he was about six years-old and Mother led him and younger brother Tom down the stairs, through their shop into King Street, up the short but sharp incline of Church Hill and over the big road where hundreds of people had gathered in front of the Sessions House. Behind it rose the massive walls of Knutsford Prison. Shouldn't such a lot of people be making more noise, he had thought. Everything that morning was so still and bare, just like his cell now. As the gloom lifted revealing a grey threaded sky, a bell tolled and a tremor of expectancy ran through the crowd. A few minutes later someone shouted: "Look, there." His mother pointed high to the roof of the building. "Yes, there. The black flag." It flapped momentarily, wrapped itself around the pole as though for comfort and then hung limply as the spectators dispersed.

Mary Ann Parrott grabbed Tom's hand and pulled him away. James followed. She seemed upset. What was it all about? James was burning with questions but there was no time. They trooped back down to King Street. Mary Ann would spend the day mending clothes, sewing hems, and helping husband Thomas in their draper's shop. With hard work, it made them a decent enough living although they had known one or two rocky spells. Competition was fierce. Every town had drapers and tailors aplenty.

"Grim was it?" he asked. She stayed silent.

Back at the gaol, the surgeon, flanked by the prison chaplain Reverend William Truss, and watched by the governor, moved forward to inspect Owen McGill as the hangman James Berry stepped down from the platform. They let him dangle for a moment but, on release, it took only a cursory examination to conclude he had died instantaneously from a broken neck. A thick neck, too, the gaol's medical officer was to note in his report, but nowhere near strong enough to withstand the rope. Only a five feet drop but you could not have wished for a cleaner end, could you Owen? As warders began to disinfect the concrete floor and to dismantle the scaffold, erected in a shed in the prison yard, the surgeon tidied up the body and set about writing his post-mortem analysis for the coroner who had to stage a formal, if brief, inquest. He could not foresee any hitches. Job well done by the public executioner Berry who had arrived the previous Saturday and had gone about his gruesome work with meticulous care. He heard a warder asking the chaplain: "How long do we fly the flag for?"

According to the surgeon's report, McGill had been despatched properly and 'humanely' as to the letter and spirit of the law. This was, in 1886, Knutsford's first execution, having taken over the responsibility from Chester, and after such a successful debut, this peaceful, pretty parish would now be firmly established as the hanging capital of Cheshire.

McGill, a 39 years-old farm labourer from Birkenhead, was a quiet, religious man who had beaten his wife to death. He took his sentence at Chester Assizes and his subsequent punishment without complaint, only to say that he wished his neighbours had intervened when, as he battered her head in, she screamed for mercy. One neighbour admitted he heard the sound of 'beating' but thought it was Mrs McGill cleaning a carpet. Although the hanging had aroused great excitement, the Reverend Truss thought the townsfolk had behaved decently, as befitting Knutsford. Perhaps the Press would act in like manner. Still incensed at one report which claimed that people had jeered and jostled McGill when he first arrived at the prison, the chaplain had written a brief but strong letter of protest to the newspaper, upholding the town's reputation for restraint and gentility as epitomised in Mrs Gaskell's writings.

Three more executions quickly followed. In 1887 Thomas Bevan, a 20 years-old iron moulder, for stamping his aunt to death all for a few shillings; and in 1890 Richard Davies, aged 19, who with his 16 years-old brother George killed their abusive father; and Felix Spicer for murdering his two sons. But the crowds waiting to see the black flag hoisted were diminishing. Mary Ann Parrott, for one, pushed such events out of her mind, although she could not smother the tolling of the parish church bell which stood between their home and the Sessions House and gave 15 minutes warning of each execution.

Mary Ann had had enough of death, losing her mother, husband and father-in-law within the space of three years 1885-88. It seemed to her that death was shadowing her family and now, if the police had their way, her son James would follow in the footsteps of McGill and the others, a 50 yards handcuffed shuffle from the condemned cell to the scaffold. It would be the North-West's first hanging of the Edwardian era, although James Berry would not be the executioner.

An emotional man (and therefore not, in the opinion of the Home Office, the best suited for hanging people) he suffered nightmares and, having hung 131 murderers including five women, he had quit in 1891, turning to drink, then to God and was campaigning fervently against capital punishment by the time Mary Ann's first-born awaited Judgement Day.,

Knutsfordians were rightly proud of their town. Small, intimate,

deeply conservative, it was the headquarters of the Cheshire Set, a group of some of England's most affluent and powerful families who owned vast tracts of the surrounding lands and chunks of the town itself – including the Egertons of Tatton Park and the Leicester-Warrens of Tabley where the Cheshire Yeomanry was founded in the late 18th century. Death duties, Parliamentary and social reform, along with the decline of agriculture, were eating away at the wealth of Britain's artistocratic families but in Knutsford at the turn of the century this elite remained extremely influential. The Tatton Estate, particularly, played a major role in local life. While the park itself was a mere 8,000 acres, the whole estate covered 40,000 acres, holding 80 tenanted farms, with nurseries, shops and houses. It was a major employer.

By virtue of this group and their connections, Knutsford enjoyed a level of political leverage which a small market town rarely possessed and, because of its significance in the county's judicial process, it boasted one of the finest courthouses outside London and a huge, if ugly, prison able to hold 600 convicts – more than 10 per cent of the area's civilian population. In the mid-1880s it took over from Chester as the County Gaol, housing many hardened criminals, and, with it, the mantel of stretching a few necks. But the courthouse and prison, and the workhouse just beyond them, were hardly tourist attractions. Usually, you only went there if you had to. What traditionally enticed visitors to Knutsford were its literary associations, intriguing blend of architecture, and pleasant walks and bicycle rides along lush country lanes.

Until John Bould came face to face with his stone-hearted killer.

As news spread of a brutal murder in Mrs Gaskell's 'Cranford' they poured in from all parts and when Parrott appeared in the dock for the first time, simply to be remanded while investigations continued, 400 spectators piled into the courtroom after queuing for hours outside. "Perhaps we should issue entrance tickets next time", said the Clerk to the Justices, Leicester Caldecutt.

No-one could get their head around this crime. Disgust was matched by fascination. Bould was the most unlikely victim, Parrott the most unlikely assassin. And this law-abiding, historic town the most unlikely scene for such horror. Mrs Gaskell would be turning in her grave. How did it all come to be?

Yet, unwittingly, Knutsford had harboured murderers before. In the 1750s Edward Higgins used a house overlooking the Heath – an expanse of common land in the centre of the town – as a base to cover his activities as a robber. Masquerading as a country squire he travelled the length of England, breaking into houses, and during one burglary in Bristol he left two women dead. Captured at Caernarvon he was hanged – although not immediately seen off. During the post-mortem a few hours later he slowly opened an eye only for the surgeon's assistant to quickly apply a coup de grace. Whether with an instrument or with his hands is unknown. 'Highwayman' Higgins, though a common thief and murderer, became part of Knutsford Romanticism, featuring in a poem by Mrs Gaskell's friend,

Samuel Coleridge.

A decade following Higgins's bizarre exit, a woman named Mary Heald who worked on the Mere estate a couple of miles outside Knutsford, got rid of her husband by dosing him with white arsenic. Convicted at Chester Assizes she was sentenced to death by being burned at the stake, a penalty reserved for women who murdered their husbands. It carried a whiff of the old offence of witchcraft. Sentence was carried out on an old pyre site at Boughton near Chester. Whether she was burned alive is unclear. Usually, in such executions, the executioner killed the wretched woman either with a blade or by strangulation before lighting the bonfire to the cheers of a football-sized crowd.

In 1786 Knutsford was stunned by another poisoning. This time a farm labourer in the adjoining village of Mobberley decided he had had enough of his wife, much preferring the charms of a neighbour with whom he was consorting, and also turned to white arsenic for the solution. Not that Peter Steer was very clever about it. After drinking heavily in one of the town's ale houses, he marched into the chemist of John Howard to demand a bottle of the poison. As Howard handed it over he asked for the customer's name. "Heald," replied Steer, possibly influenced by the Mary Heald case or, more likely, aiming to incriminate a fellow farmworker named Heald.

Steer staggered home and next morning adulterated his wife's porridge with the arsenic. "This tastes queer," she said. "Let me taste it," said her daughter, only to be stopped by Steer who insisted his wife finish her bowl. Which she did and died in agony two days later. There was no chance of 'porridge' for Steer. They hanged him at Chester, the judge ordering his body to be handed over to a surgeon to be 'atomised'.

But those mid 18th century crimes quickly blurred in the township's collective memory. Newspaper coverage was limited, both Steer and Heald came from outlying parishes and were not well known inside the town and the court hearings and executions were all held in Chester. The Bould murder was very different, committed within the recently assigned Urban District Council boundaries, indeed only half a mile from the very centre of town, and allegedly by a man born at home in King Street, christened at the parish church, and now incarcerated in the prison. The three buildings were almost in a straight line. If convicted, Parrott would travel less than 300 yards from birth to baptism to execution.

The rapacious Press ensured all Britain possessed intimate details of the case and, with the inquest and preliminary case evidence being heard in the Sessions House, the district found itself enmeshed in a web of intrigue and gossip. Theories abounded. Robbery, a love triangle, a row over money or maybe Parrott was a psychopath hunting for a victim and Bould happened to be in the wrong place at the wrong time. Another more sinister motive took hold that either Bould or Parrott was involved with a secret society.

The whole thing was scarcely believable. As Mrs Speakman might have stated: "We don't have murders in Knutsford."

Emily Speakman and her stockbroker husband Murray had an elegant, capacious house on Heath Side, close to where Mrs Gaskell spent much of her childhood. From the front windows they could look over the common. The Heath was a large quadrangle of coarse grass, sandpits, gorse and a few trees. Here General Lambert's Parliamentary army had camped after retreating from a battle at Warrington in 1651, here was where the aristocracy had staged horse racing and cock-fighting, here was where Highwayman Higgins had constructed an underground escape tunnel – so legend had it – here was the venue for the famous Royal May Day Festival and here was one of the town's most prestigious residential spots, featuring substantial homes for merchants, solicitors, financiers, and those of 'private means'.

The Speakmans lived well, employing two servants, recruited via one of the many domestic help agencies in Chester. The poor farming communities of mid-Wales provided a rich harvest for these agencies and the cook, Jane Pickstock, and her friend Mary Jane Francis both originated from the Welshpool area. Mary Jane was responsible for the general housework, doubling up as a waitress when the Speakmans entertained.

Usually the conversation over cocktails or dinner followed a similar pattern to most middle-class households. One of the big local topics was Richard Harding Watt, a wealthy and well-travelled businessman who also classed himself as a progressive architect and was busy changing Knutsford's skyline with Italian style structures. The Speakmans and their guests also debated the state of the financial markets and the new taxes on sugar and coal, the recent death of Queen Victoria, the progress of the Anglo-Boer War in South Africa, the arguments of the Suffragists, what to do about the Irish, Marconi's experiments and the menace of the unions. Weavers and spinners continued to agitate for better conditions, miners in the Lancashire town of Burnley were on strike. So much instability as the new monarch Edward V11 launched his reign.

There was much to be said for living in Knutsford in this or in any other decade. A cosy, charming place for the well-heeled, lying conveniently between their offices in soot-blackened Manchester and the frenetic maritime trading houses of Liverpool. Conditions for the poorer sections of the community were markedly different, but everyone felt safe. While the Cheshire Quarter Sessions sat regularly in the Sessions House, the judges dealt mostly with criminals from well outside the town. Cheshire then included much more populous and poorer districts, Birkenhead in the west, the weaving towns of Stalybridge and Stockport in the east, where crime was fuelled by poverty and alcohol. Knutsford was not crime free. No town was. But the magistrates of the Petty Sessions who dealt with local misdemeanours had very few serious issues to contend with.

It all changed that Easter Sunday. In the Speakmans' house, Mary Jane, close to collapse, leaned back on a kitchen chair, handkerchief pressed to her forehead, like a distressed heroine on a Victorian theatre stage. Emily Speakman stood over her, wondering what on earth to make of it. It was not that she lacked empathy. She had spoken sharply but out of shock. She sat down, needing to gather her thoughts. Jane Pickstock, who had been fussing around, trying to take some of the angst out of the situation, offered her a cup of tea which she meekly accepted. A few hundred yards away, John Bould lay on a mortuary slab waiting patiently for the workhouse medical officer Dr George Smith to make the first cut.

As for Parrott, he would remain at large for 13 days until April 20 and, so, on that hellish Easter Sunday evening he returned home to King Street, had some supper, a quick word with his mother and calmly climbed into the bed he shared with his younger brother John to sleep soundly through the night. He might well have been to church. No hint that he was a killer. At least that was what the Parrott family told the world as the case unfolded.

CHAPTER 2

*'The detection of crime relied a great deal upon
the guile of individual officers' – Simon Dell
(The Victorian Policeman, 2004)*

SERGEANT William Pierce knew a bit about murder
and felt quite proud of it. Only the previous month he
had investigated the death of a farmworker and won
a conviction. While not mentioning him specifically, the
judge Mr Justice Mayhew at Chester praised the police for
expediting the case, and he had received a brief 'Well done'
handshake from the Chief Constable of Cheshire, Colonel
John Hammersley. Admittedly, it had been a simple enough
issue and, yes, the charge of murder had to be reduced to
manslaughter. Even so....

There had been some difficulties, mainly in piecing together
the statements of several witnesses, all Irish labourers who
had been drinking at a country pub, about four miles
outside Knutsford. Walking back to their farm in the dark,
one of them, John Hyland suddenly attacked Martin Mullan,
punching him to the ground and kicking him in the ribs
before the others dragged him off. Mullan was badly hurt,
that was obvious, but conscious. They left him lying in a barn
reckoning he would be stiff and sore for days but basically
alright. Sadly, a few days later Mullan collapsed and died
from serious internal injuries.

Hyland readily admitted the attack but denied intending
to kill or even seriously harm him. And, no matter how
much he questioned him and his drinking pals, Pierce was
unable to compose a clear picture of the incident. The two
men appeared to have a history, something about Hyland
complaining that Mullan had once deliberately stood on his
leg but it was sketchy material to put in front of a jury. The
medical evidence could also be contested because of the time
gap between the assault and Mullan's death.

"We'll have him for murder, then leave it to counsel to sort out," his superiors advised.

Pierce was worried about giving evidence before an Assizes jury. He anticipated severe cross-examination so it was a blessed relief when the prosecution and defence lawyers got their heads together and settled on the lesser charge of manslaughter to which Hyland would plead guilty. No need for a trial. No need for Pierce to climb into the witness box. Mr Justice Mayhew gave 21 years -old Hyland five years penal servitude.

That was in mid-March 1901. A few days earlier, on March 11, Pierce had received even greater recognition, being raised to the Second Degree of Freemasonry at a meeting of the de Tabley Lodge in Knutsford's Royal George Hotel. Among those who welcomed him into their ranks were a local barrister Lance Bentley, the Clerk to the Justices Leicester Caldecutt, and Thomas Jackson, a clerk in the law firm of Ashworth and Inman, all names which would feature in the Bould murder investigation. There was nothing unusual about a policeman becoming a Freemason. Quite the reverse. It was a vital rung of the career ladder. Chief Constable Hammersley joined the Freemasons in the mid-1860s along with Henry Cornwall Legh, a member of one of Knutsford's ancestral families, while they were serving in the army.

Three weeks after the conviction of Hyland, Pierce found himself at the forefront of the Bould murder inquiry and this time there was no escape – his role in it was to come under the most intense public scrutiny. For the moment though he quite enjoyed the spotlight. Reporters pestered him for information. One, a young sprog on the local paper, was particularly irritating. Some of his copy appeared in the Manchester papers as 'Our Knutsford Correspondent'. Speculation, mostly. "You can put your notebook away. I'm not allowed to give you anything," Pierce told him. "You'll have to wait for the evidence."

Pierce's own notebook was filling up as quickly as the reporters'. The first entry was dated April 7 'approximately 7 25 p.m'.

That Easter Sunday evening, Pierce was in his usual seat

in the gaol's chapel when the door opened behind him, letting in a cool draught of air. Half-turning, Pierce glimpsed Constable Fred Davies. The chaplain stopped in mid-sentence as Davies, trying to be discreet, leaned over his sergeant's shoulder and whispered. Pierce's eyes widened. He stood up, nodded to the chaplain and walked out quickly, Davies following. A body? In Mere Heath Lane? On Easter Sunday?

"Who found it?" Pierce demanded.

"Bloke called Daniel. I told him to go back and wait."

The police station was close by and within a couple of minutes they were in the yard hitching up a pony and cart. Ordering Davies to stay at the station, Pierce tightened his cape, grabbed the reins and negotiated the quiet streets at a steady trot, then into the lane, a nursery on his left, Tatton Park to the right. Soon he was staring down at a thick-set man, tangled up in a hawthorn hedge, apparently dead. Nearby was a woman, trembling and soaked by the rain, only drizzle when he went into chapel less than an hour ago but now heavy and unremitting. Two men who identified themselves as Hugh Daniel and George Toft stood side by side as though on guard. Puddles were forming at the edge of the roadway. No-one said a word and, apart from the steady plop of rain on Pierce's shako, it was eerily quiet.

At first glance there seemed no reason for the man to be in this position, on his back with his head and shoulders resting against the hedge. The right leg was drawn up underneath the left and the only immediate signs of violence were a few scratches on the face, probably caused by his falling into the hawthorn. Asking Daniel to look after the pony, and motioning the others to stay where they were, Pierce stepped off the road and onto the verge to make a closer examination. All he could see of any significance were some holes or tears on the man's right jacket sleeve. Strange. He also noticed one of the trouser pockets was turned out and empty. If anything, it was this which made him suspect a crime. And then, as he stood, stroking his chin, the woman spoke. "He's dead, isn't he? I heard shots."

Pierce turned on her sharply. "Shots? What sort of shots?"

Daniel butted in: "Me and George heard them, too. We were

coming up the lane and found her. In a bit of a state she was."
"Yes," added Mary Jane Francis, "when that man was trying to have his way with me."

Pierce had been looking forward to a quiet Sunday evening at home after the chapel service. Nothing ever happened on a Sunday in Knutsford. Now he had a body, talk about gunfire, and a dishevelled woman claiming to to be the victim of some kind of indecency.

Not yet the Sherlock Holmes of the Cheshire Constabulary – although he was to become so – the sergeant was a robust, fairly resourceful bloke who stuck to the principles of police work. Cause of death had to be ascertained. Suspicious though it was, nothing could be taken for granted at this point. He certainly would not be accepting the woman's claims without corroboration – she could be 'one of those' for all he knew – and the poor bloke might have had a heart attack and hurt himself stumbling into the hedge.

The priority in this situation, not that he had ever come across anything like this before, was to get the body to the mortuary without making a big fuss of it. Standard procedure. News would travel fast, people were coming out of the churches and while Mere Heath Lane stretched away from the centre, he could see the potential for a crowd to build up. And that meant trouble.

"Any idea who he is?" he asked.

George Toft answered. "I've seen him around. Try John Cross, the tailor in Albert Street."

"I will. Help me get him onto the cart," he ordered. But Daniel demurred. "You can't just throw him onto that. There's nothing to cover him for one thing." Pierce hesitated. Daniel was right. Even the sight of him driving the cart through the town on the Sabbath, particularly Easter Sunday, was bound to raise questions and if anyone glimpsed the body, well, it did not bear thinking about.

Daniel came to his aid. "Sergeant, the Flatters aren't far away. I could nip up Tatton Street and get them to do it."

And that is how the author's grandmother to be and her family were dragged into a murder story which, for the following four months, held the whole of Britain in thrall.

Henry Flatters was a well-known carter, operating from a yard at the rear of the family home at 12 Tatton Street. Not Knutsfordian by birth, he had migrated from the banks of the River Trent in Nottinghamshire, and by 1901 had lived in the town for almost 30 years, had married and brought up several children. Later, the business evolved into the Flatters' Removal Co with a motorised van, but when Daniel came knocking on his door that night it was for the use of his horse and cart. "It's a body," Daniels informed him. "In Mere Heath Lane."

The Flatters' cart was well built, lined, and could be covered up. Henry quickly readied it and, with his 17 years-old son George alongside, he steered a course along the back of Tatton Street's terrace until they could emerge onto the road and traverse the junction with Garden Road into Mere Heath Lane. The brick boundary wall of the huge Tatton Park estate was on the right with small fields and coppices sandwiched between it and the lane. Just beyond the cricket ground on the left they saw Pierce waving them down and, as they dismounted, he pointed to the body. "I need him in the mortuary quick as you can."

Shifting Bould was no easy task. He was well-built. The verge was slippery, the rain coming down harder, and part of his jacket was pinioned by the hawthorn. His right hand gripped his hat, doubled up. Unable to get around his back because of the hedge, they heaved on his legs and shoulders, dragging him into a horizontal position so that he stared emptily into the darkening sky, and lifted him carefully into the cart. Somehow, despite the rough handling, he had kept hold of the hat, a Trilby of cheap felt material. Pierce prised it out of his fingers, placed it over his face and helped to cover him completely with a canvas tarpaulin.

"Now away with you," said Pierce. "I'll follow." The names and addresses of the witnesses were in his notebook. Daniel, a Tatton Park gardener of King Street; Toft, a printer, also of King Street, and Mary Jane Francis, a domestic servant, of Heath Side. Although sopping wet and upset, and maybe as daft as a brush for all he knew, there was something about her. And it was nice to hear a Welsh accent, reminded him of his Flintshire upbringing. Game as well, he had to admit, refusing to withdraw her crazy, unseemly tale about a sex beast on a horse.

"No," Mary Jane had spluttered, wiping rain off her nose. "No. I will not forget all about it, sergeant. I will be pressing charges."

Pierce told all three to present themselves at the police station to make statements although, from their conversation while waiting for the Flatters, he reckoned they would be of little help. Clambering onto the police cart, he warned them against rumour spreading 'until the facts can be established'. Pierce sounded confident. He always did. It did not become a police sergeant in the Cheshire Constabulary to show doubt. And, at such an early stage, he could not have imagined the hurdles which lay in his path.

Rattling into the workhouse, opposite the police station at 7 50pm, he found that the Flatters had already helped to offload the body into the mortuary where he met Dr Smith, the workhouse's medical officer. Together, they stripped the body. As they neatly piled up the clothes, they discovered a pocket watch, a pipe, a twist of tobacco, a broken penknife, a handkerchief – and a string of bullet holes. Blood had oozed from a chest wound, there were punctures in his right arm and in his back and shoulder. George Smith grimaced. "It would appear someone didn't like him," he muttered.

Any fan of TV cop drama can see that the investigation was already badly flawed, at least from a modern vantage point. No attempt to preserve the integrity of the scene of crime (SOC), no SOC forensics, no photographs, the most cursory of medical examinations, and no immediate order for an all-out hunt, both for the murderer and his weapon. Etc. But this was 1901 when most police forces had few resources at their disposal,

In moving the body as quickly as possible, Pierce was only following the guidelines. He might have roped off the scene, but without men to protect it, what was the point? A picture might have been useful, but crime photography was generally limited to taking images of prison convicts, partly because it was so expensive. (A few months later, Kodak launched their mass produced and cheap Eastman camera). Fingerprints? Ah, therein lies a tale which will be examined later in this book.

What about setting up an immediate manhunt? After all, Smith had found bullet holes in the body. It looked like murder. But, maybe he was jumping the gun. It might have been an accidental shooting. Lots of people had guns. Gamekeepers in Tatton Park, one of the largest estates in the country. Poachers. Someone hunting rabbits. It was stretching it, of course, but Pierce had to consider all the possibilities. He did not want to be accused of creating panic with a premature verdict and so he kept it brief and factual when he rang HQ in Chester's Foregate Street.

Telephones were still a rarity in Britain where the network was rolled out so slowly that in an 1895 comparative table of phones per 1000 inhabitants, London was ranked 13th in the world with Stockholm, Paris, Vienna, Copenhagen and several American cities well ahead. The Cheshire Constabulary had used phones in the larger towns like Crewe and Altrincham since 1880 but the Knutsford force did not get one until 1889. 'Knutsford 16' was a candlestick model, without a dial, and Pierce had to crank it to alert the exchange operator and to ask to be put through to Chester.

Whether murder or not, Pierce, along with Constables Fred Davies and John Turner promptly got to work and made some progress. Pierce knew that the story would be all over town by morning despite his warnings about 'rumour mongering', and the Press would soon be clamouring for details. Imperative therefore that certain 'need to know' individuals had it first. Superintendent William Leah, stationed at Chester and the county force's top deskman, would contact the coroner who lived in Macclesfield on the east side of the county, but Pierce felt he had a personal responsibility to inform the local heirarchy, particularly as most of them belonged to the same Freemasons' Lodge as him. Caldecutt, the court clerk and one of the North-West's leading masons, was one. He would pass the news on to other senior lawyers and top magistrates like Francis Ashworth, the shipping merchant who lived in a Richard Harding Watt's villa.

Pierce and his colleagues also had to quickly establish the dead man's identity and they did so easily enough, by taking Daniels' advice and knocking on the door of John Cross, disturbing him as he got ready for bed, but a brief description of the man was all he needed to reveal the name of John Bould, that he had worked for him as a journeyman tailor since the New Year, and that he believed he lodged in Swinton Square with the Engbersons.

"Why are you asking about him?" said Cross. "He's not a criminal, at least he doesn't come across like that. He's a quiet sort of bloke."

Pierce put his notebook and pencil back in his pocket, patted it and turned away without answering. Swinton Square, a cubby hole of cottages separating King Street and the lower swampy ground called the Moor, was a few minutes' walk away. Close to midnight, and beyond the gaslit King Street where the lamps cast an eerie green glow, it was pitch black. If there were to be a murder in Knutsford he could imagine it in a rough, gritty area like this, with its unhealthy smell that the breeze and rain failed to dissipate. Less than a couple of hundred yards away was a small sewage works, squeezed between the Moor and the railway, but many of the cottages at the back of King Street had earth closets - and you could tell. This was the other side of Knutsford. An 1899 council report had labelled several parts of the town as 'insanitary'.

Pierce was thankful for his police lamp. Not that he felt fear. A powerful, solidly built 31 years-old, the sergeant who had started working life as a brickmaker, could handle himself. But the oil lamp, which he could attach to his belt, was a reassurance on this dark, unforgiving night. He located the Engbersons' home, knocked and waited. Almost immediately a slightly built woman opened the door.

"Mrs Engberson?" said Pierce.

"Oh no. It's John, isn't it? Something's happened."

Charlotte Engberson had been unsettled. Had stayed up when her husband Bernard went to bed. "I've been so worried. He should have been back ages ago."

Pierce looked at her carefully. Why should she be so concerned about a lodger? Maybe he had not paid his rent. Otherwise she seemed unduly fretful, the left hand clutching the right wrist, her neck stretching up, her face strained. Mr Engberson, pushing his shirt into his trousers, came to the door. "Come in," he said.

The cottage was typical, small, with little furniture of note and the smell of soot. This one at least seemed well cared for, benefiting from a lodger's rent. Pierce tried to keep things vague, that he was simply enquiring about Mr Bould and did they recognise these items?...He produced the pipe, tobacco, handkerchief and knife he had removed from Bould's clothes and laid them side by side on the pine table. Mrs Engberson obviously did. "Oh!"

Her husband asked: "Where's his purse?"

As they talked, Pierce found it impossible to keep the truth from them. They had vital information. Mrs Engberson exclaimed: "I knew something bad had happened. I just knew." She leaned against the mantlepiece, forehead pressed into her hands. Both were shocked but managed to be helpful. Yes, they agreed, it was John Bould the sergeant was talking about. Quite tall, about 5 feet 7 inches, maybe 5 feet 8 inches, dark hair, well nourished. Kept himself clean. The last they saw of him was after supper that evening when he went for a walk, saying he was going to post a letter to the Society of Tailors in the East Cheshire mill town of Ashton-under-Lyne. It contained a £1 postal order for subscription arrears. He would also have had his purse with him. Yellow, pigskin, well worn. And he had a sister, Teresa, in Burnley. They were always writing to each other and seemed very close. Did they have an address? Yes.

Bernard Engberson agreed to go to the mortuary – 'just to make sure', said Pierce, confident as they strode out of Swinton Square that he had a solid lead to lay in front of the Chief Constable when he arrived to take charge of the investigation. Robbery – that was it. Bould's trouser pocket was turned inside out. The purse was missing. As was the letter with the postal order, although it was probable that Bould had already posted it. And if it was robbery, then it logically followed that it was murder, although he would leave it to the Chief to voice that conclusion. Which he did when he and Superintendent Leah turned up at the station after taking the first train from Chester on Monday morning. "But," added Colonel Hammersley, "we need to be careful about what we say to members of the public and, particularly, to the Press. We have to maintain calm."

You can understand his low-key approach. Police had to gather as much relevant information as possible and, to achieve that, they had to suppress wild talk. Of course, the main job of the Press was to stimulate as much wild talk as possible.

Engberson had looked carefully at Bould before confirming: "It's him alright. Charlotte will take this hard." By the time Teresa Neagle reached Knutsford late on Easter Monday the town was in uproar. Shops were shut for the Bank Holiday but the streets were filled with people and the buzz of excited conversation. Police were knocking on doors and reporters asking questions.

Stepping off the train which had steamed through the south Manchester suburbs and then into the Cheshire countryside, Miss Neagle was met by Pierce and another officer who escorted her 300 yards along Love Lane to the mortuary where Dr Smith and the giant Roman Catholic priest Father John Roche were waiting. Roche had not been in Knutsford long but had quickly made his mark, simply through his height, six feet six inches. He dwarfed the sergeant who at five feet nine inches was just above the national average. Beside him, Neagle seemed like a child. Pierce detected a note of familiarity about the way they greeted each other but made no comment.

Bould's head peeked out from under a sheet which, she felt, had not been laundered very well. She shuddered, lowered her head, made the sign of the cross and uttered something which Pierce could not make out. After giving a formal statement at the police station she was met outside

by friends ready to accompany her to St Vincent's Roman
Catholic Church. Pierce watched them walk away, hurrying
to keep pace with the long striding Roche. He had been
impressed by the diminutive Miss Neagle. Though Burnley
in East Lancashire to Knutsford was not a simple journey,
with changes needed at Bolton and Manchester, she had
responded promptly and, while tired and upset, she had
behaved in a dignified manner throughout.

As for the dead man, previously known officially as 'the
deceased', well at least he now had a name. And a religion.
Identified by two witnesses, one being his next of kin –
it seemed there were no other surviving members of their
family – this obscure tailor, born in Staffordshire but who,
according to his sister, regarded the Derbyshire town of
Glossop as his home, could soon be presented to the world as
the victim of a terrible murder. The world would ask 'Who
did it?' and 'Why?' and Pierce would struggle to answer.
Leah had thrown cold water on to the robbery motive, not
a bucketful, just a couple of drops but sufficient to make
everyone re-consider.

"He was as poor as a church mouse," said Leah. "Even if he
had a few shillings in his pocket why would anyone want to
shoot him for it?"

The superintendent was clever. Pierce could see that the
Chief put great store by his opinions. He decided to keep his
head down and stick to the basics of harvesting evidence.
Superintendent John Okell had also joined the team, heading
up the day to day enquiries and noting their progress in
a journal. But, for now, the stars of the show were not
police officers. John Bould was to become famous. Mary Jane
Francis was to have her 15 minutes in the spotlight too, and
others were hovering in the wings.

Cheshire policemen of the early 20th century with their shako headwear - how Sergeant Pierce and his constables would have looked. © The Museum of Policing In Cheshire

CHAPTER 3

*'Oh it was an awful time, coming down like a
thunderbolt on a still sunny day when the lilacs were
all in bloom' – Elizabeth Gaskell (Cranford)*

UNTIL Easter Sunday 1901 George Rowe had enjoyed
life immensely. An ingenious, industrious man, he
owned a boot polish firm in Altrincham named
Blyth and Platt and while it had certain cash flow problems
he knew he was onto a winner, mainly because of his self-
designed mass production process which simply outgunned
any rivals. Rowe, son of a Manchester fish and game dealer,
had also married well. His wife Gertrude (Gertie) came
from the Pritchard family, headed by Manchester alderman
William Bridgett Pritchard, whose full-length portrait hung
in the city's Town Hall, a richly coloured oil painting redolent
of Britain's self-esteem, which, driven by the words of
Rudyard Kipling and the music of Edward Elgar, was to reach
its apex in the coming years under Edward V11.

Gertrude's four brothers were all surgeons and doctors, one
of whom, Harry Washington Pritchard, was temporarily
lodging with her, George and their young son Walter at their
home in Altrincham, when the thunderbolt struck. If the
lilacs were not quite in bloom, it was certainly an awful time
for the Rowes.

"What do you mean, the police want to see you. Why?"
She felt sick with anger and fear. Rowe had told her of an
'incident' when he and Harry had returned home on Easter
Sunday evening, soaking wet and smelling of drink, but now
he was talking of guns and having to go to Knutsford to
see the police. Not just the police, actually, but the Chief
Constable of Cheshire.

"It's only a   precaution," he reassured her. "A body has
been found and we were in the vicinity at the time. Sheer
coincidence, but the police are asking for help and any
possible witnesses so we have to see them."

"We?"

"Not you, Gertie. Harry and I. We will have to make statements I suppose."

Rowe cursed his bad luck. He and Pritchard, along with their friend Harry Yarwood, had ridden horses the eight miles from Altrincham into Knutsford on Easter Sunday afternoon to take 'tea' at the Royal George Hotel. They had done it before. Tea, of course, was a euphemistic description for a drinking bout, this one was a little send-off for his brother-in-law who was serving as a field surgeon in the Anglo-Boer War and, after a short leave, was planning to return to South Africa the following weekend.

On their way home, around 7pm, they had trotted down Mere Heath Lane where, he had subsequently heard, a man was shot dead. He told Gertie what she needed to know. There was a lot more to it, of course, but hopefully he could sort that out. Rowe took a train to Manchester to visit a gunsmith of his acquaintance.

Meanwhile, the search for a murderer and his weapon intensified. Witnesses were interviewed, police reinforcements drafted in from other parts of Cheshire. Colonel Hammersley had a reputation for quietly encouraging his men and for shrewdly utilising very limited resources, but it was Superintendent Leah who did the paper work, liased with other forces, and collated the evidence to be presented to the coroner in deposition form. Superintendent Okell, the oldest and most experienced officer, directed operations 'on the ground'.

The Cheshire force did not have a specialised detective unit at that time, unlike Manchester where Jerome Caminada had established himself in the late 19th century as the role model for Arthur Conan Doyle's super sleuth character Sherlock Holmes. Caminada, head of the city's CID, was unorthodox, going to great lengths to study criminals and their behaviour. Hammersley had to rely on his uniformed officers, some bright, others little more than plodders. He was not sure where Pierce slotted in just yet, although Okell seemed to hold him in high regard.

In reviewing police methods of that era it is easy, 120 years on, to criticise but, despite the success of Caminada and the exploits of his fictional doppelganger, investigative work was still in its infancy and has to be considered in the context of slow communications, slow transport and Victorian propriety. Few phones were readily available. Messages went by hand, by telegram or by a postal service which could collect and deliver on the same day, sometimes within hours in some districts, but which was still cumbersome in terms of police work. As for getting around, that meant waiting for a train, harnessing a pony and trap, jumping on a bicycle or slogging it out on foot. For the great majority of sergeants and constables it was the latter.

Of course, the criminal was hindered by the same restraints. No getaway cars. And not many places to hide. In fact it was not until the introduction of motorways in the 1960s that British 'crims' really spread their wings. (When the Kray twins tried to muscle in on the Manchester scene they travelled from London by train – and were quickly seen off by the local warlords).

Hammersley's force focused initially on a five miles radius of Knutsford, particularly Tatton Park, yet, despite all their local knowledge and all the assistance that the townsfolk offered, they stumbled along with little joy. On Tuesday April 9, Hammersley made a cautious statement to the Press, containing the phrase 'supposed murder', when, in fact, he knew it could be nothing else. Police were 'puzzled' opined the Manchester Guardian, because of the absence of a motive. John Bould was simply John Bould, a poor but honest tailor. No-one, it seemed, could have any reason to blast him to Kingdom Come. Without a motive (disregarding all the nonsense being bandied about), without the murder weapon, without anyone who had actually seen the shooting, and without anyone coming forward to confess, the Chief was more than puzzled – he was deeply concerned. The murderer was still at large and quite possibly still in Knutsford. He warned his men that they could come face to face with an armed killer, possibly a mad one, possibly one utterly cruel and black-hearted. Either might not think twice about adding a bobby to his list.

If Hammersley thought that the full post-mortem carried out by Dr Smith on that Tuesday would be of help, he was wrong. While it illuminated some points, it acted like a faulty gas lamp mantle on others, creating shadows and flickering ghosts. Some of it, partial and inaccurate, had already appeared in a couple of newspapers. He wondered how. Smith would have to present his findings when the inquest opened the following day, April 10 – that should be interesting. What Hammersley, nor anyone else, anticipated was that when the subsequent newspaper headlines screamed 'Extraordinary Evidence', it was nothing to do with gunshot wounds, but with 'The Scandalous Tale Of The Servant And The Three Horsemen'. Although this proved only a sideshow to the main event, it entertained millions throughout the spring and summer of 1901. Sadly, it was in fact a sordid episode which led to humiliation and tragedy.

While the police already felt frustrated they were pleased at one aspect, the response of the public. The dossier of witness statements was growing. Mary Jane Francis, Hugh Daniels and George Toft had signed off theirs within 24 hours of the incident, and others who had been in Mere Heath Lane that evening had also come into the station to give their accounts. John Parkes, who had been canoodling with his lady Jessie Groucott; Thompson Flood and his wife Mary who had been escorting a couple of young children, and The Three Horsemen, Rowe, Pritchard and Yarwood.

But, like Smith's post-mortem report, their accounts highlighted some things and blurred others. Witnesses of the same incident could always be relied on to give differing reports, but usually a picture emerged. Here, the statements merged into a grey shroud of vagueness punctuated by ambiguities and anomalies. Nothing hard, nothing direct for the police to act on.

Pierce was suspicious about Rowe and Yarwood, not so much Pritchard. Rowe came into the station that Tuesday morning, stating he had an appointment with the Chief Constable. He seemed very sure of himself. Yarwood, he had more time for. One of the lads, sporty in his youth, still up for a laugh, a game of bowls, and a good time. But Constable

Davies had heard something about him, that after drinking in Knutsford he had been known to pull out a gun and fire into the air. Crack! Crack! Crack! Yes, Pierce could easily imagine Harry doing something daft like that. He would have to have another word with him. As for Rowe, the Chief had looked after him, accompanying him down Mere Heath Lane to specify 'points of interest'.

Apparently, The Three Horsemen had engaged a barrister to represent them at the inquest. Interesting, thought Pierce. Rowe and Pritchard were brothers-in-law, middle-class you could say, but Yarwood was a village blacksmith. An unlikely trio. What tied them together?

It is a bit late but perhaps the author can help on this issue.... Rowe and Pritchard had family connections. Imbued with the Victorian spirit of adventure and enterprise, Rowe was an ideas man, who had borrowed money to boost his boot polish company and was also involved in designing eyelets for shoe laces, improving pneumatic tyres and the streamlining of cars while Pritchard was a volunteer field surgeon, putting himself at risk while treating wounded soldiers in South Africa. One of the heroes of Imperial Britain.

At first glance, Harry, a wheelwright/blacksmith in the village of Dunham Massey (a few miles from Knutsford) seemed the odd man out. But Yarwood was not just a red face at a hot forge. He was a former athletic star, winning sprints in front of big crowds all over the North-West and in 1897 at the age of 46 he dominated his local sports day, held on a field close to his smithy, coming second in the 200 yards and first in the 100 yards. Partly through his service with the Cheshire Volunteers, he had many contacts in different levels of society, was often seen on horseback – in January 1901 he was fined five shillings for riding on the footpath – and was useful with a rifle. In earlier years he had practised on the Volunteers' range on the Moor, the furthest target at 600 yards being placed close to Swinton Square and King Street.

Despite 48 hours of intense effort, the police had little new to give the growing and ever more demanding Press corps. What seemed certain, however, was that the incident was a one-off, not, as feared by some, the start of a murderous rampage by an armed madman. He could strike again but only if cornered. For the moment he was lying low.

After the drama of Easter, Knutsford tried to get back to normal. Shops and offices re-opened on Tuesday, the hammer of building work could be heard from Legh Road and Drury Lane where Richard Harding Watt's 'follies' were under construction, and the scents of warm bread and freshly ground coffee from Watson's store competed bravely with the stench of smoke and sewage. King Street, as ever, was busy. Knutsford's lengthy main retail artery wound its way from the railway bridge to the junction of Tatton Street, Garden Lane and Mere Heath Lane, incorporating shops and trades of all descriptions, along with offices for the professional classes, and any number of pubs and ale houses. Some of the buildings were three storeys high, the street was narrow, and on a gloomy day, a sense of claustrophobia crept in but the town's heart beat strongest here. Some tried to push the murder aside with a 'life has to go on' outlook but the growing presence of police, reporters and curious visitors made it difficult.

Any criminality would most likely be encountered here although when police were needed it was usually to sort out drunkenness. The Rose and Crown, one of only two pubs in the town to have a licence for music, was one of the rowdiest places, although the best spot to see a fight, women as well as men, was outside the Golden Lion in the Market Place which, like Swinton Square, lay on a slope between the street and the Moor.

No-one could accept that the murderer, as well as the victim, had walked down King Street every day. It could not be that local. As Mrs Gaskell said when writing about a sudden spate of robberies: *'Cranford had so long piqued itself on being an honest and moral town that it had grown to fancy itself too genteel and well bred to be otherwise and felt the stain upon its character at this time doubly. But we comforted ourselves with the assurance which we gave to each other that the robberies could never have been committed by any Cranford person; it must have been a stranger who brought this disgrace upon the town'......*

Mary Ann Parrott, for one, reckoned that The Three Horsemen must have had something to do with it. She had heard about Yarwood flaunting a gun, and that one of his friends was involved with the military. Surely, it was more than coincidence that they were in Mere Heath Lane at the same time as the shooting. But you had to be careful not to say too much. She had heard her sons chatting about it and hushed them up. John went off to the Post Office to start his round. It was a good job, a postman. Only 16 but tall for his age, and his uniform, cap and coat gave him added status. Tom would have been proud of him. Her husband had died in 1887 at the age of 35. Tubercolosis. Common, but still a shock – particularly the debts he had left. Their oldest son James was a different kettle of fish. You never could tell what he was planning and now he was off again, this time saying he had a job in Altrincham eight miles away and was going to board there rather than take the train each day.

James Crossley Parrott smiled as he walked out of the front door of the shop, leaving his mother pedalling the Singer. He turned left towards the station. Yes, he needed a break from Knutsford. It was his home town but it did not feel like it.

CHAPTER 4

*'Sure, it is a dreadful thing to take innocent
people's lives' – John Bould*

HERCULES Campbell Yates was seething. As he sat
down to breakfast at his home, The Rookery, in the
Bollington Cross area of Macclesfield, he once more
read the Manchester Guardian, flattening the pages down
with an impatient hand, his frown deepening with every
sentence.

'There seems no doubt now that the man John Bold *(sic)* who
was found dead on Sunday evening was murdered. The post-
mortem examination yesterday by Dr Smith revealed the
fact that five shots had been fired and that all of them struck
the unfortunate man. Dr Smith, it is stated, believes that the
murder was committed by a man who, standing about three
feet away from Bold had emptied a revolver of five chambers
into his body.....'

Yates curbed the temptation to throw the newspaper across
the room. The Clerk to the Justices, Leicester Caldecutt
had told him of a similar report in the previous evening's
Manchester Courier and now here it was encored in the
Guardian and, no doubt, in papers across the country. "We'll
see about the good doctor," he told his wife, as he shrugged
on an overcoat and took his top hat from her. "How dare he."

Yates was bound for Knutsford. Everyone there, indeed
everyone in the North-West, referred to him and knew him
only as Mr H C Yates, the Cheshire coroner and on this
Wednesday morning the main man. A coroner had extensive
powers. He could direct police action, put down lawyers,
order witnesses to speak up or else, and make doctors regret
that they had ever opened their mouths. H C Yates was about
to open the inquest on John Bould and he was determined to
make his mark.

Mary Jane Francis was up and about early that Wednesday.
There were chores to be finished before she set off for the
Sessions House. She would not be working at Heath Side

much longer. Mrs Speakman had treated her kindly enough but her attitude had changed dramatically once she realised that the maid had deceived her. And soon it would be public.

At the scullery sink, she pulled the curtain behind her for privacy, and washed herself with a bar of Sunlight soap previously used to scrub the linoleum covered floor. She thought about cleaning her teeth but could not find the tin of powder – Jane must have put it somewhere - and so contented herself by rubbing them with a piece of damp cloth. Her hair hung loose for a few moments while she dabbed it with a pomade of lavender oil, then she piled it up on the top of her head and neatly pinned it. She tidied her clothes, put on her hat, adjusted it to a more jaunty angle with the help of a mirror, and set off. Taylor, the bricklayer who was carrying out some work at the Speakmans', muttered something as she walked past. Something derogatory, probably. Others had made comments, too. But she had got over the initial shock of Easter Sunday and was feeling more like herself, confident, chirpy even. Knutsford was a nice place, Spring was here, and she hummed a song as she walked purposefully along Toft Road. She would show 'em, toothache or not.

George Rowe and Harry Yarwood had travelled to Knutsford together by train. At the Sessions House they met their barrister Ambrose Jones. Rowe tried to diguise his anxiety with a show of bombast. "She's lying. Who's going to believe her?" Yarwood laughed. "Only your wife maybe," but the joke bombed. Rowe had gone through a harrowing 24 hours at home, explaining his interview with the Chief Constable, the trip along Mere Heath Lane, and questions about his old revolver. "Nothing is going to happen," he told Gertie. "It is an inquest, that's all." She refused to be placated.

Yarwood effected to treat the whole affair lightly. He had done nothing wrong, had nothing to worry about, and quite enjoyed his friend's discomfiture while patting him on the shoulder and assuring him: "A storm in a teacup. Nothing more." Ambrose Jones agreed, although, privately, he was not so sure having seen the woman's statement. He smiled wryly. At 10 45am, Jones left them to enter the courtroom.

They remained seated on one of the wooden benches lining the corridor. Teresa Neagle sat opposite, straight backed, eyes closed. The Engbersons stood nearby, looking nervous and out of place. In, through the main door, strode Francis. She averted her gaze from Rowe and Yarwood, sat alongside Neagle, and calmly fiddled with her hat. A clerk took their names and, as he opened the door to return to the courtroom, they heard Leicester Caldecutt call: "All stand for the coroner." The inquest was to begin.

Compared to modern times, the speed with which this hearing was set up is surprising. As a crime reporter, the author came across hundreds of inquests which were opened and adjourned, usually to allow relatives to sort out death certificates so that the body could be released for burial and it could be several weeks, even months, before the full inquest was held giving police and doctors plenty of time to organise their evidence. But, although Bould had been dead less than 72 hours, the coroner was calling an array of witnesses, a jury had been selected and the main court of the Sessions House made ready.

Yates, whose father and grandfather were judges, dealt with an average of 270 inquests a year. By 1901 he had served 20 years as coroner, and was to continue in the role for another 30. He was also the chairman of Cheshire Quarter Sessions and there was little which could catch him off guard. However the newspaper leak of the post-mortem findings had ruffled him and worse was to follow. First, a surge of people pushing and shoving to get into the public gallery. Then the news that the barrister Jones was holding a watching brief on behalf of Rowe, Pritchard and Yarwood, all followed by some startling evidence. Before that, though, the coroner gave Dr Smith a public dressing-down laced with sarcasm.

"It is needless for me to go into the details of the case as it has been given very efficiently in the newspapers," Yates told the jury in his opening remarks. "I must, however, refer to one point. The newspapers have published the result of the post-mortem... it was most improper because the medical evidence is perhaps the most important we have in the case. I can only hope it was the imagination of some writer and that it was not furnished by the medical man."

A murmur ran through the public gallery. Faces turned towards the doctor. Thankfully the coroner had a lot to get through and he moved quickly on. "Call the first witness."

Teresa Neagle, describing herself as a housekeeper of Padiham, Burnley, stepped into the box. The following 15 minutes highlighted the lack of care in establishing evidence, and giving it, which characterised The Knutsford Murder case throughout.

Neagle said she was Bould's sister. She obviously considered herself as such but, in fact, she was his half-sister, born in Cork, Ireland. Her mother was also Teresa Neagle, who moved with her daughter to England in the 1850s and wed Richard Bould, a labourer, in Stone, Staffordshire. John Bould was their son.

Coroner Yates asked Neagle for Bould's age. She replied: "I don't know exactly, but about 35."

It was one of many guesses about the murdered man's age. In the 1901 census, conducted only six days before he was shot, Bould was said to be 30. Who provided the census taker with that information is unknown, it might have been Bould himself, it might have been the head of the household Bernard Engberson. No matter, it was grossly inaccurate. Numerous Press articles claimed vaguely that he was 'in his thirties'. Yet Bould was born in 1857 and died at the age of 44. His half-sister, said to be close to him, thought he was almost 10 years younger than that.

Bould did not look his age. A muscular man, he kept himself fit with regular walks and a fairly disciplined teetotal diet but it seems strange that Teresa Neagle got it so wrong. Eventually, Bould's age proved of little significance. Greater disparities were in the offing but Neagle's contribution was an early example of the imprecision which pervaded this investigation.

Encouraged by the coroner she offered more detail about Bould.

No-one had any bad feeling about him. He was single and did not have a love affair – as far as she knew. He was against all secret societies and......At this point, Superintendent Leah jumped to his feet, asking for permission to put a question to the witness. The coroner agreed. Leah gathered himself: "What reason do you have for saying that he was against secret societies?"

Neagle, an Irish Roman Catholic, understood why the polite enquiry about Bould's history had suddenly taken a sinister turn. What they wanted to know was whether he was a Fenian. She handled it adeptly. "Some years ago we were reading about the Phoenix Park murders and he said to me 'Teresa, sure it is a dreadful thing to take innocent people's lives.'" Looking around the court, she saw Father Roche – how could you miss him? He was a reassuring figure, known to her and John when he was in charge of a church in Stalybridge where they had worshipped some years previously.

He nodded in her direction. It was a good answer, she could tell from the sudden silence. As though everyone was paying respect to the dead. Leah was not entirely satisfied. "Is that the only reason?" but pushed it no further when she replied: "Yes."

Leah himself was a member of a secret society, the Freemasons, but his questioning underlined the general anxiety about Irish nationalism and working class agitation. Nearby Manchester was a hotbed, but one of the most radical towns in Britain was Ashton-under-Lyne with which Bould was extremely familiar. Neagle's denial failed to quell growing support for the theory that there was something 'fishy' about it all. Bould might well have been an agent for the nationalists, using his job as cover to glean information. Knutsford, after all, was a legal and military centre, the historic base of the Cheshire Volunteers who retained a major presence in the town.

A picture of Bould was emerging, not a full-length oil, as befitting the likes of Alderman Pritchard, more of a pencil line sketch, but enough to show him as a peace-loving, even gentle man. This image was embroidered by the Engbersons. Almost a saint, he was, according to Charlotte. Honest, straightforward, liked by everyone, usually stayed in, content to read a newspaper. Oh, yes, she remembered now, there was a man he did not like, named Lockland, who worked at Slater's tailors in Knutsford where Bould had also been employed for a while. Apparently they had argued but she did not know why.

Here was the first mention of someone who might have had reason to kill Bould. A possible suspect. Lockland was an Irish tailor who moved from Knutsford to a boarding house in Chester sometime in March. Did he return to Knutsford to shoot Bould? Drinkers at the Golden Lion had told the police of a stranger lurking around the Market Place on the Saturday night, 24 hours before the murder, but, as he had not been seen since and could not be traced, they had crossed him off the list of possibles.

H C Yates was now in full flow, pumping questions at Charlotte Engberson.

"Did he ever express any fear of this man?"

"No, sir. He always said he was not afraid of him."

"He did not like him, that was all?"

"Yes, sir."

"Did Bould ever carry a revolver?"

"No, he did not like such things. It was only on Sunday morning he told my husband that there should be a law against carrying them."

Someone at the back of the court muttered: "Poppycock." And, as the coroner admonished him with a stern look, another voice whispered: "No-one is taking my gun."

While he was ready to stamp down on interruptions, the coroner appreciated the reaction to Bould's statement. The right to bear arms was as cherished in Britain then just as much as it has always been in the USA. Only the previous year, the last of Victoria's reign, the Prime Minister Lord Salisbury said he would 'laud the day when there is a rifle in every cottage in England'. The army was being stretched by the Anglo-Boer War and with ever present fears of a conflict in Europe, the PM was keen to ensure that Britons could defend themselves. Rifle clubs had mushroomed and, in Knutsford, the Volunteers staged target practice on part of the Moor. Gun law was virtually non-existent. You could buy any type of firearm, from a small 'derringer' pistol which could be hidden up a sleeve, to a Gatling (a rapid fire field gun) without a background check.

'Anyone' says criminologist Colin Greenwood, 'be he a convicted criminal, lunatic, drunkard or child, could legally acquire any type of firearm.' Salisbury referred to rifles, but an argument had developed over the surge of revolver and pistol sales, inspired by the success of the Colt Company. Lloyds newspaper ran an editorial warning of the dangers of the revolver, when in the hands of 'reckless characters from America and the Fenians who have sown weapons of violence in our poorer districts.'

The Knutsford Murder, a revolver shooting of a seemingly poor, innocent man deepened the political struggle over firearms. And the inquest into the killing, though only an hour or so old, had thrown up two possible motives – a personal dispute and a political assassination. And the 'Extraordinary Evidence' was still to be given.

"Mary Jane Francis." The court usher was at the door beckoning her inside. She rose carefully, drew in breath, and followed him in, refusing to meet the stares of Rowe and Yarwood, one sour, the other amused. Once through the door, she was momentarily confused. So many people. So many heads turned towards her. The usher took her arm to guide her down the stone steps into the well of the court and then up into the witness box. She took the proffered bible and card and read out the oath in her clear Welsh accent. No need to tell her to speak up, thought Caldecutt in his seat directly below the coroner. But she was too busy looking around. "Please face the jury and direct your answers to them," he ordered. Francis adapted her stance. She knew her place. Like most other employers, Mrs Speakman did not allow familiarity with her servants. But this was her day, she would have her say and there was nothing Mrs Speakman or anyone else could do about it. And, now feeling more settled in the witness box, and in her own mind, she determined not to be over-awed by the occasion. For almost 20 years she had worked in the homes of the well-off, some wealthier than the Speakmans, and particles of their self-assurance had rubbed off on her.

'Face the jury', all men of course. Women occupied a fair percentage of the public seats, a group seated with a priest, a huge man, and others dotted around, hardly working ladies on a Wednesday morning, and not of the Speakmans' class either, something in between, some with old fashioned plumes in their hats. But the coroner, the court staff, the solicitors and their clerks, the policemen – all male. While the women's rights movement was gathering momentum it would be a long time before they got the vote, and much, much longer before they made an impact in the judicial process. Francis noted that most others were dressed in black, as befitting an inquest while she wore a jacket of grey and blue, puffed up slightly at the shoulder, and a charcoal grey skirt which tapered towards the ankles. At just over five feet tall, her trim figure was almost lost in the massive witness box, a pulpit of polished mahogany.

Questioned by the coroner who had use of the written statement she had made to the police, her early evidence was deeply important, recounting her departure from the Speakmans' house on Easter Sunday at 6 20pm, intimating she was going to church with the cook Jane Pickstock. However it was an excuse. While Pickstock answered the bells for evensong, Francis went to a surgery in King Street for some medicine she needed. By then it was a little after 6 30pm. The plan was to meet up with Jane when she came out of church and they would return to Heath Side together at 8pm as expected. Until then she had well over an hour to kill, and so she decided to take a walk on a loop route along Mere Heath Lane and onto the parallel Manchester Road taking her back to the Heath. Not far along Mere Heath Lane there were haystacks in a field on the right, and nearby a gate from which a man emerged, shutting it behind him. She did not know him.

Prompted by Yates, Francis described him as "pale-looking, sallow. He was wearing glasses."

Yates: "Do you mean spectacles or what are called nose-riders?"

"I should say spectacles. He was wearing a coat, a dark one. An overcoat. He was respectably dressed, I should say well dressed."

"A quiet man?" the coroner inquired. "A quite inoffensive fellow?"

"Yes. He had rambling eyes."

This was the first time the public had heard a physical description of a possible suspect. The hum of whispering voices swept along the back of the court. Francis sensed she had made an impression but the coroner was eager for her to continue.

Walking slowly along the lane, she was overtaken by three men on horseback. A minute or so later she caught up with one, who had dismounted. Although she did not know at the time she now believed his name was Rowe. He bade her good evening and mentioned it was very wet – "it was pouring" – and she replied but, as she went to pass, his horse became restless.

"I was terrified and told him I was afraid of horses and I asked him to go along. He said: 'You need not be frightened of the horse; there is a man with it,' and another of the men came back and took hold of the horse and tied it to a gate."

Glancing at her statement, the coroner paused for a few seconds. His tone sharpened when he resumed the interrogation. "Then what happened?"

Mary Jane Francis needed no encouragement. Gripping the rail of the witness box, she raised her chin, looked at the coroner, then back to the jury: "He put his arm around my waist. I said: 'Will you please keep your hands off me?' He was a perfect stranger to me and he behaved rather roughly."

Yates leaned back. "Did you resent it? Did you box his ears as he deserved? Did you hit him?"

"No, I did not. I was firm with him and I screamed. Then he let me go."

It was here that the clerk, Caldecutt had to intervene. The court was in ferment. Some reporters were trying to get away from the Press bench, aiming to be first to a phone or to grab a messenger, the spectators seated in the raised public gallery or standing along walls were in uproar, members of the jury were shouting questions at the witness, and Ambrose Jones, the barrister representing The Three Horsemen, was on his feet waving a slate coloured file tied with red ribbon. Caldecutt bawled: "Silence in court. Silence."

While 'around my waist' might have been a coy way of describing it does not matter. This allegation was as serious and as sensational as it could be. A domestic maid claiming that on a public road, a so-called 'gentleman' had indecently assaulted her, watched by another man who had offered her no assistance. On Easter Sunday. In Knutsford. Victorian morality had always been clad in hypocrisy, but there were no closed doors here. Scandal loomed.

Yates commented: "I hope the police will take note of this."

Leah nodded in assent. Jones said loudly: "I have a very different complexion to put upon this." He demanded that Rowe should have the chance, there and then, to make a public denial on oath, but Yates refused point blank and, with a wave of the hand, displayed some exasperation. The coroner had erred in allowing Francis to give such detail. Better to have ruled that it was irrelevant, that this was not a criminal trial but an inquest simply to certify the manner of death. Now the whole murder investigation would be clouded by a sex controversy.

When things had calmed down, Francis continued but with almost every sentence she raised the noise level.

Again, perusing her statement, Yates looked up and asked: "Did you hear the sound of a pistol?"

She took a breath. "I heard two shots fired. Rowe had his arm around me. I could not say whether they were gun or pistol shots. They were loud reports. I said to Rowe 'Did you hear those shots? They must be shooting birds on a Sunday'. But I don't think he replied."

When Rowe released her, she turned to walk back towards Knutsford and just after going around a bend she saw a man lying in the hedge. Whether he was dead or alive, she could not discern, but there was a 'strange man' bending over him with his hands on the other man's chest. Apparently alarmed by her approach, he ran off towards town, his long overcoat almost tripping him up.

"I could not see his face and I cannot say whether he was dressed like the man I saw at the gate earlier." Francis was answering confidently. She seemed sure but Yates pressed hard.

"Can't you say whether he had the same overcoat?"

"No, this man had a grey overcoat."

"So had the other man, hadn't he?"

"No, a dark one, dark grey."

"Could you say if he was wearing spectacles?"

"No."

At this point, Yates emitted a sigh and held up Francis's statement. "To the police I see you say you believe it was the same man but now you can't say?"

"No, sir. I cannot say it was."

Only two days had elapsed since giving her statement to the police and something had made her change her mind. Yates wondered if she could be trusted. Within a matter of minutes, he was not sure how many, 10, possibly 15, she had seen one man coming through a field gate (what was a well-dressed man doing in a field when it was pouring with rain?) and another leaning over a body in a hedge. In between Bould had been gunned down and she had been assaulted. Her story would be enshrined in headlines but it was pitted with doubt. Leah aggravated the situation asking for Rowe to be brought into court for Francis to identify him. Which she did, providing Jones the opportunity to cross-examine her and he was just getting warmed up when the jury foreman intervened. "This isn't relevant," he said.

Exactly. The coroner himself should have sorted it out but, as he admitted later, he was reluctant to halt counsel in mid-flow and the preliminary hearing ended with an unseemly argy-bargy between Yates, Jones and Leah about what should or should not be the way to proceed and whether the police were likely to charge Rowe with an offence. Leah refused to commit himself and Jones stated: "I simply say, on behalf of the three men, that they totally deny any impropriety having taken place."

Francis butted in: "Well, they would, wouldn't they, sir?"

Yates heard laughter at the back of the court. He had had enough, adjourning the inquest for a fortnight.

The court emptied quickly with wide-ranging reactions. Rowe was fuming that he had been refused permission to swear on oath that he was innocent; Jones felt he had been insulted by the coroner; Leah and Okell who had sat beside each other all day were more puzzled than ever; and Yates returned to Macclesfield fearing this case would be the most difficult of his career. Francis, who had blossomed under the spotlight was suddenly left to her own devices.

Trudging back to Heath Side, where the next day Emily Speakman would be talking to her about her future, or lack of it, she suffered a sense of anti climax. Where was the elation, the justice done emotion she had imagined for herself? In court, she had enjoyed the attention but, as the questioning intensified, she had wondered whether she should have been in the dock, rather than the witness box. One juror had leered at her, and she had not expected to be so close to Rowe again. Three days ago he had his hands under her coat, groping at buttons, and...she remembered his hands, the filthy fingertips, as though he had stuck them in a tin of blacking. What might have happened but for those gunshots? Mary Jane, the maid, was used to working long hours, never complaining of tiredness, not that anyone would have listened. But Francis, the witness, had to admit she was exhausted. Naturally a slow walker, she almost came to a stop before, at the corner of Toft Road and Heath Side, she jerked herself back into life. The Speakmans were holding a dinner that night and she would be waiting on.

At newspaper offices throughout the country, sub-editors were sticking headlines on their reporters' copy. The words 'remarkable evidence' cropped up in several articles.

Remarkable indeed, considering Francis had thrown a huge spanner in the wheel. Not with her allegations against Rowe, but by suggesting that the 'well-dressed' man at the gate and the 'strange' man leaning over the body were different individuals when, originally, she had thought they were the same. Why the change of heart?

Several issues have to be taken into account.

Firstly, the statement she gave to the police was primarily oral, Hammersley asking questions, Pierce taking notes which he wrote up and handed to Leah. Basically this method existed for many decades and was open to genuine mistakes, misunderstandings and/or abuse. Neither Pierce nor Leah was corrupt but the sergeant was later to exhibit a worrying approach to this aspect of police work.

Secondly, Francis made her statement less than 24 hours after a harrowing experience. It was essential to extract one from her as quickly as possible but what was her demeanour? Was she still distressed? Excited? Were words put in her mouth at a time when she was hardly thinking straight?

Thirdly, while there were weaknesses and anomalies in her evidence, which will be referenced at a later stage, she appeared essentially forthright and honest. However, in court and sometimes under pressure, she tended to vary the detail. At one stage she said, no it was not the same man, but at another point, she merely said she could not be sure. Clarity was lost in an emotional, sometimes boisterous hearing.

Fourthly, no-one asked her about her eyesight. She did not wear glasses but how good was her vision? How could she differentiate between a dark grey overcoat and a light grey overcoat with the daylight fading and the rain hammering down? No-one bothered to inquire.

Perhaps instinct told her it was the same man but, between making the statement on Monday and giving evidence on Wednesday, she had thought about it and decided she could not provide a cast iron guarantee. Maybe someone put a doubt in her mind. In any event, it made life for the police much harder. One man, described with certainty as having glasses, 'rambling eyes', and good quality clothes was easier to track down and a prime suspect. But now, apparently, there were two men, and the one leaning over the body was identified only by a long, drab coat.

Our Knutsford Correspondent worked overtime that Wednesday night. He could make his name with this story, and a lot of cash. While the inquest had been adjourned until early May, and Sergeant Pierce and Doctor Smith had clammed up, there was nothing to stop him having a chat with one or two others. The Speakmans would be his first port of call, and he could perhaps nab Teresa Neagle before she returned to Burnley. Yes, still plenty to go at...

The imposing Sessions House, Knutsford, now over 200 years old

CHAPTER 5

'...every bullet hath a lighting place' – George Gascoigne, (Fruits Of War, 1575)

ONE thing was clear in an increasingly complex case – John Bould met his fate at the hands of a determined killer. Dr Smith's post-mortem proved it. Five shots at close range. And eight wounds, three of the bullets going straight through him. The phrase 'riddled with lead' came to mind, not that he read those vulgar yellowbacks, of course.

George Henry Smith, appointed medical officer of the workhouse in 1900 and rapidly climbing the tree of Knutsford society, put his report into a file in his desk and locked the drawer. No doubt he would need it again when the inquest resumed and, no doubt, the coroner would be carefully examining him.

Smith was still smarting from H C Yates's public reprimand. He had not been given the chance to answer. Yes, he had spoken to a reporter but only off the record and on condition that it was only for 'background', not to be used immediately. He had been as shocked as Yates when he saw it splashed across several papers on Tuesday evening and Wednesday morning. Can't be trusted, these Press guttersnipes. Badmashes – the Urdu word remembered from his Indian childhood suited perfectly. Standards of journalism had certainly fallen in the last few years. That fellow Harmsworth was to blame. How did the Prime Minister describe the Daily Mail, ah yes, 'a newspaper run by office boys for office boys'. Although, Smith had to confess, Lord Salisbury had been quick to congratulate the Mail and its young owner after they had helped him win the General Election of 1900, the last of the Victorian era.

Born in India but hurriedly evacuated at the age of eight when the 1857 rebellion began, the doctor had been educated at Aberdeen University and had served in various parts of the world, including West Africa, before settling in Knutsford in 1892. He had been around, had seen death in many forms, but had never come across a body so perforated with bullets. Only a cursory inspection was needed that Sunday night to establish that Bould had died from a wound in the region of the heart, but his full examination on Tuesday morning revealed much more. The killer had fired five times from close range, possibly as little as three feet away, that he had aimed at the upper part of the body, and that Bould had thrown up his arm to try to deflect the first two bullets.

Bullet one hit him in the right forearm, two and a half inches from the wrist, going straight through and causing an exit wound directly opposite;

Bullet two entered higher on the same arm and exited above the right elbow;

Bullet three went into Bould's back, between the shoulder blade and spine, passed between the fourth and fifth ribs, and re-appeared two inches from the left armpit and six and a quarter inches from the top of the shoulder;

Bullet four caused worse damage, entering near the left armpit, puncturing the rim of the left lung and coming to rest at the joint of the third rib and the breastbone. But, Smith believed that Bould was still alive at this stage;

Bullet five was the one which did for John Bould. A full frontal shot between the fourth and fifth ribs, slightly fracturing the fifth rib and embedding itself in one of the cavities of the heart. This had caused the chest wound which he had seen straight away when he and Sergeant Pierce stripped Bould's body in the mortuary. The 'immediate cause of death'.

Eight holes altogether. Smith's explanation was that as the killer pulled the trigger Bould lifted up his arm and twisted his head away in an almost automatic defensive response. He partly succeeded, the first two chunks of lead scything through his arm. As he turned away, the gunman continued to fire. The fourth bullet tore a hole in one lung and left him gasping for air. And then came the coup de grace. Smith's report presented Bould as a strong man who might have survived for a few seconds, 30 at the most, but, basically, it was the quickest of deaths.

Pushing aside the absence of motive, Smith wondered what sort of man could commit such a terrible deed. "It is not easy to kill," he told Pierce, "if you are not used to it, as a soldier is. It is even harder if you are face to face with your victim."

His judgement was based on normal human responses. Many would-be killers have lowered their arms at the last moment, unable to go through with it. The other side of the coin is the psychopath. Cold, free of emotion. In 1965, for example, Ron Kray strode into The Blind Beggar pub in London, put a pistol to the head of a rival, George Cornell, shot him and calmly walked out. Kray ensured that one shot was enough. Bould's death was a much more messy affair.

Imagine the scene. Two figures in the rain. The shooter pulls out a revolver and the right-handed Bould, reacting as though bothered by a wasp, whips off his hat and tries to swat it away. Two cracks of the gun, his arm damaged, he is turning away trying desperately to evade another wasp sting but feels an impact in his back and then another in his left side. It robs him of breath and he crumples. But he might still survive, if his assailant is merciful. *Crack!* The final shot.

At the opening of the inquest, Smith had produced to the coroner one bullet – the one which had lodged between a rib and the breastbone. Of the five fired it was the only bullet ever retrieved.

John Bould's death certificate, showing: 'Cause of death: Internal haemorrhage caused by a bullet entering the heart. Wilful murder against some person unknown'

John Bould was laid to rest on Friday April 12 1901. Though he was a Roman Catholic, the burial service took place at St John's, the parish church of Knutsford, opposite the Sessions House, 300 yards from the mortuary and 120 yards from Swinton Square, his home for the last four months. A sizeable crowd saw him on his way. Father Roche led the proceedings, aided by the long-serving vicar, Henry Barnacle. The mourners included members of the St Vincent's Roman Catholic Church in Queen Street where Bould had worshipped. There was no graveyard there, and the opening of the municipal cemetery was not due until the following year, hence his internment at the parish church.

A fine day, so it was, with a light breeze. A good day to be placed 'Underneath', the term used on many memorial stones in the graveyard. Mourners in black moved slowly, heads bowed. Police and prison officers stood to attention, and officlals from the Urban District Council and other organisations paid their respects. Father Roche spoke of the 'hand of Satan'. Superintendent Leah commiserated with Teresa Neagle who wiped tears from her eyes to reveal a sharp glint. "Those who live by the sword will die by it," she said, glancing past his shoulder at the Sessions House.

After an uneventful life, John Bould had found fame in death. And though there was nothing in his pockets he took something of note with him. A bullet. In his heart.

Among the onlookers was Mary Ann Parrott. The new grave was close to that of her husband Tom and his father James who had died in 1887 and 1888 respectively, a double blow which had left her fighting to bring up five children. It proved too much which is why James had had to go away for a few years. Nowadays his moods and silences disturbed her, but things had brightened up recently thanks to an inheritance from his grandfather's estate.

Mary Ann had known Bould. One side of Swinton Square butted on to the rear yards of the King Street houses. Occasionally she heard him chatting with one of the Engbersons. No doubt, he would have overheard some of her family's conversation. He had even approached her on one occasion, saying if she ever needed a hand with the business he was available. Some hope. There was hardly enough work for her, never mind anyone else. Fortunately, the kids had grown up, and all earning money, although James moved from job to job.

Perhaps the new century was Mary Ann's time. The 1890s had been tough. No man in the house and a constant battle to keep her head above water. But the 1900s promised better. A new monarch on the throne, James had handed over part of his inheritance to shake off some debts, and Spring blossom scented the air. Of course she felt sorry for Teresa Neagle. All Knutsford did. After all the excitement of the last few days, the town was sombre and reflective. She would wait until the funeral party had gone and then pay her daily visit to Tom's grave. Maybe, too, sometime in the summer, she would place some daisies on Bould's.

Glancing around the graveyard she spotted the Engbersons standing by the west door. An odd but likeable couple. Someone said he was a Jew who, with his parents and siblings, had fled from Russia to escape persecution. The family had settled in Islington, London, but Bernard and Charlotte had come north for some reason, making Knutsford their home. He was a highly skilled tailor. She had seen samples of his work, indicating strong, supple fingers and excellent eyesight. Always polite, Mr Engberson. Charlotte had been badly affected by losing two sons in infancy, the second Gerald, only last January, just after Bould had arrived in the town. She seemed to enjoy having the newcomer around. Bernard had been working away in Northwich, returning home at the weekend. Not that Mary Ann thought anything was amiss. Charlotte obviously needed company and the sober living, stay at home Bould provided it. Perhaps, too, he was good wth their young boy, eight years old Bernard jnr.

The service over, Mary Ann changed her mind about visiting Tom's grave and almost bumped into Bernard Engberson who had stopped suddenly by the gate and was turning back. Apologising, he walked past, heading towards Toft Road. Charlotte called "Bernard" but he either did not hear or ignored her. She seemed upset, stood still for a second and then hurried away.

Mary Ann was glad to get home. Although the weather was clear, and the heavy curtains tied back, the shop was dark and uninviting. It had not always been like this. Tom Parrott had decided that, unlike his father who farmed 60 acres a few miles south of Knutsford in Holmes Chapel, the outdoor life was not for him and, instead of a plough he would use a needle and thread to earn a living. For a while he prospered. Originally he had rented the King Street premises which acted as their draper's shop and as their home but when the chance came in 1881 to buy the freehold at an auction, he grabbed it, laying out over £800. More cash was spent on alterations, the old stock sold off cheaply. Mary Ann was worried about the debt but Tom reckoned it would be worth it in the long run. Specialising in silk brought from nearby Macclesfield, Tom labelled himself as a 'silk mercer', attracting a clientele of ladies, if not middle-class then aspiring to be so. The Parrotts became well-known and respected - as long as they understood that they remained trades people, nothing more. Social mobility was to the fore at the birth of the Edwardian age, but the swaggering upper classes still lorded it.

The Parrotts might have climbed a little up the ladder, but Tom's ill-health, coupled with the fact that they had her widowed mother Hannah and her younger sister Annie living with them caused cash flow problems. Hannah died in 1885. Then Tom became ill. Tubercolosis, a killer disease, not helped by the conditions in the shop, where dust and soot mingled with miniscule flecks of material. He died in the winter of 1887 aged only 35 coughing blood to the terrible end. With only a few days left, he called in his friend Tom Jackson, clerk to Inman and Ashworth solicitors, to sort out a will. Everything went to her, but everything was less than nothing. Debts had piled up. Within a year Tom was joined by his father James snr who, long retired and widowed, had given up the farm and had been living with them. Another will, and again, little or nothing for her. Most of the bequest went to his oldest grandson, James Crossley, to be invested until he reached 21.

Following the death of James snr, she had to quit their King Street home, and move to new premises a couple of hundred yards away in Princess Street. And look at the trouble that caused! A labourer whom she paid to transport their goods helped himself to an overcoat, an ulster and a silk top hat left by her father-in-law and kept for sentimental reasons. What a rogue.

He claimed that she had given him the clothing, his not guilty plea forcing her to go into the witness box, – and he received six months.

As the last decade of the 19th century got under way, Mary Ann was struggling. Business was up and down. On her own with five children she was in danger of going under. Thank goodness a place was found for the boy. And James had been so co-operative. No fuss at all. He had not changed over the years, either. Hardly says a word, never complains. Oh yes, there were problems with him, but she owed him a lot.

Mary Ann's train of thought was broken by her daughter

Mary planting a pot of tea on the table. 'Bineham's best'. Bineham's grocers was where her younger daughter Edith worked and where they claimed to package the 'finest leaves from Ceylon'. Edith occasionally brought home a few ounces for her mother who liked it weak, so that fresh pots had to be made rather than let it stew on the stove. Sipping from her cup, Mary Ann wondered how James was getting on with his new job. She had not heard from him all week. No need to worry though. He could look after himself.

About the same time that Mary Ann had her feet up with a cuppa, Bernard Engberson was talking earnestly to Sergeant Pierce. "The doctor said there were no signs of violence on John other than the bullet wounds," he said.

"That's right," Pierce answered curtly. He was in a dilemma over the post-mortem but had to be careful about what he said in public.

"But," Engberson went on, "there were bruises on his face. I saw them in the mortuary. You saw them. It looked like he had been hit with something. And scratches."

Pierce was anxious to end the conversation. "He fell into the hedge. Scratched himself on the thorns and he could easily have banged his head as he went down. If the doctor thought it was anything to be concerned about he would have said so."

Engberson was not satisfied but there seemed no point in arguing. After leaving Charlotte he had caught up with Pierce at the corner of Love Lane near the prison. Not the best place to confront him with lots of people around but Engberson had thought about it long and hard since the inquest hearing and felt he had to say something. So there, he had said it, and to little effect. Pierce, however, was also concerned.

By the time Engberson identified the body in the early hours of Monday morning bruising had started to emerge. Engberson must have good eyes, he thought, to discern it in that dimly lit mortuary. Doctor Smith obviously thought it of no consequence and Pierce had been content to let it go, death was from a bullet not from someone hitting him in the face. Even so, the sergeant feared it was a detail which could come back to bite them. Discolouration of the skin, a few hours after death – the post-mortem stain- was normal, but not on the face.

Back in Swinton Square, the cottage was quiet. Bernard junior was still at school, Charlotte barely spoke. The kitchen chair that John usually occupied to read the paper was tucked under the table. Engberson recalled how considerate he had been towards Charlotte when the child had died in January, yet he often showed a disregard for the fairer sex, calling the Suffragists 'trouble-makers' and while he had reluctantly decided to pay up his subscription arrears to the Amalgamated Society of Tailors and Tailoresses, accepting the union's growing power, he had opposed the formation of a female section in 1900. Yet women were attracted to him. Easy to see why. Tall, thick dark hair, broad shoulders. Kept himself neat and tidy. And he preferred to listen rather than talk. Charlotte had bustled around him, making sure he was comfortable, taking care over his food – he loved her version of Irish stew – and treating him almost like a child really. Maybe that was it. A man to be mothered.

The bruises which so concerned Bernard Engerberson were on Bould's nose, an eye and on the forehead which he described as a deep pulpy spot. "They would appear to have been made by a hard, blunt instrument," he added in a statement to the Press. Engberson had voiced his anxiety to the young reporter who had knocked on his door optimistically asking for an interview. The Speakmans' door had been opened by Mary Jane Francis and immediately slammed in his face by Emily, and Teresa Neagle had brushed him off at the railway station on Monday morning, saying she had a train to catch and, if she did talk to the newspapers, it would only be when she got back to Burnley.

But nothing makes a good newsman more determined than repeated knock-backs. He had seen Engberson's animated conversation with Pierce after the funeral and reckoned Swinton Square worth a visit. To his surprise, Engberson was eager to talk. Pierce read the subsequent article with growing exasperation and slammed the paper down on the table, startling his mother-in-law Sarah, now in her 80s and virtually blind for the last 10 years. He excused himself and strode out to seek Doctor Smith. He needed some reassurance on this issue before telegraphing an update to Chester HQ.

Our Knutsford Correspondent was not the only reporter preening himself over a nice 'angle'. One from the Burnley Express had managed to get hold of Teresa Neagle at the house where she worked in Padiham and she had spoken of her 'brother' in glowing terms, claiming he was 'a courageous man with a chivalrous nature'. According to her, he was fit and active, not in any way nervous or timid, and would have given 'a good account of himself in a fair fight', which, obviously, it was not. But that was only the lead-in to the bombshell. Miss Neagle, wrote the reporter, is 'perfectly confident in her own mind as to the manner in which her brother met his death but it was impossible to give publicity to her opinion as it would implicate persons against whom no suspicion has yet been entertained. It is perfectly clear that the assailant was thoroughly accustomed in the use of firearms, in any other case it is unlikely that he would have succeeded in lodging five bullets in the body of his victim.'

This pronouncement gave the murder another sinister aspect. 'Persons against whom no suspicion has been entertained'. Who could she possibly be referring to? An expert with a gun? There were many in that part of Cheshire, with its Volunteers, gamekeepers and poachers and rifle clubs.

Police felt that her comments were unhelpful – just muddying the waters. And, it seemed she was ignorant about the type of weapon that was used. Military trained men would usually rely on service revolvers, accurate in the hands of an experienced shooter, but heavy and difficult for anyone else to control, particularly when aiming five shots in quick succession. But the bullet which Dr Smith showed the coroner was a .32 calibre delivered at point blank range from a comparatively lightweight weapon. Police had failed to find it despite an extensive search of the area and, without it, they had little to go on.

Hammersley and Leah had returned to HQ, ready to act if anything new cropped up but also having other work to attend to, leaving Superintendent Okell in charge with Pierce at his side and assuming more and more of the workload. Frustration was creeping in but one clue they could chase up was that of the Man At The Gate, the well-dressed chap wearing specs, as described by Mary Jane Francis. A possible suspect. But no-one could say who he was. Well, no-one they had spoken to so far. In fact there was someone who recognised him, but who would have thought a dainty 11 years-old girl could be the vital witness?

CHAPTER 6

'Journeyman: qualified artisan working for another; sound but undistinguished workman' – Oxford English Dictionary

ONE of the busiest parts of Knutsford was the coal yard, sloping down one side of the railway station. Huge heaps of the black stuff ranged down the yard, a wooden shed served as an office and merchants like Beswick's shovelled it into one hundred weight sacks to be delivered by horse-drawn waggons to every building in the area. On wind free days in winter parts of 'picturesque' Knutsford could hardly be seen for smoke. The interiors of even the best houses had a sooty smell – a typical middle-class household burned a ton of coal a month - and fog quickly turned into smog in the lower reaches of King Street and the alleys and squares leading down to the Moor and up into Princess Street. On such a day neighbours and friends were transformed into ghostly figures, heads down, gliding past each other like strangers. People died in winter. Tom Parrott, for example, wheezing for breath, and little Gerald Engberson, barely a year old and cold in the bed. The workhouse was a lethal place to be, accounting for half the burials in the parish church between January and April. But, in the darkest days of winter, Charlotte Engberson opened the door to a ray of light in the form of a robust looking journeyman tailor.

John Bould had first learned to sew at the family home in Stone, Staffordshire, coached by his mother. From the age of 14 he served a long apprenticeship, after which he was able to join the Society of Tailors and to charge a daily rate. He moved around looking for work and came knocking on the Engbersons' door three weeks before Christmas 1900, showing a reference from a Mrs Rhodes, of Edward Street, Glossop with whom he had lodged previously. Father Roche at St Vincent's Church could also vouch for him, if necessary, he added. Charlotte told him not to worry about that, the room was his for 7s 6d a week, with board, and he was most welcome. Bould proved a Godsend, not just the extra money, but for his company. And when, in the New Year, Gerald was taken from her and her husband took up a job in Northwich, Bould filled the gap. The perfect lodger. Regular in his habits, clean, uncomplaining, reserved but chatty enough to lift what otherwise would have been a dull existence.

The funny thing was that Charlotte felt safe in every way with Bould around. A decent looking bloke – she could imagine some of the gossip. But it was nothing like that. Bould was a confirmed bachelor, tending to be dismissive of women generally, but not of her, always treating her with a cordial respect, and not of his sister. From the number of letters they exchanged, they seemed very close. What Charlotte enjoyed most was 'doing' for him, cooking the food he liked, tidying up around him, patting cushions into place. He would sit at the table reading a newspaper, making the occasional comment, while she busied herself. But he would never sit for long. If not working, he would announce: "Right, I'm off for my walk," and away he would go, for an hour or more. It helped his digestion, he said.

As Spring approached, his walks got longer. Sometimes she stood at the door, shaking out a mat or a blanket, but noting his direction. Sometimes, down the incline towards the Moor, usually upwards into King Street when, although quickly losing sight of him, she knew he would head towards Tatton on a route taking him right along the street, past the Post Office, the Royal George and the Angel before entering Mere Heath Lane which wound its way through pleasant countryside alongside Tatton Park. "A grand walk on a fine evening," he told her.

And then, this. Some called it a tragedy. Others, a mystery. But, for Charlotte, it was devastation.

The events of that Easter Sunday would stay with her for the rest of her life. She remembered how he had lifted his jacket from the back of the chair, how he had put it on, how he had extracted a letter from it, addressed to Mr W Leonard, Secretary, Society of Tailors, Cotton Street, Ashton-under-Lyne. Containing, he informed her, a postal order for £1 as part payment of subscriptions arrears. Made a bit of a show of it really. And, then, how he had smiled. "Cheerio." And, off up towards King Street. It was about 6 45pm, supper cleared away, and he would be out most of the evening. Bernard might go to bed before he returned but she would wait and keep the fire in for it looked like rain and he would be wet. She never saw him again. Worried out of her mind, she was, by midnight, and then her worst fears realised when the police banged on the door.

"He was an honest, straightforward man?" the coroner had asked of her.

"Yes."

"And did he ever speak of a love affair?"

"No. He had no sweetheart, as far as I know. Indeed, he had a dislike for the female," she replied. But he had looked at her in a certain way, she was sure of it. Sometimes she had jealously wondered if Bould might be meeting someone on his long excursions.

While Teresa Neagle was giving her controversial views to the Burnley newspaper, Pierce was holding a difficult conversation with Dr Smith about the facial bruising. Smith had already put him off once but when Pierce finally collared him he led him into his office and instructed him in precise terms that he would not entertain any more questioning about his report. Having already had a rocket from the coroner, he was in no mood to accept criticism from someone like Engberson who knew more about hemlines than corpses. Rather theatrically, he pulled out a paper from his file. "Look carefully," he said, tapping it with a finger. "Cause of death. Internal haemorrhage caused by a bullet entering his heart. That's what will be on the certificate. Nothing more to be said."

Pierce let it go. The doctor was right. The investigation was stuttering almost to a halt. Ignore Engberson. Forget Neagle. They desperately needed a real breakthrough, not a shoal of red herrings.

Little changed over the next few days. Knutsford life carried on as usual with the caveat that residents were warned to make sure their doors were bolted at night and not to wander alone along the lanes. But the police had the sinking feeling that the murderer was an outsider who had got away. If he were local, surely someone would have spotted something awry. Some out of character behaviour, nervousness, perhaps even blood on his clothes. Knutsford was a closed shop where everyone knew each other's business. Impossible to protect or hide a killer for any length of time and it was now well over a week since the shooting.

The railway timetable for Easter Sunday showed a train leaving Knutsford at 8 30pm in the direction of Manchester. Pierce could envisage him jumping into a carriage even as the train started to move, or even casually walking into the ticket office, hat pulled over his face, and asking for a single to Altrincham, or Manchester, anywhere really, and calmly mingling with other passengers on the platform or even in the waiting room. Their target, he was convinced now, was brutal, but as cool as a cucumber. Altogether a tricky customer.

But, if he had used the railway as an escape route, then what chance had they of nabbing him? He could be anywhere in the country by now, even abroad, Ireland maybe.

They had chased up the letter Bould had posted. It had arrived at the home of the Tailors' Society secretary, Mr William Leonard, who confirmed it contained a 20 shillings postal order and a brief note explaining it was to cover some of Bould's subscription arrears. They knew Bould in Ashton-under-Lyne, not well, but he had lived and worked in the area over the years. Okell wanted to follow this up – Ashton was a town full of radical mill workers and Irish nationalists and Bould might have had enemies there, but he accepted it would stretch their scant resources and would probably be a thankless task. Anyway, Knutsford itself had enough Irish to worry about. Tailors, hawkers, labourers, many with Irish origins, still wandered the country searching for jobs following the mass migrations of the 19th century and Knutsford attracted its fair share.

Another possible clue had also come to nought. During the search for a weapon, a constable had shouted: "Something here!" But not a gun – a two ounces empty pepper packet, damp but clearly labelled 'Hugh Fay and Co, cash grocer's'. How on earth had it got there? The Engbersons discounted any possibility that it was Bould's. Fay's had branches in various parts of Manchester and also in Salford. Superintendent Leah contacted the Manchester force and asked them to help. As a result Constable Charles Cummins popped into one of the shops not far from the Newton Street police station and discovered that a man who might fit the bill had bought the item a few days before Easter. But, pressed, he could not give a detailed description, just that he wore a suit, was clean shaven and carried an overcoat.

"Could be one of thousands," remarked Okell when he saw Cummins' report. "It doesn't take it any further." Later, the packet of pepper deserved more attention, and did not get it. For the moment, though, no-one could argue with Okell's verdict and, with that, came the full recognition that the police had nothing. Still no motive, no weapon, no direct witness. There were haystacks in the fields along Mere Heath Lane and Pierce had to smile because they were looking for a needle in one of them.

Yet it would have been a totally different story if they had interviewed all the witnesses at their disposal.

Mary Jane Francis, The Three Horsemen, John Parkes and his 'girl' Jessica Groucott, Hugh Daniel and George Toft, Thompson Flood and his wife Mary. Ten. All providing detailed accounts of what they saw. Parkes and the Floods had also talked of a man in Mere Heath Lane behaving rather strangely, but could not positively identify him. No proof then that he was the same figure seen by Mary Jane. It was all so vague. If you had pointed out to Pierce that there were other witnesses he would have laughed. Children were to be seen not heard.

It had been a pleasant Easter Sunday at the Floods' cottage just inside Tatton Park, a mile and a half or so along Mere Heath Lane from the town centre. The Tatton joiner Thompson Flood and his wife Mary had entertained three children, sisters Dorothy and Nora Jackson and their eight years-old friend Arthur Betteridge, as well as their toddler son Noel. After tea, the Floods walked the children back along the lane, intending to meet the sisters' father, Tom, at the junction with Garden Lane. Thompson pushed Noel's pram, the girls held hands, dancing and skipping along the verge. What they saw, both proceeding towards Knutsford and on the way back, was intriguing but inconclusive until 12 days later, Friday April 19, and a chance remark over breakfast at Orchard Cottage, home of the Jacksons.

Orchard Cottage, on the corner of Bexton Road and St John's Road, was geographically at the centre of Knutsford's justice system, with the police station, prison, courtrooms, workhouse and offices of the district's Board of Guardians grouped closely together, ideal for a busy solicitor's clerk like Tom Jackson. He originated from a large and well-established Knutsford family. There were Jacksons all over the town and, while he had dearly wanted a son to carry on the name, by 1901 he and Annie had five girls, Dorothy aged 11, Norah (10), Fanny (5), Edith (1) and Bessie (3 months).

Dorothy, Norah and Fanny had to go to school that Friday, the Egerton school built by Lord Egerton of Tatton, on Church Hill, just behind the Market Hall (which he had also paid for) and opposite the parish church. Over breakfast Tom mentioned to Annie that the best chance of solving the case was to find the mysterious man from Mere Heath Lane. No-one knew who he was.

"Oh, I do."

Dorothy had broken off from chatting to Norah. Tom and Annie, astonished, stared at their daughter who, unconcernedly, had gone back to her bowl of porridge.

"Pardon," said Annie.

"I know who he is. It's James Parrott."

Tom pushed back his chair. "Are you sure Dot? Why didn't you say so before?"

"No-one asked me but it's him."

Tom Jackson still had to be convinced. "But your aunt Mary didn't recognise him."

Dorothy looked at him sulkily. Father sometimes got like

this, talking like a teacher. "She doesn't really know him, does she? Anyway he looked straight at me. It was James Parrott."
Jackson shot out of his chair. Instead of school, Dorothy Jackson spent most of the morning at the police station. Mrs Pierce gave her a glass of lemonade. The sergeant asked her some questions and wrote it all down in his notebook. Then, she told Norah, and their friends Louisa and Daisy Flatters when they met in the girls' schoolyard later, "he patted me on the head and said I was brave and clever, so there."
Louisa looked doubtful. "What if that James Parrott finds out you told on him and he shoots you?"
A shadow flickered across her sister Daisy's face. Like the shadow which flitted across their front window in Tatton Street on Easter Sunday evening as she sat at the table, reading the neatly decorated card Lou had given her. Someone going quickly, running. Half an hour later a banging on the door, and her father and brother suddenly rushing away with the cart. Now Dot was talking about police and lemonade. Such excitement! But she had also heard her brother George saying: "He's got a gun and he'll use it again if he has to." Daisy hoped they caught him soon and put him in prison so that they would all be safe.
Dorothy's intervention did not prove that Parrott was the murderer. Not by any means. But, if they could tie it up with the other evidence to show that it was he bending over Bould's body, or, at least, that he was the Man At The Gate, they would have enough to question him and to search his home. They relayed the news to Chester. Leah promised to be right over.
Tom Jackson was in the thick of the action. After Dorothy's interview at the police station, he nipped along Love Lane to the Inman and Ashworth office on Heath Side and related the story to his employers. "Is she sure?" asked a shocked Edwin Ashworth.
"Yes," said Jackson. "It's hard to believe, I know. My own daughter. But you know how I trust her. She's not making it up. Good Lord, as if Mary Ann hasn't had enough to cope with."
Late on Friday afternoon, having been schooled by Okell and

Leah to be careful, not to cause unnecessary alarm, Pierce strode into the Parrotts' shop. The two superintendents thought it better for a familiar face to do the job. Two constables, Davies and Turner, were posted outside, front and back.

"Good afternoon Mrs Parrott. Is James around by any chance?"

Mary Ann sighed. She fully believed he had changed his ways. What was it now? Riding the train without a ticket?

"No, I'm sorry Sergeant. He's away working."

Pierce cursed silently. She thought he was in the Altrincham area somewhere, but was not certain. He had gone off without telling her much (as always) but said he would be back, probably at the weekend. Mary Ann looked bewildered. Pierce told her to keep him informed. He could do little more. The protocol was now to ask someone from the Altrincham station to make enquiries and, hopefully, find where Parrott was working or living.

The answer came back before mid-day on Saturday. Parrott was working at the Groves and Whitnall bottling plant in Altrincham's Market Place, while lodging at a house just off Victoria Road, close to the railway station. On the other side of the tracks was Mill Street where a certain George Rowe had a boot blacking factory....a small world.

Pierce made another visit to Mary Ann Parrott. She had received a postcard from her son, saying he would be back late that night. Why did the police want him? Refusing to be drawn, Pierce made his exit. Okell, who had been impressed by the sergeant's diligence, left him to it. Arrangements were made with Altrincham and at 9.30pm the sergeant received a call from them - Parrott was at the station. His train would arrive in Knutsford at 10 10pm. Pierce buttoned his tunic, donned his shako, checked the lamp hanging from his belt, and the whistle attached to a lanyard around his collar, said to to his wife: "I won't be long," and marched out to meet and greet a man who, for all he knew, was dangerous, armed and probably not too keen to be hanged.

The Floods, an artist's sketch. © Reach PLC

CHAPTER 7

'Good evening young man. I need to have a chat with you. Do you mind coming to the police station?' -
Sergeant William Pierce, April 20, 1901

B EFORE leaving for further duties in the Anglo-Boer War, Dr Harry Washington Pritchard made a public pronouncement, along the lines of: 'I know nothing.'

Pritchard was keen to refute the malicious rumours shrouding the case and leaving a black cloud over his family, one of the most notable in Manchester. The story of The Three Horsemen had ignited almost two weeks of innuendo and suspicion which his father, Alderman William Bridgett Pritchard, and older brother William Bridgett junior, were anxious to dispel. Their good name was at stake.

Pritchard, due to board a Liverpool ship bound for The Cape and given licence to miss the inquest when it resumed on April 24, had already provided a written statement to the Chief Constable but, on the eve of his departure, thought it a good move to go public.

After a preamble in which he wanted to make it clear that he should not be 'confounded' with Mr W B Pritchard (MRCS) of 272 Oxford Street, Manchester *(his brother)*, Pritchard said he, his brother-in-law George Rowe and a mutual friend, Harry Yarwood, had ridden to Knutsford for Sunday tea 'as was their frequent practice'. Leaving the Royal George in the early evening they rode at walking pace through the streets. Yarwood was on a restless horse, a hunter.

"The next thing that happened," he said, "was that I went on ahead because my horse was pulling and trotting and, consequently, I got a bit in front of my brother-in-law and Yarwood. I did not see anybody in Mere Heath Lane until I saw Miss Francis. It was raining very hard and she was putting on her cloak. I said to her, jocularly, 'Shall I help you?' She said something in reply which I did not catch and laughed. I trotted on with my head down and did not look back at all.

"There was a gatekeeper's cottage on the side of the road and I saw two men come out of a gate what abuts the road, 20 or 30 yards from the cottage. I continued on and, at the end of the lane, I saw two or three people but took absolutely no notice of them. When I got to the hotel at Bucklow Hill (*the Swan*) I dismounted and went in for shelter. About five minutes later Mr Rowe and Mr Yarwood came up at a trot. I invited them to come in for some refreshment but they answered, no, it was too wet and we rode straight home."

When asked about what might have happened between Rowe and Miss Francis, Pritchard told the reporter: "I don't know anything." But he said Rowe had told him he had spoken to her, a casual remark about it being so wet, while he was off his horse, wiping his saddle and while Yarwood waited for him. Just as Rowe re-mounted and they rode off, Yarwood heard shots in the distance.

Pritchard's account seems straightforward. The men he saw near the cottage were Hugh Daniel and George Toft, on their way into Knutsford and the people he encountered at the end of the lane were probably the Floods, completing their return trip and nearing their home in Tatton Dale.

Clearly, Pritchard had nothing to do with the murder nor with the alleged assault on Mary Jane. He was well away from all the action. But his statement did not absolve him in the eyes of the conspiracy theorists who still claimed that Bould's death was an assassination, planned by men with military experience. Nor did it smooth over the ruckus in the Pritchard/Rowe household. If Pritchard thought he had cleared the air, he was mistaken. He knew nothing, but someone did – perhaps George Rowe - and when he sailed for the Cape to re-join the Field Ambulance Unit of the East Lancashire Regiment he left behind a simmering stew of questions and recriminations.

What really stirred the pot was the brief encounter at Knutsford railway station on Saturday April 20 between a sturdily built police sergeant and a wisp of a young man named James Crossley Parrott. Pierce had told the station staff that he was simply meeting a witness. He wanted everything to look normal. The '10 10' steamed in, clanked to a halt, and a couple of carriage doors opened. Out stepped Parrott.

"Parrott!" Pierce called out. Parrott turned, shrugged his shoulders, put a hand in his pocket and waited.

"Good evening young man," said Pierce. "I need to have a chat with you. Do you mind coming to the police station?"

A remarkable show of bravado, or simply Pierce's phlegmatic character. Whichever, it must go down in criminal history as one of the coolest ways of dealing with a possibly armed killer. Pierce, on his own and without any back-up, had no way of knowing whether Parrott was gripping a revolver butt in his pocket. He did not search him. They walked out of the railway station, turned right up the hill, across Toft Road, and along Love Lane around the back of the prison. Even at a steady pace, it took five or six minutes. Parrott could have made a run for it at any moment. Or pulled out a gun.

And then something even more incomprehensible. Pierce opened the door of his police house, invited Parrott into the kitchen, sat him down at the table and asked his wife to brew some tea.

As Parrott made himself at home, the sergeant sat opposite and launched the most important interrogation of his career so far by asking pleasantly: "Now Parrott, have you any objection to informing me where you were on Easter Sunday evening?" Pierce may have hoped that, full of remorse and with a cup of tea in front of him, Parrott would break down and confess. Not so. He had an alibi.

Basically, the first of two stories which Parrott gave to the sergeant was that on Easter weekend he had visited his brother Thomas Holland Parrott, who had a job in Liverpool and was lodging there. He stayed with him on the Saturday night and on Easter Sunday morning he took a train to Manchester and then walked the 16 miles to Knutsford. He was used to long walks. Approaching Knutsford, his route took him along Manchester Road, past the Blue Bell farm and straight into the town. He went to the railway station, then to the nearby Sword and Sceptre (aka Legh Arms) for a quick drink, and then home. No – he was not wearing an overcoat.

No - he did not have a revolver with him and had never owned one. No – he was never in Mere Heath Lane.

The detail of that conversation comes later but the upshot was that Pierce asked Parrott to stand and told him: "James Crossley Parrott, I am arresting you for the wilful murder of John Bould."

This, the author believes, is the only time that an alleged murderer has been arrested after having a cup of tea in a police sergeant's kitchen.

Parrott's immediate reply was one of total innocence. "You are on the wrong track. I did not do it." But Pierce had no hesitation in leading him across the yard and placing him in the cell block, or 'bridewell' as it was nicknamed. Parrott was lying, he was sure of it. As the clock ticked towards midnight, Pierce set the justice process in motion, calling Chester HQ, ordering Constable Turner to pull in a few locals to form an identity parade for the following morning, and then leaving Constables Davies and Jones in charge of the office while he strolled the 30 yards along Bexton Road to Tom Jackson's house. His 11 years-old girl would be needed to pick out Parrott at the parade. And Tom would sort out his solicitor to act on Parrott's behalf.

This, the author further suspects, is the only time in a murder enquiry where one man has supplied an essential prosecution witness from his own family and also an advocate for the defence from the firm which employed him. To complete the circle. the Jacksons were also closely connected to Mary and Thompson Flood and to the Parrott ensemble. Now James was on a murder charge and 'Little Dot' Jackson could help to send him to the gallows.

Parrott's arrest late on a Saturday gave the police a little leeway before the news broke in the Press. But it could not be kept completely quiet. Mary Ann was at the police station immediately, demanding an explanation from Pierce, and one of the railway porters John Webb who had seen Pierce and Parrott walking off the platform was soon recounting the tale to regulars in the Sword and Sceptre, one of whom was Our Knutsford Correspondent. However it was too late to get into the morning papers.

On Sunday morning, Tom took Dorothy around to the police station, through a crowd of onlookers and through the yard gate, his arm around her shoulders. Pierce, Okell, and a couple of constables were waiting. Dorothy was told not to be afraid, but to go into the next room where she would see some people. All she had to do was to point out the man she saw in Mere Heath Lane and whom she had later said was James Parrott.

"That's all," said the sergeant. "It will be over a jiffy."

Dorothy was interested, not afraid. In the adjacent room she saw a number of men, six or eight standing in a line, but took only a moment to pick out Parrott who looked straight at her, as he had done that night. She pointed. "Him," she said. Parrott smiled. Pierce said: "Are you sure?" and she nodded.

Later her father commented: "It wasn't difficult, was it?"

"No," said Dot. "I know him, don't I? Anyway he was the only one with spectacles."

Pierce was on a roll. Things were moving in the right direction. After arresting Parrott and locking him up, he had traipsed down to King Street to knock on Mrs Parrott's door. Although the early hours of the morning, lights were showing and she opened up immediately. She looked weary and worried. Pierce felt sorry for her, but could not afford to show it.

"I need to search the house, Mrs Parrott," he said tersely.

In the hall a long, dark brown overcoat hung from a hook. He took it, rifled its pockets and pulled out some small change, a few postage stamps and a replica revolver, a toy gun as it was later described, not capable of firing bullets. Interesting, but probably not relevant. Mary Ann looked on anxiously. "Where does he sleep?" he demanded, sounding more aggressive than he wished. She led him up the stairs but stayed outside the bedroom while he rooted around. Pierce found two boxes, one made of tin and fastened with a couple of nails which he prised open to uncover:

a yellow leather purse, containing a farthing and a half farthing similar to coins owned by Bould;

a notebook with betting entries;

a pawn ticket for a swordstick, with the name of Parrott's

uncle Alfred Islip on it;

an empty leather embossed gun case with the serial number erased but bearing the logo the Colt Firearms Manufacturing Company, London.

He took the items and overcoat back to the station and, although disappointed that there was no sign of the gun, Pierce was pleased with himself. Even more so when a few hours later, shortly before the identity parade, he interviewed Parrott for a second time, again in the kitchen of the police house but slightly more formally than the previous evening and with far more success.

As Parrott emerged from his cell to get a wash and tidy himself for the line-up, he glanced at the overcoat which Pierce had laid provocatively across the table. It appeared to spark something. "Oh sergeant," Parrott said, casually. "I told you wrong last night. I had that overcoat on when I walked from Manchester. I borrowed it from my brother. And I made a mistake in saying I came down the Manchester Road past the Blue Bell farm. I came down Mere Heath Lane..."

Pierce's recollection was that Parrott blurted out this revelation almost by chance. When he sat down to answer further questioning, he continued to re-organise his original alibi for several minutes. Why? Probably because he knew by then of Dorothy Jackson's intervention, placing him close to the murder site. When he saw the overcoat he also realised that Pierce had searched his home. Best to come clean about his movements, although he continued to deny the central accusation.

It suggests a nimble brain, and, as the case progressed, it became evident that the lightweight Parrott, who could walk long distances and run fast, could think quickly on his feet.

According to Pierce, Parrott came out with one admission after another in that most extraordinary interview. Firstly, the coat. Parrott had originally claimed he was not wearing one, therefore could not be the killer. Now he recalled having borrowed it from John who, although five years younger, was much taller.

Then, the route into Knutsford. Coming from Manchester, a walker had a clear choice - to continue along the main thoroughfare, Manchester Road, taking him past the Blue Bell Farm on the left, then past The Heath on the right and into the town centre; or at the Swan Hotel, Bucklow Hill, to turn left for a more winding and picturesque stroll along the lane bordering Tatton Park. Eventually the lane and the main road ran parallel, separated by farmland. If in Manchester Road, Parrott would not have had a clue as to events in the lane and could not be linked to the murder. But, now, with Dorothy Jackson pointing the finger, he was saying: "Oh, yes, I was in Mere Heath Lane."

While that went some way to 'clarify' the situation, his next admission really spiced up the confessional.

"And I forgot to tell you," he went on. "I have had a revolver. I bought it some months ago from Colt's with some cartridges. "

Undemonstrative as he was, Pierce features tightened with the tension of that moment. All he needed now was for Parrott to tell him where the gun was. It seemed that, after weeks of frustration, everything was coming together. And he, Sergeant William Pierce, had cracked it. But, almost immediately, any euphoria was quickly doused. Parrot added: "I paid about £4 for it but I sold it the last Saturday I was in Liverpool to a sailor in the street for 50 shillings."

When later he looked through his notes, written in pencil on blue foolscap paper, Pierce rocked back in his chair and, privately, made his own admission, "We haven't got anything like enough."

Now the public focus switched from victim to alleged murderer. Mary Ann Parrott soon got fed up with people knocking on her door to inquire after her health and: 'Oh, is it true that they've arrested James?' She spent some time at the police station, asking to see him, and handing over some food – he did not eat much, but she could not stand the thought of him surviving on gaol rations. Thankfully, Tom Jackson was as helpful as ever, promising it would be alright, he would have the best possible solicitor and barrister, Edwin

Ashworth and Lance Bentley working for him. James, he said, would appear before the magistrates the next day and would be remanded in custody. The police needed her to make a statement and they might also ask his brother John.

Parrott's revised story spurred Pierce and his constables into action. Among a list of new witnesses were Mary Ann and John Parrott, Robert Lee, the licensee, and others at the Sword and Sceptre, and porters at the railway station. Superintendent Leah was to contact officers in Manchester and Altrincham to verify Parrott's claim of arriving in Manchester on Easter Sunday and then walking to Knutsford, taking him through the city and the districts of Stretford, Sale and Altrincham. Leah also had to ring the Liverpool force, to check Parrott's story that he had spent the Saturday before Easter Sunday at the house in Walton where his brother, Thomas Holland Parrott, was staying. Also, he wondered, could Liverpool possibly locate a certain seaman? No, he did not have a name. No, he did not know which ship he served on. But, it was important to find him. Perhaps a few bill posters in the docks area?

With Parrott back in a cell, and behaving like a model prisoner, Pierce and Okell got their heads together. They had a mass of evidence but all circumstantial, nothing which would guarantee a conviction and, with pressure mounting on every side, they had no time to lose. The inquest was set to resume on the coming Wednesday, April 24 and while his first appearance in court today was little more than a formality, they could not expect the magistrates to continually remand Parrott in custody while they searched for more clues. Some day soon, probably no more than two weeks away, they would be ordered to present Parrott for committal, meaning they needed to produce enough evidence to warrant sending him for trial at Chester Assizes. With such a tight deadline, Pierce's main worry was that, having shredded his original story Parrott now appeared to be one step ahead all the time. He had made certain admissions but strenuously denied the charge.

"Get on to the girl Francis," Okell suggested as he and Pierce debated the best way forward. "When you first saw her she said she thought the man leaning over Bould was the same she had seen earlier at the gate, and we know now that that was Parrott because Tom Jackson's girl has identified him. Francis seems to have changed her mind, keeps saying that now she can't be sure. Let's have another chat with her. Show her the overcoat. What else have we got?"

Pierce was a methodical man. He lined up the exhibits on the office desk, the coat, the toy gun, the purse, the betting book and the gun case and pointed to each one in turn.

"John Parrott has confirmed that the coat is his and that he let James use it that weekend when he went to Liverpool. He also says the toy gun is his too. Now that James has said he wore the coat, it's only useful to us if one of the witnesses can recognise it properly.

"The purse is a possibility. I don't know about the coins. The book has got a record of bets. If we can find he has lost money heavily, that could be a motive for robbery, but we're already doubtful about that because Bould was poor.

"As for the gun, perhaps the Colt Company tomorrow will turn up a record of selling one to Parrott, but, as you can see, the serial number has been rubbed off. They sell thousands of guns so it might take a while for them to find what we need. Parrott says he erased the number because he was thinking of using the case to make a jewellery box."

Okell looked at his sergeant. "What do you make of that?"

"It's difficult, sir. He seems to have an answer for everything. It's not that he is denying having a gun."

"No." Okell grimaced. "He had one, just happened to sell it to some sailor he bumped into in Liverpool. Hardly likely is it? But it's not for him to prove anything. It's up to us."

Without the murder weapon, the police faced all sorts of difficulties. In its absence their best chance lay in persuading Mary Jane Francis that her instinct was correct, that her immediate impression that the man bending over Bould was the one she had seen earlier, Parrott. Another avenue to pursue was the pigskin purse. Could it be definitely identified as Bould's? Pierce took it to Swinton Square to show to the Engbersons. Charlotte handled it carefully. "It looks the same," she said. Bernard agreed but neither could say for certain. "What about the bruises?" he asked. Pierce sighed and left them. Normally he would have marched up Church Hill to get back to the station but people were just leaving church, a number coming in his direction, and, partly to avoid being waylaid by questions and comments, he veered right to stride along the relatively quiet King Street. He passed the Royal George where the Three Horsemen had enjoyed Sunday afternoon 'tea' and where, only a few weeks earlier he had been inducted into the de Tabley Lodge, ensuring that if he stayed in the force long enough, without making too many mistakes, he would one day be promoted to inspector. At the White Lion corner he turned left up Minshull Street, glancing into Lance Bentley's office. Bentley would have been at church, showing – or, rather, ordering – people into their correct places in his role of churchwarden. Pierce recalled a story he had heard about Bentley actually kicking someone out of a service because they had sat in someone else's pew. Apparently the best ones were rented by the elite and no-one could use them, even if they were empty. Bentley would serve Parrott well in court.

At the top of Minshull Street, Pierce thought about popping in to see Henry Flatters, the carter who had helped remove Bould's body. He had not had chance to speak to him since, although Constable Davies who lived opposite, chatted to him regularly. Pierce also remembered that he had to sort out a licensing matter with Annie Jackson, mine hostess at The Feathers. There had been a row over the piggeries at the rear of her premises, someone claiming it was unhealthy. Even in the midst of a murder enquiry he had routine matters to deal with. But now was not the time. He continued through Northwich Street, past the White Bear and onto Heath Side.

Mary Jane Francis said she wanted to help but that night....it was getting dark, she was upset, it was a long way away. How could she be sure that it was the same man? Yes, she had thought so at the time. Now, thinking about it, she could not swear to God. She sat at the table, fist clenched.

"I'm sorry sergeant. People keep asking me about the man who was shot, poor soul, but what about me? I was molested. Will that man be arrested? People are saying all sorts of dreadful things about me. I thought Knutsford was a nice place. Not now, I don't. My family want me to go home."

Pierce expressed sympathy. "I'm sure they know best. But for the time being we need you here. The coroner might need you again, and we will certainly want to have another chat."

Jane Pickstock tried to show him out by the rear door but Pierce, who had heard Mr Speakman grumbling about 'another interruption' insisted on leaving through the front. This was a murder investigation. But, as he marched back to the station, hoping a good Sunday dinner would be waiting for him, the doubts mounted. He had drawn another blank.

In his cell, Parrott stuck a spoon into a shepherd's pie brought by his mother. He ate slowly, sparingly. Mary Ann had often gently chided him for his lack of interest in food. "You need to build yourself up, James." Once, she said irritably: "If you're not careful you'll go the same way as your father – you're as thin as a rake." She regretted it instantly, of course. James had merely smiled. He quite enjoyed making people lose their temper.

The pie was well-made but cold. He messed around with it, pushing bits around the dish, contemplating. Tomorrow he would meet his lawyer, Bentley. Introductions would be unnecessary. Bentley was one of Knutsford's top nobs, into all sorts. He assisted the vicar, the Reverend Henry Barnacle at each church service. He was a member of the recently formed urban district council and, as such, heavily involved in planning issues. He and Tom Jackson were as thick as thieves. The grave of Bentley's two young sons sat close to that of Parrott's father and grandfather in the parish church yard. Parrott mused about the interplay of Knutsford society, yet, although born in King Street and baptised by Reverend Barnacle, he often felt outside of it all. Mind you, there was good reason for that. Was it his fault, this sense that he did not belong anywhere?

Except perhaps in a cell?

The Knutsford police station of 1901, now a private
residence. The entrance to the yard and cells is on the right

CHAPTER 8

*'In the dock he bore himself with nobility and
betrayed no outward concern for the gravity of his
position.' - Manchester Guardian, April 1901*

P arrott was an overnight hit. Newspapers throughout
Britain trumpeted the arrest in similar style to that
of the Manchester Evening News who headlined it as
their main story: 'The Knutsford Murder, Sensational Arrest'.
Pierce let him read his copy. He held it close to his face but
seemed unconcerned. So much so that Pierce caught him
glancing at the racecourse betting odds on the adjacent page
and snatched the paper away. 'A strange bird,' he said to
himself. A young man charged with murder should surely
be showing signs of stress but Parrott was quiet and polite,
giving nothing away. Just the occasional twitch at the side
of his mouth, otherwise impassive. In court that morning
he had stood in the dock, upright and attentive, one hand
behind his back, only changing stance once to lean over the
brass dock rail and mutter something to Tom Jackson who
passed it on to Lance Bentley. All his family were there, Mary
Ann, his sisters and brothers, yet he scarcely gave them so
much as a blink.

Parrott had been steered into the smaller, number two
court at the Sessions House where 100 people jammed into
the public gallery, and hundreds more lined the corridors,
covered the cobbled frontage, and spilled out into the road.
Queues had formed outside the court an hour before the
scheduled 11am start, and Leicester Caldecutt, the clerk,
had to push his way through the crowd to gain admission.
It was almost 11 30am when the hearing got under way.
For a minute or two while documents were sorted and the
courtroom settled down, Parrott stayed seated. Caldecutt
told him to stand, automatically silencing the remnants of
whispered conversations in the gallery, and the prisoner
obeyed, moving to the front of the dock.

"James Crossley Parrott." Caldecutt's voice filled the room.

"The charge is that you, on the seventh of April 1901 in the township of Knutsford, feloniously, wilfully and with malice aforethought did kill and murder one John Bould."

Only then did the enormity of it all strike home. Mary Ann's shoulders sagged. For a few awful seconds all that could be heard were the muffled sobs of her daughter Edith, a shifting of feet in the public seats, and a squeak from his leather cushioned seat as Lance Bentley rose to indicate that he was acting on the defendant's behalf. No plea needed to be taken at this early stage, and Parrott stayed silent and upright, appearing to stare into the distance. Superintendent Leah, temporarily acting as prosecutor, asked for a remand in custody for two days based on evidence of identification, at which Dorothy Jackson made her first of several appearances on the public stage over the next three months.

LITTLE "DOT" GIVES HER EVIDENCE.

Dorothy Jackson in the witness box - an artist's sketch. © Reach PLC

'Little Dot' as the Press christened her, gave a nerveless performance, smiling at her father and confirming that she had seen Parrott both in Mere Heath Lane and at the identity parade. Wearing a white frock and a wide-brimmed straw hat, her 'rosy cheeks and golden curls completed a pretty picture out of harmony with the surroundings' wrote the inspired Manchester Evening News reporter. He also described Parrott as 'a slightly built young fellow, a mere boy in appearance with a thin, fair moustache and short sandy hair'.

Bentley did not question Dorothy, reserving his cross-examination, and the magistrates Francis Ashworth and Major Thomas Davies ordered Parrott to stay in police custody until at least the following Wednesday when he had the option of attending the resumed inquest. Colonel Hammersley, holding a watching brief, promised Bentley that he and his solicitor would have every opportunity 'within the law' to talk to their client. It was, as those in court work termed it, a quick 'up and downer'. Over in a few minutes, setting the pace of the case over the next 10 days. Speed, rather than accuracy and completeness, was the hallmark of The Crown versus James Crossley Parrott.

Later, after a short conversation with his legal team, Parrott was led back to the police station where Pierce had to negotiate another bunch of spectators, some of them from the workhouse opposite.

Mary Ann had appeared with another meal for her son but he seemed more interested in the newspaper until Pierce re-possessed it. "Never known anything like it," he grumbled to Constable Davies. "He's just come out of court charged with murder and there he is looking up the odds."

"He's a gambler," Davies offered. "That notebook with all the racing entries. And his brother says that he went to Haydock races on Easter Saturday and lost money."

Pierce was anti-gambling. One of the curses of the working class – he frequently lectured family and junior colleagues on it. Newspapers were a disgrace, giving betting so much publicity. He was not on his own. Some papers printed race odds on their main news pages, stoking up criticism from the Anti-Gambling League.

Pierce had heard about the Knutsford races of old, a grand annual event on the Heath where big money changed hands. Thankfully, in his view, it had come to a halt in 1873.

He would not have enjoyed policing something like that, with all its attendant evils. No, the biggest event nowadays on Knutsford's social calendar was the Royal May Day procession and the crowning of the May Queen, and that was bad enough, for amid all the innocent pageantry, there were the usual troublemakers, sodden with drink.

And that was another blot on working class life. Booze. Britain was awash with it. Pubs and beer houses all over the place. Knutsford, a small town, boasted 26 licensed victuallers, eight beer sellers, and nine off-licences.

Pierce did not mind a man having a glass of ale after a good day's work, but too many lived by it. Weak stuff, yes, but at tuppence a pint, even the poorest paid labourer could sup his fill before swaying home to demand his supper and play hell if it was not ready. Life for some women was hard. He thought fleetingly of Mary Ann Parrott, face straining, as she watched her son in the dock that morning. And maybe he himself had not been that easy to live with over the last few days. It would not do any harm to praise his wife Anne for the liver and bacon he had attacked with a vengeance at dinner time. She had a way with liver and bacon.....

Lance Bentley was jubilant. The case would eventually go to trial, and a more senior barrister would soon enter the fray, but for now, he had control of it and he had quickly made his mark that morning. Of course, it helped that two close associates of his were the magistrates, Ashworth and Davies. There had seemed no point in questioning Dorothy. Bentley had seen her grow up, initially when the Jacksons lived in the Freeholders' Cottages on Love Lane, and then at Orchard Cottage which was just around the corner from his own home. A delightful little girl and no need to put her through cross-examination - Parrott now fully acknowledged his presence in the lane. But Bentley felt that he had stamped his identity on the affair. He was forthright, speaking in an authoritative but respectful manner. And, maybe, just maybe, he could steal the thunder of leading counsel by halting the case before it reached Chester. The evidence gathered so far was painfully thin and, if the police had a card up their sleeve, then he would like to see it.

The gun was a possibility. Parrott persisted with his excuse that he had sold it to a seaman in Liverpool on a Saturday night after visiting Haydock races. Vague, but of virtue because it would be impossible to disprove unless it was found – and that, now, was unlikely.

Whether Parrott was a murderer or not, Bentley sniffed some personal glory. And why not? Here was a man who challenged for the title of Mr Knutsford, who had worked tirelessly for the town, was secretary of the Conservative Association, and various other organisations, and the future chairman of the urban district council. Indeed, he would soon take over from a certain Francis Ashworth, Justice of the Peace, who had held the post for three years. But that was all on a local scale, with this case his name would be plastered over all Britain, especially if he could engineer Parrott's early discharge.

Bentley had channeled all his energy into public life following the death of his and Mary's first child, Lance jnr, aged four, in 1875. They were delighted when Mary gave birth to a second son Henry Lance but he, too, died in his fifth year, joining the brother he never knew in a grave at the side of the path leading to the parish church's west door. That was in 1887, a fortnight after Parrott's father Tom had been buried nearby. Luckily the Bentleys also had daughters who survived into adulthood.

That Monday night, Tom Jackson visited Parrott in the police cell, then Bentley at his house Hazelmere in St John's Road, a round trip of about 300 yards.

"He is sticking to it," Jackson reported, tapping his bowler against his thigh.

"Right, unless they find the gun and pin it to Parrott, we have a chance." Bentley was bright and breezy.

"What about the purse?" asked Jackson. He sounded less optimistic. "It looks like the one Bould had. He would have had it in his pocket, maybe the one that was turned inside out. Parrott says the one they found in his house is his, not Bould's, but I'm not happy about it."

Bentley patted his jacket sleeve. "If the police have got something up theirs, you should see what I've got up mine."

Strolling back to Orchard Cottage, Jackson wondered whether Bentley's cavalier approach might go awry. It was no time for games. He had promised Mary Ann that all would be well, a rash pledge, accepted, but she needed a crumb of hope. Dorothy broke into his musings. "Father, did James Parrott kill that man?" He might have struggled for an appropriate answer but she did not wait. "Because if he didn't, Daisy Flatters says I'd better watch out. The man who really did it might come for me."

Jackson told her to take no notice of Daisy Flatters. If James was innocent, and he was still to reach a personal verdict on that, then the murderer must be an outsider, well away from Knutsford now. No-one could hide a killer for long in such a tightly knit community. Anxious to lighten the conversation, he asked her how the dance practice was progressing.

"Very well," said Dorothy, giving him a twirl and a roll of her arms.

He laughed. "You'll be the star of the show."

Dorothy laughed with him. A lively youngster, the apple of her father's eye, and over the next 10 days he would watch proudly as she danced between leading roles in the witness box and the Royal May Day festival, enthralling spectators all the way. Meanwhile, he had work to do. Parrott's arrest had invested sudden impetus into the case. Police were stepping up their enquiries into his past, whether there was any history between him and Bould. In Liverpool bills were posted around the docks, requesting information about the mysterious sailor whom Parrott claimed had bought his gun. In Manchester, Constable Charles Cummins, armed with a description of Parrott's features, went back to various branches of Fay's the grocers to make another check about the sale of pepper to a man who vaguely resembled him, and in London an officer from Scotland Yard visited the prestigious offices of the Colt's Firearms Manufacturing Company in Pall Mall.

People who did not know Parrott quickly became better acquainted with him thanks to the Press and, in the absence of photographs, its capacity for descriptive writing.

Reporters were encouraged to go into great detail, although occasionally they got things wrong, as in his age.

'....he is twenty years of age but he looks a mere youth, whose slender build with pale, thin features suggest no great physical strength.' That is how the Manchester Guardian viewed him on his first appearance in court. Their report continued: 'He wore glasses. In the dock he bore himself with nobility and betrayed no outward concern for the gravity of his position.'

This blend of fact and subjective comment characterised most reporting of the day, particularly in the popular Press, and could be deeply influential. By Tuesday morning, hundreds of thousands of readers had a sympathetic portrait of an alleged murderer. No more than a young lad. And needs spectacles! How could he possibly have shot a man to death? And it says here in the paper he showed 'nobility'.....

This freedom of the Press was in stark contrast to court reporting in later times when a paper and its reporter who gave away details likely to prejudice a trial could be hauled before a judge and punished for contempt. It was serious stuff, demanding rigid adherence to the rules, whereas the author's 1901 predecessor would have scribbled a pageful of words, or battered them out on a heavy, black typewriter, a new Underwood if he were lucky, with his editor demanding more 'colour'.

Pierce was worried about newspaper intrusion, but there was nothing he could do about it and, to be fair, the police took advantage of the Press when necessary, making various appeals for information and, of course, they had their own paper, the Illustrated Police News. What he disliked was the public getting the wrong idea, that Parrott's mere physique automatically placed him among life's innocents. It did not always work like that. Both he and Superintendent Okell would confirm that, having dealt with the Davies brothers 10 years earlier. Appalling, that was...

Richard Davies was 19, his brother George, 16. They lived near Crewe in Cheshire, and, with their mother, were subjected to long-term bullying and abuse from their father, a merchant. Eventually the brothers agreed to kill him, which one of them did with a hatchet, as they rode alongside him on their horse and cart. Leaving him by the roadside, they claimed that they had been waylaid by two men, but Okell and Superintendent Jesse Leah – father of the current 'Super'– quickly saw through it and brought them to trial at Chester where they were sentenced to death. Despite their youth the law gave the judge no choice, although the jury recommended mercy, and a national outcry followed. Public opinion, generally, was that George, at least, should be spared. He was little more than a child and looked it. But petition after petition to the Home Secretary and to Queen Victoria fell on deaf ears, the counter argument being that while their father was a brute he did not deserve to die. Murder was murder and, despite the difference in ages, the brothers were equally culpable.

Richard and George Davies were on Death Row at Knutsford Prison. Crowds gathered outside. Many were in tears at the thought of a small, 16 years-old boy going to the scaffold. With a few days left, the Home Secretary relented and reprieved George, death being commuted to life imprisonment. Some, including members of the jury, continued to fight for Richard but there was no escape. Deeply religious, he wrote two moving letters to his family. In one, he told his mother: 'I never struck my father on the night of his death. I never had the axe in my hand.' In the second he implied that his brother, whose fresh-faced youth had earned so much sympathy, was the real killer.

'I am glad that George has been reprieved,' he wrote, 'though he will live a hard life. But, dear Mother, I thank God I have told the truth, although I have not been able to prove it on earth, but dear ones, God will prove it at our next trial, which will be the great Judgement Day, if it is not proved sooner. I hope George will confess it some day and then you will see.'

The public executioner James Berry hung him at Knutsford with a six feet drop. To the end he protested his innocence. The surgeon Dr Theodre Fennell pronounced death as instantaneous and, agreeing with him, the coroner, H C Yates recorded that the hanging was carried out as 'humanely as possible' within the law.

Judge for yourself. This is exactly what happened, and what, with little amendment, threatened James Parrott. Davies, remember, was only 19, still a youth, even in the days when children could legally start work at age 13.

A large crowd gathered outside the gaol gates at 7 30am that morning April 9 1890. Ten minutes later a group of reporters were allowed in and led along corridors by the prison governor, Captain Price, to the condemned cell. Already waiting by the cell door was the chaplain, Reverend William Truss, in his surplice and holding a prayer book and at 7 50am the prison bell began to toll. At 7 55am, Berry appeared with the acting Under Sheriff Walter Gregg. They entered the cell, tied Davies's arms behind his back and brought him out, his face pale and his lips moving in prayer. A procession formed, a warder on either side of Davies, the chaplain and governor in front, the under sheriff, executioner and reporters behind. The prisoner's head was bowed but he walked steadily, continuing to murmur a prayer. Stepping into the open yard, which they had to cross to reach the hanging shed, Berry suddenly moved forward and placed a white hood over Davies's head, guiding him the remaining 40 yards.

"We went into a rather small room with whitewashed walls," an observer said. "A rope dangling from a blackened beam over two black painted trapdoors revealed this was the place where Richard Davies would breathe his last. Berry led him to stand over the drop and deftly pinioned his ankles. Then, while the rope – a new one sent from the Home Office - was being adjusted the poor youth exclaimed: 'O Lord, to Thee I commend my spirit; receive it for Christ's sake.' The last word had barely escaped his lips when Berry touched the lever and the body of Richard Davies disappeared into the pit."

In his autobiography, Berry explained the exact preparations for a hanging. He thought the public should be aware of the care he took.

'For successful working the rope must be strong, and also pliable in order to tighten freely. It should be as thin as possible, consistent with the strength, so that the noose may be free running, but it must not be so thin as to outwardly rupture the blood vessels of the neck'. (Berry later cut up his rope and sold it in sections).

The scaffold was erected and dismantled – carefully, so that it could be used again - by Home Office engineers. It consisted mainly of a heavy cross beam, bolted, and with hooks for the rope; a platform with two three inches thick oak trapdoors over a brick built pit. The door hinges rested on a draw-bar which, when activated by the hangman's pull of a lever, released the trap. Berry used the 'long drop' method which involved weight and distance calculations, designed to instantly sever the spinal cord, avoiding strangulation. In Richard Davies's case, the body was left to hang for a while before being cut down. Fennell claimed that the actual execution, once Davies had stepped onto the trap, had taken five seconds. Berry said he had met his end bravely and with great self-control. But this was one of the executions which gave him nightmares for years and persuaded him to quit and to campaign against capital punishment. Davies was a journeyman tailor.

Pierce figured that, when he faced a jury, Parrott might well win a sympathy vote. On the other hand, if convicted by sheer weight of evidence, he would certainly be hanged. No amount of petition signing would save a 21 years-old man who had pumped five bullets into another, so deliberately, and, seemingly, without provocation. Unless..the possibility of insanity suddenly popped into Pierce's rationalising. The hangman waited in the shadows yet Parrott perused the horse racing news. Strange to say the least, but insane – not in his book.

In the build-up to the resumed inquest, the word 'strange' featured regularly as journalists dug into the prisoner's antecedents. 'Our Knutsford Correspondent' used his contacts well during this period. Knutsford born and bred, he played football and cricket for local teams, consorted regularly with councillors, lawyers and traders in the White Lion and The Angel, and on Friday nights joined the riff-raff of his youth in the Cross Keys and the Rose and Crown. "Get some background on him," he was ordered.

It was fairly easy. A quick trawl of the shops where managers and assistants were eager to offer some inside 'gen' provided sufficient material for a holding story, little more than speculation and gossip, but enough to satisfy the evening paper news editors until he could grab hold of someone of more substance later in the day. Bentley maybe. He always liked to see his name in the paper. Caldecutt might be worth a visit, too. Just before Easter the reporter had compiled an article about the coming cricket season, referring to the Clerk to the Justices as one of the town's sporting champions. Surely that was worth an interview, perhaps to discuss the arrangements for the resumed inquest?

Back in the office, the reporter shifted the cumbersome Underwood into position, inserted three sheets of A5 copy paper interspersed with two of red carbon and typed out his story. Though his fingers sped over the keys, it was a laborious exercise. Each page had to be numbered, with only one paragraph on the first – the 'intro' – and no more than three on subsequent sheets. The top copy went into the editor's tray, the two carbons were jabbed onto separate spikes, lethal metal rods on wooden bases, for future reference. Satisfied with his morning's work, he ambled up the street for a well-earned draught at the White Lion.

The article which appeared in the regional daily Press was based on the words of the Knutsford Correspondent but included contributions from reporters in other towns where Parrott had previously worked, including Ashton-under-Lyne and Altrincham. The overall picture was that of a loner, kept himself to himself, only spoke when necessary (and, sometimes, not even then), was as 'tight as a drum' with his money, and – according to one of the locals – 'was a bit queer', referring not to sexuality but to his peculiar habits. One man who had lodged in the same house as Parrott when he worked briefly in Ashton said: "He was morose. Sometimes a whole week would pass without us hearing his voice. He was very careful and ate only the simplest fare." But, while Parrott had no close friends, neither did he have enemies, and no-one thought him capable of killing in cold blood. "He wouldn't say boo to a goose," remarked another ex workmate.

The police felt the Press was leaning far too heavily on Parrott's side, but on the Tuesday of that week, one story appeared which seemed to justify his arrest. 'Police have made a dramatic breakthrough', claimed the Manchester Courier with the discovery of a revolver in Tatton Park. Pierce received a call from Chester HQ telling him to make sure that Parrott read it, and so, despite misgivings, he told Constable Davies to give him the paper, open at the relevant page, along with his evening meal. Davies made small talk while he observed Parrott's reaction.

"Did he say anything?" Pierce asked him a few minutes later.

"No. There was something in his face for a second or two, I don't know. He sort of raised his eyebrows. He read it all the way through and didn't say a thing. He started looking at other stuff so I took it off him. He's still eating. What's all this about finding a revolver?"

Pierce shrugged. "You know what the papers are like."

Obvious, he thought. The story had been planted. By whom, he could not say. But if they thought it would provoke Parrott into saying or doing something injudicious, they were wrong. He would not break easily. When Davies retrieved Parrott's supper plate, half of the mutton and potato pie Mary Ann had delivered was still there, cold and greasy. "Mother always gives me too much," he had explained, wearily.

In the office Davies found Pierce and Okell discussing how things might proceed when the inquest resumed the next day. "No wonder he hasn't grown properly," remarked Davies. "He doesn't eat anything."

The three officers were all of a good height, between 5 feet 8-9 inches, and 'of proportionate build', as the Constabulary records stated while Parrott was 5 feet 3 1/2 inches, having grown only a fraction since the age of 16. 'All skin and bone' his mother would say, a diminutive, almost fragile figure compared to others of his generation, who had benefited from an era of improved diet. The basics remained – cheap cuts of meat like pigs' feet (tastier when stuffed with herbed breadcrumbs), bread, potatoes, porridge, jam and treacle, tea and 'dripping' for frying. But the growth of imported tinned food provided more variety than ever before, although it depressed the home-produced market, and fish and chip shops were rapidly gaining popularity. Fat was good. Sugar was beneficial, despite a new tax on it. Though the aesthetic cadre of Victorian Christianity admired an athletic figure, many traditionalists considered too skinny a frame as undesirable. It was not manly. It posed a health risk. How could such a slight body fight off TB, or any disease? And it smacked of poverty, considered the worst affliction of all.

Parrott's perceived vulnerability was underpinned by a vision problem which required rimless spectacles. His hair was tidy, flopping a little over one side of his forehead, and he was clean shaven apart from a flicker of a moustache, hardly visible from a few yards away. 'Now't but a lad,' it was said. Okell, however, reminded his colleagues not to be taken in by appearance. "Looking at him, you'd have thought butter wouldn't melt in George Davies's mouth but, I tell you, he is lucky to be picking oakum in Parkhurst rather than underneath with his brother."

Richard Davies was buried in the grounds of Knutsford Prison. Parrott, then aged 11, again accompanied his mother in the hushed crowd outside the gaol on the morning of the execution. Mary Ann had signed petitions clamouring for George's reprieve, but now, as the black flag rose once more over Knutsford, she wondered whether it was right to hang anyone, never mind a 19 years-old. James did not hold her hand this time. Emotionally, if not physically, he was changing quickly. By pure chance, he had lost his father three years previously, and he wondered why the Davies brothers had deliberately got rid of theirs. They deserved to die, but he did not dare articulate his thoughts to Mother.

They went home to the smell of fried bacon. His sister Mary had a panful on the stove. She dished it up with some bread soaked in the fat. He ate greedily.

CHAPTER 9

'The court was crowded, the proceedings being watched with intense interest by large numbers of the Knutsford people among whom both Bould and Parrott were well known' – Manchester Evening News, April 24, 1901

WEDNESDAY, April 24. Blue skies, a light breeze. Perfect for a little trip into the Cheshire countryside to escape the city suburbs, wander along pretty lanes, breathe in the fresh air. Not so. The early morning Cheshire Lines trains from Manchester carried hundreds of visitors to Knutsford eager to hear more of murder most foul. They joined the galumph of townsfolk to the Sessions House only to find the doors locked. "You'll have to wait – the jury have gone to inspect the murder site," a constable told them.

The inspection did not take long. As the jurymen were all local, they knew Mere Heath Lane quite well and, while Pierce was able to point out the exact location and position of Bould's body, there was nothing else to indicate the brutality of Easter Sunday. Grass, weed and hawthorn had grown quickly in the fortnight since. By 11 20am they were back, and at 11 30am, with all those directly involved in their places, the doors opened. The Manchester Courier reported: '..there was a rush more suggestive of a demand for entry to the popular parts of a theatre than a solemn court of law. The men of course were able to secure the best places and the members of the weaker sex, of whom there were many, were forced to keep in the background.'

In all the pushing and shoving one woman stumbled only for an alert court usher to save her from a nasty fall on the stone steps. Coroner Yates sighed and tutted but allowed time for the commotion to ease. By his side was Chief Constable Hammersley. As they peered down from their elevated Bench, they saw immediately in front of them, Lance Bentley, another barrister Ambrose Jones – representing

The Three Horsemen – and Parrott, with Pierce standing close by. Although Parrott could have been mistaken for a junior clerk, helping Bentley or Jones, Yates recognised him immediately. They last met three years previously and Parrott had hardly changed.

Parrott was exercising his right to hear the evidence. Dressed in the grey checked tweed suit he had worn constantly, he was groomed neatly, as always, and was free of handcuffs, presumably because the police had no reason to think he might try to bolt. As the coroner started to speak, Parrott took off his glasses, wiped them with a white handkerchief, put them back on, and looked steadily around the court. The family were all there. He half raised a hand in a vague acknowledgement.

Yates began by admitting a problem. It would be impossible to complete the inquest that day because witnesses had to be brought from London and Manchester, for what he did not say. He would deal with as much as possible and adjourn. For Parrott's sake he read over the evidence produced at the original hearing before asking the clerk to call the first witness.

Caldecutt's voice boomed out from his station directly under the Bench. "Call Teresa Neagle." Shrouded in black, she stepped up into the box and took hold of the Bible. Bentley had half expected her to give Parrott the evil eye, but the top half of her face was disguised by a veil and it was difficult to discern who she was looking at. But her brogue was light and easily understood. She had little of relevance to say except to identify a letter she had sent to her brother and which had been found in the Garden Lane nurseries by a passer-by, Fred Copeland. Caldecutt had the letter passed around the jury, though the coroner remarked: "There is nothing of importance in it."

"Why bother, then?" thought Bentley, anxious to get to the meat of it.

Neagle re-joined her group in the gallery. Father Roche was again prominent. Pierce glanced at him. So tall. What had he been fed on? Apparently his congregation had paid for a special bed to be constructed for him.

Charlotte Engberson was up next. Bentley, who tended to lounge in his seat, pulled himself upright. Pierce stiffened. Colonel Hammersley took a breath. In the next few seconds she could virtually condemn Parrott to the rope. Caldecutt handed her the pigskin purse, recovered from Parrott's home. "Tell me," said the coroner deliberately, "have you seen this purse before? Is it the one which John Bould possessed?" Charlotte took it carefully, turning it in her fingers, seemingly unaware of the rising tension around her. "It is something of the same," she replied. "I saw him put something similar on the table when he was counting his money."

Hammersley silently swore. 'Similar' was not sufficient. Pierce had reported that she was almost sure it was Bould's. Before the coroner continued, the Chief Constable jumped in: "Do you believe it is the same purse?" Pressed, Charlotte hesitated. "I can't swear to it as I never had it in my hand."

She was well used to handling different materials. Her husband was a tailor, she was competent with sewing thread and needles. If she had ever picked up John's purse, felt its texture, its character almost like a fingerprint, then she would have felt qualified to say for definite. Perhaps in different circumstances she might have been persuaded to pronounce it as the same, but this was a courtroom, and Mary Ann's son facing a death sentence.

Bentley saw his chance. Rising to his feet he inquired of her: "It is a very common type of purse is it not? There are hundreds of thousands of them." Relieved that someone understood her position, Charlotte answered: "Oh yes, it is hard to swear to one of them." And with that, Bentley flicked the ace out of his sleeve. Pulling a purse from his waistcoat pocket, he held it high in the air. "Why, it is something similar to my own!"

Chuckles turned to laughter when one of the jurors shouted: "But not so well filled perhaps."

Even Parrott smiled.

Some wondered why Bentley used a common item like a yellow pigskin purse when he could afford something much more elegant. But he would never be asked about it. With no further questions of Mrs Engberson, he sat down, satisfied, gave Tom Jackson a wink. Caldecutt called the court back to order, but, for Hammersley, the damage was done. A cheap trick although he had to admire Bentley's opportunism.

Charlotte Engberson hardly knew what to think as she left the witness box. She had wanted so much to do right by John Bould, yet she could not imagine saying anything which might lead to Parrott being eventually convicted. Pierce stared hard at her. Mary Ann looked grateful. Bernard laid a comforting hand on her shoulder as she returned to her seat, but all she wanted was for it all to end. Just a nightmare, that's what it was. When they got home, John Bould would be sitting at the table, reading the paper, and he would say : "Oh, hello," and then little else for the next hour as he turned through every page. The quiet life resuming.

Dorothy Jackson made another appearance, this time evoking sentimental murmurs among the audience, rather than the surprised oohs and aahs of her debut. The onlookers included many friends and relatives of the Jacksons, all there to give her moral support. Her strides to the centre of the court were accompanied by smiles and whispered encouragement. Little Dot looked at her father. At his friend Mr Bentley. At another friend Mr Caldecutt – she wished they would stop talking about cricket all the time, it seemed a very complicated game – and she felt right at home.

Repeating her previous statements, she said she saw Parrott in Mere Heath Lane that evening as she, her sister Norah and Arthur Betteridge were being walked home after spending Easter Sunday at the Floods. It was him, she said, pointing to Parrott, wearing a cap and spectacles, standing by a gate near a haystack. Again Bentley did not cross-examine. The fact was that Dorothy's value to the prosecution was waning, even though she remained a charismatic figure to the public.

From the police viewpoint the early stages of that morning's session were acutely disappointing. Teresa Neagle's letter to Bould was dismissed as of no worth by the coroner,

Bentley oozed confidence, and Charlotte Engberson had been entrapped by the lawyer's stagecraft with the purse. Accepted, the inquest was not the criminal trial. Evidence could be changed, new facts brought into play as the case progressed through the criminal courts, but, in that way, the defence could benefit as much as the prosecution, and Hammersley was unhappy. Perhaps Mary Jane Francis would redress the balance. Pierce had visited her again at the Speakmans' house, pushing hard for her to reconsider, and to re-engage with her original impression that the man at the gate and the man leaning over Bould were one and the same - Parrott. She had promised to think about it. "I'm optimistic," Pierce said. "She's a good girl really."

Others had also referred to Mary Jane as a 'girl', assumedly because she was working class, off a farm, and a domestic servant since the age of 14. This demeaning term was endured by millions of females 'in service'. In fact she was a mature, intelligent woman, aged about 30. Pierce was not the only one who thought he had the right to turn the screw on her. Various members of the town's Establishment had stuck their oars in and, all week, the 'girl' had heard voices urging her to be careful, to be certain of her facts, to make an error could have grave consequence. No-one did anything wrong, no-one told her to lie, indeed it might all be counted as sound advice, but gradually it weighed so heavily on her that, try as she might, she failed to bring the detail into sharp focus. Maybe it was one man. Maybe it was two. The words of her favourite song came into her head: 'Oh Mr Porter what shall I do?'....Emily Speakman did not like it. "Disgusting," she rasped, when she walked unexpectedly into the kitchen and found Mary Jane singing it. Laced with sexual innuendo, Marie Lloyd's music hall hit jeered at the hypocrisy of 'respectable' Victorian society. Mary Jane heard it for the first time on a rare evening out a few years back when, while working in Liverpool, she and another servant visited the Empire in the city centre. What a night that was! So much noise, everyone laughing, cheering, singing.

Back in the witness box for the second instalment of the inquest, she caught Pierce glaring at her from across the court. And there was Parrott, sitting nonchalantly alongside his solicitor and barrister. Yes, she said in answer to the coroner, he was the 'Man At The Gate'. Yates then raised the issue over which she had received so much 'advice'.

"Can you say whether he is the same man whom you subsequently saw standing over the deceased?"

Pierce's shoulders tightened.

"No sir." Even Mary Jane was surprised by the manner of her response. So quick, so assertive. "No sir, in consequence of the distance I was from him, I cannot swear."

Pierce felt distinctly uncomfortable. The packed courtroom was warm, sunlight slanted through the tall, narrow windows directly behind the Bench, but it was embarrassment more than heat which caused him to sweat. He could sense Hammersley's disapproval. Just to rub it in, Yates repeated the question. And, again, Mary Jane answered: "No, I cannot swear to that." The coroner raised his eyebrows at Hammersley, leaned back and slowly twirled a fountain pen around his fingers. The police chief shuffled some papers. Parrott cleaned his specs again. She noticed how he carefully folded his hankie before putting it back in his waistcoat pocket.

The Clerk told Mary Jane: "You may leave the witness box," and she stepped down, aware of the gaze of the assembled Press and of difficult days ahead. Pierce's face looked like thunder. Rowe and Yarwood were waiting to give their evidence and, no doubt, would dispute her integrity, and she anticipated a disagreeable conversation with her employer once back at their Heath Side home.

Over the next few hours, the courtroom grew warmer and the evidence more complex. The bulk of it was a time and motion study, the what and when of events in the lane. Analysed from a modern stance, it is also a study of a fragmented investigation in which vital pieces of the jigsaw were missed, ignored, or put aside.

This inquest was developing into a three part soap opera over a period of three weeks, April 11-May 3. Midway through this Part Two, it threatened to get bogged down with saturation coverage of times, distances and places. While crucial to the case, it was hard for the onlookers to digest. They had come expecting something dramatic or controversial. Thankfully, Dr Smith, embellishing his post mortem, provided the first ingredient, Harry Yarwood the second.

Smith explained that the victim and the murderer were on about the same level at the time of the shooting, that the revolver was pointed at Bould's head 'probably the face' and that he had put up his arm for protection, accounting for the wounds to the wrist and forearm, and that, as he turned away from the gunman, he was shot in the back. The final bullet was full frontal, tearing open his chest.

Yates asked: "You think that death would be instantaneous?"

"Yes," said Smith, "within 30 seconds."

Coroner: "And the fatal shot was the last?"

"Yes."

From the public seats it was impossible to gauge Parrott's reaction – if there was any. Yet they still tried, peering over the balustrade. The shuffling and whispering caused Caldecutt to order "Silence in court!" Parrott, in fact, remained immobile. Pierce could not work it out. Surely there should be some show of emotion. Smith had depicted a grisly scene. The last moments. The final bullet. One or two jurors, hand-picked, experienced men, looked shocked. He could hear a woman weeping – he wondered if it was Mary Ann or Teresa Neagle, though Bould's sister was made of teak. But Parrott..nothing.

The sound of a man's boots ringing out on the stone floor brought the court back to business. A hefty man, used to heavy work with metal and horses, but with the quick confident stride of the athlete he once was. He almost bounced up the steps into the witness box and there were knowing smiles at various points of the room. The Joker in the Pack. George Henry (Harry) Yarwood.

It is difficult to dislike someone who makes you laugh, no matter what their behaviour or attitude. Intentionally or not, Yarwood transformed the murder inquest into a farce. Tears were rubbed dry, frowns turned into smiles, laughter rebounded from the grey walls. Oh, how they laughed. And Yarwood escaped unscathed both from his reprehensible actions of Easter Sunday and his pathetic excuse.

Yarwood, he told the court, went to Knutsford with George Rowe and Harry Pritchard for Sunday tea 'as was their custom'. They rode there from Altrincham. Everyone suspected that 'tea' was a euphemism for a drinking session, but the waitresses at the hotel, Lizzie and Annie were not called to give evidence and no-one at that stage queried it. Leaving the Royal George, where stables lined the cobbled yard, they pointed their horses along King Street and into Mere Heath Lane. Pritchard went ahead and, after a short while, Rowe stopped and dismounted while Yarwood waited 60-100 yards in front. Twisting around in his saddle he saw Mary Jane Francis approach and reach the spot where Rowe had halted by a field gate. Then he heard firing and, about the same time, the sound of Rowe's horse trotting up behind him.

Consulting the statement Yarwood had made to the police, Yates asked: "You heard two shots?"

"Oh no," Yarwood stated. "I heard three, four, five shots in quick succession. I should think they were from a revolver, from the direction of Knutsford about 400-500 yards from where I was."

Someone gasped. The coroner paused to let it all sink in. A murder heard but not seen. A man lying in a hedge in the last throes of life, his killer standing over him, hidden by a bend in the road, but with two men on horseback only a brief canter away. At that moment, all Yarwood and Rowe, or just one of them, had to do was to urge their mounts back towards Knutsford to take a look and, while it was too late to save Bould, they would have seen the murderer and, at least, been able to follow him or to give the police a description. But neither did. They continued along Mere Heath Lane as though nothing had happened. Yarwood admitted that he did not mention the shots to Rowe. (Rowe later claimed he had not even heard them).

To give Yarwood his due, the sound of shooting in the vicinity of Tatton Park, and in the farmland around Knutsford, was not unusual. Gamekeepers and farmers had guns and used them. But – rifles and shotguns, not revolvers. And not on Sundays. Particularly Easter Sunday when the chimes of church bells should have been the only disturbance to the general peace.

Against this background, Yates asked him: "Did you take it *(the shooting)* as a common occurrence?" Back came the first ridiculous reply: "No, but I forgot, for the time being, that it was Sunday."

The coroner smiled. "I take it you had not been to church?" producing chuckles all around. Yates was pleased with his little jest. The pantomime had begun. "No," said Yarwood, grinning. "It would have been better if I had." Though not a great joke, it broke any remaining tension and the court collapsed. A few remained stoney-faced, the Parrotts, Teresa Neagle in deep mourning, Mary Jane Francis fighting for her good name, among them, but most joined in the fun. Good old Harry. Even Pierce had to work hard to control himself.

Bentley wanted to know whether the rumour was true that Yarwood was in the habit of carrying a revolver, coming into Knutsford and firing it off at the roadside. "No," he replied with a dismissive gesture of the hand "it is not true." Again, there was laughter. Yarwood had a way about him. Ambrose Jones, representing The Three Horsemen, then took over the narrative. Surveying the court to make sure everyone had his attention, and keeping his tone pleasantly light, he said: "Many things have been rumoured – it's not true, is it, that you have confessed?"

"Not yet," Yarwood answered with emphasis while nodding at Pierce who, this time, could not stop a chortle which he tried to disguise with a fake cough. The room was in uproar now. If Yarwood had added: "Actually I am the murderer," they would have slapped him on the back and told him he was a right card. In fact, the last question to him was extremely serious, which battened down the mood within the room.

The coroner: "When you heard shots why didn't you turn back?"

Sadly, the answer was an affront to common sense. "I did not think about it being Sunday night. If I had thought of that I could have been there before the man had got 50 yards away."

Yarwood's explanation defied logic and belied his own intelligence. He, Rowe and Pritchard had expressly gone to Knutsford for 'Sunday tea' as they had done regularly. And this was Easter Sunday. But even accepting his daft reasoning, the rest of his story was, like Bould, full of holes.

Normally, if shooting was heard in the Mere Heath Lane/ Tatton Park area it came from long barrelled weapons with discernible intervals between each blast. What Yarwood described was completely different to any day, never mind a Sunday, and far more sinister. Very few people, other than soldiers, would ever have heard anything like it. Not only five shots, but a quintet 'in quick succession', which few firearms of the day could achieve unless in the hands of an expert, and the fact that Yarwood certified it as a revolver indicated a knowledge of weapons that he had gained in his younger days in the Cheshire Volunteers.

So why did Yarwood ignore it? He was not a coward. Granted he was un-armed, but he was assured, powerfully built, had soldiering experience, was a skilled horseman and had a friend with him. Yet he rode away. Without a word. And the murderer was running, his overcoat flapping around his calves, running for dear life, fearing maybe that at any second he would be charged down by the cavalry. In the space between the horsemen going one way, and the killer going the other, was a domestic servant, soaked to the skin, trembling with the shock of being assaulted, hardly knowing which way to turn, and the body of a journeyman tailor.

Mary Jane listened to Yarwood, biting her tongue. As well as his evidence about the shooting, he told the court that he had not seen any 'impropriety' between her and Rowe, and he had not heard her scream. Liar, she thought. Her bile rose as Yarwood passed in front of her, looking for a seat and deliberately smiled at her. She hoped that Rowe would make some form of admission from the witness box but it was a forlorn hope. Yes, he admitted, he did say something to her – "I could hardly remember what, something about it being a very wet night. I wiped my saddle with my sleeve, mounted and rode on. She was still standing there. I trotted up and overtook Yarwood, he was 60-100 yards away and I was in sight of him all the time."

The coroner: "Is there any truth in the statement that anything improper took place with her?"

"No, certainly not."

Mary Jane felt heads turning towards her. She bent hers for a few moments. Rowe went on to say how he heard about the murder the following day and returned to Knutsford where he and Colonel Hammersley visited the scene of the crime and the gateway where he had dismounted, the hoofprints still visible in the mud. He said nothing of his revolver, and was not asked about it. Evidently, the police had decided it was not the type used.

Yates adjourned the inquest until May 3, picked up his documents and walked out. Four magistrates, including Francis Ashworth, replaced him on the Bench, Parrott was ushered into the dock and further remanded in custody without any more evidence being taken. The only change was to transfer him from the police station to the prison where the regime was stricter. No more newspapers or friendly chats with the bobbies, and the food – well, his mother would sort that out, not that he was too bothered. As for the cell, to him one small room was like any other. Just a place where he could sit and think, be himself.

Mary Jane was soon back at Heath Side, swapping her jacket and skirt for her black and white waitress's outfit as the Speakmans were entertaining. Jane Pickstock, frowning, handed her an unstamped letter, addressed simply and mis-spelled to 'Miss Frances', the 'F' blurred by an ink blot, and the seal of the envelope slightly raised at one corner. For a moment she wondered if it had been steamed open, but not Jane, surely. "It came under the kitchen door," said the cook. "But I don't know who did it." Mary Jane shoved it into the wooden trinkets box her father had so skilfully carved for a birthday, long ago. "I'll read it later." Trying to appear unflustered, she busied herself by arranging some glasses on a silver tray, but she had an inkling that the note would be more of the same. More nastiness.

Rumours and aspersions about her having an affair, that she had been in the lane to meet her man, had grown in size and volume over the last week or so, initiated she suspected by the bricklayer who was pointing up a garden wall at the Speakmans' house. He had tried to chat her up a couple of times and, rebuffed, had become distinctly unfriendly. However, the handwriting on the envelope was not a man's.

As she carefully spaced the glasses on the tray, Mary Jane fell to musing about the vagaries of life. Little more than a fortnight ago, she was content. A good position in one of the most respectable homes in one of the most respectable towns in the country. Somewhere to settle down with a sense of pride. But look now! What a sadness. All because she went for a walk instead of going to church. She cursed the condition which had persuaded her to use that Sunday evening as a chance to get more medicine from the surgery. But the truth was that mistresses like Mrs Speakman did not cherish sickly maids. In service you had to stay on your toes. Plenty of others ready to jump into your shoes.

As she carried the tray towards the dining room, she caught a glimpse of herself in a mirror. The image distressed her. Normally, a pinkish tinge to her cheeks hinted at natural cheerfulness. Maybe it was the light, the sun of a fine Spring afternoon reflecting off the glass, but she looked oh so pale. She quickened her step, the tray rattling.

CHAPTER 10

'..the maintenance of religion and the estates of the realm and of the Imperial ascendancy of the British Empire continue to have a strong hold in the minds and affection of the people of this district' – Lance Bentley, secretary of the Knutsford Habitation of the Primrose League AGM, 1901

CHESHIRE police had a week to re-group while Parrott whiled away the time in the prison. The third and final stage of the inquest was scheduled for May 3, immediately followed by the committal hearing when they had to convince the magistrates that the prosecution evidence was worthy of putting to a jury at the Chester Assizes.

Already they had backed off from several lines of inquiry.

1: The Three Horsemen. Talk of a conspiracy involving Rowe, Yarwood and Pritchard had faded since Parrott's arrest. Nothing linked the prisoner with any of the trio. The behaviour of Rowe and Yarwood was disgraceful but the police eliminated them as possible murderers. Indeed, it seemed improbable that Rowe would be charged with indecency against Mary Jane Francis.

2: A Political Execution. John Bould had certain Irish associations, his Cork born sister Teresa Neagle for one, but he was not a Fenian, as first mooted. The Society of Tailors to which he mailed his subscription had many Irish born members but it was a well-established and open union.

3: The Pepper Pot Plot. During a series of mailbag robberies in the North-West, pepper had been thrown in postmen's faces and an empty two ounces packet of the spice was discovered at the crime site. Was Parrott the mailbag villain or, perhaps, a copy cat robber? An employee at Fay's, the Manchester grocers' chain, remembered a man buying a similar item but could not identify him with certainty as Parrott.

4: A Game Of Cards. Four teenagers were seen playing cards, a game of Banker, near the time and place of the murder. They must have seen something, said the gossipers, but, having located, questioned and warned them about gambling on a Sunday, Pierce was satisfied they knew nothing.

5: The Love Affair. Parrott and Bould 'quarrelled over a woman', yet the tailor never mentioned having a lady friend and the Engbersons believed he was a confirmed bachelor. None of Parrott's family or workmates reckoned he had a girlfriend, or wanted one. They appeared two of the unlikeliest womanisers you would ever meet. A homosexual link was more likely within this category, but homosexuality itself was then illegal, and a topic only mentioned when absolutely necessary. It is extremely doubtful that anyone considered it, and if they did, they would have kept their thoughts to themselves. Certainly there was no evidence whatsoever.

6: Your Money Or Your Life! Did Parrott fancy himself as a Highwayman, like Knutsford's Edward Higgins? Bould never had much spare cash – he could work for five years without earning what Parrott had pocketed from his recent inheritance. But Bould's purse had been taken and, while the theory of a pre-planned robbery carried little weight, the fact was that robbery had occurred.

As they moved cautiously up one cul-de-sac after another, hastily retreating from most, the police came under heavy shelling from the Press. Pierce rarely talked about his work to his wife, particularly with her mother in earshot – she was blind but could hear as well as most – but the more anxious he became the more he confided in her.

"We've got to make it stick now. We'd look fools otherwise," he told her. Pierce folded the stropping belt that he had just sharpened his razor on, hung it over a rail by the sink, and placed his shaving mug and brush on a shelf. "It's got to be him. There's no-one else in the frame."

"Can you prove it?" she asked tentatively. She understood his need to talk about it but she also knew that he did not relish being pushed into a corner.

"We'll have to. If we could only find that gun."

Nothing had come of their appeal for the Liverpool sailor whom, Parrott claimed, had bought the revolver off him.

Notices had been circulated in the Liverpool docks area, stuck up in the seaman's mission, pubs, shops and in lodging houses, and the city's Press had helped. Local police had chatted to sailors, dockers and other harbourside workers without result. Was that because no such seaman existed?

Parrott's tale about the gun stretched credulity. He met the sailor by chance. He could not recall exactly where and he could not fully describe him although, later, he was to provide a little more detail. The deal was the revolver and some cartridges for £1 (Pierce initially misunderstood the sum to be 50s) plus the promise of some smuggled tobacco to be handed over the following week at a pub in Manchester. Parrott lied, Pierce was sure.

Two possibilities remained – that he threw away the gun as he ran full pelt down Mere Heath Lane, or he shoved it back in his pocket to hide somewhere later. After a painstaking search of the roadside verges and hedges, Pierce plumped for the latter. So where? The problem was that Parrott had had two weeks to decide on the best hiding place. Since his arrest they had combed the route he said he had taken, calling in at the railway station and then the Sword and Sceptre. Fruitless. Officers at Altrincham had searched the premises of Groves and Whitnall mineral water manufacturers and the boarding house in Victoria Street, Altrincham, where he had lodged. Nothing.

Parrott had only worked at Groves and Whitnall for 10 days and no-one there professed much knowledge of him, least of all where he might have secreted a gun. Try the station, suggested one, he was always down there. Again, a waste of time. But it gave Pierce an inkling. Parrott liked walking – 16 miles from Manchester to Knutsford was not unusual for him – but he also rode the railway a lot. Porters at Knutsford knew him well. He had also been seen regularly at Altrincham, Sale, Stretford and at the Central Station terminus in Manchester. Not only at the stations but in adjacent pubs. At Pierce's request, Superintendents Okell and Leah arranged more searches without success. When Pierce had another idea – what if he threw it out of a train window in between stations? – he was greeted with silence.

If they could not find the gun, at least they could track its history. Parrott had openly admitted purchasing it from the Colt Firearms Manufacturing Co in London along with a batch of 100 cartridges. The case in which it was despatched was retrieved from his bedroom with the serial number rubbed off but Colt's staff had scrutinised their order book, and there it was. One of their top men, a firearms expert, was coming up to give the necessary evidence. His name was Mr Goodbody.

One political line which the police did not even start to follow concerned the 2nd Anglo-South African War between Britain and the Boers (descendants of early Dutch settlers) who controlled a huge region of South Africa, the Transvaal and the Orange Free State, and were unfairly restricting the political and commercial interests of British colonists.

That was one way of putting it. Another was: Imperialist Britain wanted all South Africa's gold and diamonds and thought that, as the world's major power, they could simply push a few rebellious farmers out of the way. It developed into a major war with the British army growing from 100,000 troops in 1900 to 250,000 in 1902 and, at its height, the cost was over £2million a month. As in the 1857 First War of Independence in India (Indian Mutiny) it fanned the flame of British Imperialism but then, as horrific stories of the treatment of civilians appeared, it developed into a political storm. Anti -Imperialists, or Pro-Boers, including Irish Nationalists, condemned the conduct of the war.

Knutsford was a hub of Imperialism. Its people backed the war. The Cheshire Yeomanry founded in Knutsford in 1798 and supported by the then Prince of Wales, were involved in the Peterloo Massacre and had grown into the 3rd Volunteer Brigade which fought in South Africa and, in the spring of 1901, were heading home to a rapturous welcome. It was an emotional time, pulsing with patriotism. Debates raged in Parliament, particularly over the detention camps where thousands of South African women and children were dying through disease and starvation, deep splits affected British society but Cheshire and Knutsford in particular remained firmly behind the government and the army.

When, shortly after the murder, the Knutsford Habitation of the Primrose League held its annual meeting in the Town Hall, Lance Bentley delivered his report as secretary in these terms: "The objects and principle of the Primrose League, the maintenance of religion and the estates of the realm and of the Imperial ascendancy of the British Empire, continue to have a strong hold in the minds and affection of the people of this district."

The Knutsford Habitation had 1067 subscribing members, 295 from the Tatton Estate, in effect the estate's entire workforce including the likes of Thompson Flood and John Parkes. Lord Egerton of Tatton was the Habitation's 'ruling councillor'. More pertinently, Harry Yarwood was elected as the 'warden', there to organise and to protect. A Mr Fixit. In a vote of thanks for the secretary, Bentley was said to be 'as well known as Knutsford itself'.

John Bould was no radical. He did not belong to a political party, nor to any secret society. He had even let his membership of the Society of Tailors fall into massive arrears – the postal order he sent on Easter Sunday did not cover the full amount owed – and he was generally regarded as a peaceful, mindful character who disliked quarrelling. But two women, Teresa Neagle and Charlotte Engberson, while emboldening his image of The Quiet Man, also hinted at stubbornness, and the ability to defend himself, verbally or physically.

Neagle insisted that her brother abhorred unnecessary violence but, 'in a fair fight' he would give 'a good account of himself'. And Engberson revealed he had argued with another tailor when they worked together at the firm of Slater's in Knutsford. "He told me he could not agree with anything he said." It seems then that Bould held certain views. According to Engberson he also carefully read a daily newspaper, and must have been fully aware of the conflict and the controversies in and over South Africa. Did he feel strongly enough to protest openly against it? If so, he was either brave or foolish.

The district's long-term antipathy towards dissent and pacifism was highlighted when in 1918, nearing the end of WW1, the government ordered dozens of conscientious objectors to be accommodated in Knutsford prison, part of which had been reconstituted as a 'labour centre'. Protests and demands that they should be housed elsewhere climaxed in a riot with a number of COs injured.

The subsequent court case was derisory, showing clearly where sympathies lay. Ten local men were charged with the minor offence of causing a breach of the peace but they were hailed as heroes – one had been wounded fighting for his country. When one solicitor, George Keogh, was reprimanded by the chairman for terming the COs as 'parasites', he responded: "Well, they have been called stronger names," and everyone burst into laughter.

Seventeen years earlier, at the time of the murder, with Victoria not long in her grave and a new king to be crowned, with Volunteers returning from the South African war as heroes, the flag of St George flew high and proud above Knutsford. If Bould spoke out of turn, would it motivate someone to kill him? In isolation, most probably not but, taking into account other matters, it was worth considering. Neagle certainly thought it of significance which is why she hinted darkly at the killer being someone who knew how to handle a gun, someone with soldiering experience, perhaps. And Parrott was not a Volunteer.

"His eyes are weak, he couldn't hit a barn door," claimed Lance Bentley when he chatted to Pierce after a briefing with Parrott at the gaol.

"Which is why he got up close," retorted Pierce. And, for once, Bentley had no answer. Later, though, he dismissed it as inconsequential. The defence case was simple, that Parrott was not the shooter. Someone else committed The Knutsford Murder and he was roaming free.

CHAPTER 11

'what makes Britain great: manliness, fair play, decency,
honour and an ability to play cricket' – Boy's Own magazine

DOROTHY JACKSON was pleased with herself. Her big day was coming up fast and she had practised hard. She and her friend Elsie Cockram were not quite up to the mark yet, particularly with the port and starboard steps, but there was time to perfect it. The Lady's Hornpipe would be a crowd puller. Her name would be in the papers again. Maybe even another drawing of her like they had in the Manchester paper the day after she had had to go to court and swear on the Holy Bible that it was James Parrott she had seen in the lane. That was a nice picture of her. She had cut it out, delicately brushed flour paste onto it and stuck it to the inside cover of her scrapbook. 'Little Dot', said the caption.

The biggest event in Knutsford's calendar was Royal May Day. 'Royal' because the Prince and Princess of Wales had attended in 1887. The 1901 version on Wednesday May 1 would, as usual, consist of a long procession of children, dressed in character costumes, winding through the streets and onto The Heath for dancing and the crowning of the May Queen. Dorothy and Edith were to perform the hornpipe on a platform in front of thousands of spectators. They had to get it right. Everyone loved the hornpipe dance. Dorothy worked hard, jigging up and down, swivelling left and right.

She would be May Queen one day, her father had promised and he ran it – well, not just him, but him and his friends. In fact they did everything. It pleased Dorothy to know that her father was so influential and popular. She wanted him to be proud of her. More practise. On the day itself, she and Edith would be accompanied by a silver band, but, here in Orchard Cottage, she went through the moves in silence except for the clattering of her tiny clogs on the kitchen floor.

Tom Jackson was hard at it, too. The success of the Royal May Day was vital to Knutsford. It attracted up to 30,000 visitors from all over the North-West, a bonanza for local traders, but also and, perhaps more importantly, maintaining the town's status as a bastion of monarchy, tradition and British values. It demanded a tremendous amount of planning all through the year and the week leading up to the event was the busiest. He needed a murder case like a hole in the head. Not only that but the town was preparing for the Volunteers' homecoming and Leicester Caldecutt was bothering him about the first game of the cricket season. "It's at the Western club and we don't stand an earthly if we can't field our best side. By the way, what do you think of the proposal to change the leg before law? Tricky isn't it?"

Jackson pushed a sheaf of papers at him. "We've got a few things to sort out before the cricket. Parrott isn't playing ball with us. And there's the Volunteers and May Day, and.."

He sighed. A warm, cheerful Spring was in the offing, the scent of fresh cut grass in the air and there was no game like cricket even if, in such a conservative town, it tended to accentuate class divisions rather than level them. He returned to his office, a desk littered with documents, and a frowning Lance Bentley.

"You haven't forgotten that we're seeing Parrott this afternoon?"

They strolled over to the prison, had a quick word with the governor Major James Nelson, and were escorted to the prisoner's cell. Parrott stood up, shook their hands, and sat down again, his back straight, hands resting lightly on his knees. Two hours later he was in the same position, having hardly moved, and having hardly spoken except to reiterate his earlier statements and to repeat: "The police are on the wrong track." Occasionally, a tremor could be seen on one side of his face and his cheeks reddened, once or twice his lips turned into the germ of a smile, otherwise it was impossible to glean anything of his emotions.

On leaving, Jackson asked: "Are they treating you well, are you getting enough food?"

"Certainly," said Parott. "I have no complaints at all and my mother brings me food each day."

"Any problems with him?" Jackson asked the warder.

"Nothing at all. Quiet as a mouse, this one is. Wish others were the same. We're short of men and some of of the older lags take advantage."

Bentley spoke to the governor again, requesting that a close eye be kept on Parrott to 'obtain information about his state of mind'.

"You consider him a risk," the Major said, surprised. "A suicide risk?"

Bentley did not want to go that far. "It is difficult to measure him. Some people say he is morose and doesn't make friends, but that doesn't mean he would harm himself. However… if he shows any signs of abnormality we would like to know." As far as the sterile interview went, Bentley was not too concerned. The less Parrott said the better. As long as he stuck to his complete denial, the evidence against him was as thin as his smile.

On his way home Jackson popped under the arched gateway of the police station yard and into the kitchen for a chat with Pierce. "Have you got anything new?"

Pierce grunted. "Wouldn't you like to know!" But he and Jackson got on well, shared knowledge, sometimes a drink and the secrets of the de Tabley Freemasons' Lodge where Jackson had witnessed Pierce's initiation in 1899 and his elevation to 'second degree' in March 1901. Both events at the Royal George were of high ceremony. Dressed all in black, apart from a white shirt, Pierce had to expose his left breast, to pull up his right trouser leg above the knee, to exchange his left shoe for a slipper, and then to have a noose called a cable tow looped around his neck. The Junior Deacon led him around the room three times and made him kneel and take an oath before introducing him to the Wardens who gave him a password. Finally, Pierce was welcomed by the Worshipful Master. It was an intimate ritual, so ludicrous to an outsider that it bound the participants ever tighter. Pierce also had to show that he could afford the subscriptions, could attend a certain number of meetings, and that he had a clean criminal record (laughs all round), but he also had to swear that he believed in God.

Now in the police house kitchen, Jackson sat at the oilskin

covered table, Pierce leaned comfortably against the sink and there was a few moments' silence before the sergeant took up the conversation. "Nothing new of note, Tom. Anyway, how is our Dorothy? Looking forward to the May Day?"

"Oh definitely. I don't suppose you're looking forward to it. Hard work for the police."

"Yes, as if we haven't got enough to deal with." Pierce slurped his tea. "Thirty thousand people coming in. Cheshire Lines have put a lot of specials on, discount prices too. The place will be bursting at the seams."

"It's our big day," Jackson interposed. "Bigger than ever this year. There's something in the atmosphere, something to do with the old Queen going, and wanting to make it good in her memory. But also it's a kind of welcome for the King, and the Volunteers coming home and - I don't know --but whatever the reason it feels special. And it pulls in a lot of business for the shops."

Pierce stabbed the air with a thick forefinger. "Yes. But also good for the ale houses and n'er do wells. Drunks, pickpockets, scoundrels of every type. It's supposed to be a day of fun but it's a full-scale operation for us." Jackson had heard it before, from Pierce and from previous station sergeants. He did not show any sympathy. Royal May Day put Knutsford in the limelight. One newspaper had said only the previous day that it made the town 'famous the world over'.

"Anyway," Pierce continued, "if we have to kick a few arses that's what we will do." He softened his vulgarity with a laugh. He was not 'a clip around the ear' bobby but this was a man's moment, a few seconds of male freedom of speech, only available when out of the hearing of the women of the house which, in Jackson's case, was well nigh impossible with Orchard Cottage filled by the chatter of five daughters.

"Right, I've got to be off." Jackson plonked his cup down. "Perhaps we can have a quiet weekend before the storm breaks."

Pierce patted him on the shoulder as he went past and through the back door. "Don't fret – the cricket season is here, so Caldecutt tells me. He's very keen, isn't he?" Jackson did not reply.

Unfortunately, neither man had a relaxing weekend. On Saturday morning, Bill Wragg, for 20 years the chief bookmaker for Knutsford's best known grocer, W D Watson, went missing. His family and employers were naturally worried but tried hard not to panic. By Saturday evening, with still no sign of him, they reported it to Pierce. By Sunday morning a full-scale search was in progress. Someone claimed they had seen a man of his description in Higher Peover, a rural parish a couple of miles outside the town, and in the afternoon they found his body in a water-filled pit in a farm field. The coroner was informed. Another inquest, to go along with that of the five months old boy found suffocated in his bed in a house in the Old Market Place, and, of course, with the next chapter of the Bould case to follow. Pierce went to bed late on Sunday night facing a crazy week of rural festivities, homecoming celebrations, and general death under the categories of infant mortality, suicide and murder. Superintendent Okell had once told him that Knutsford Station was an easy beat.

Jackson, meanwhile, learned of a new witness to the murder, a woman named Taberer who, apparently, had actually shaken Bould's body believing him to be drunk. She lived in London, and had been visiting relatives in Knutsford. This astonishing news came out of the blue from Mary Ann Parrott on the back of a chat with her friend Elizabeth Hough. No-one had even mentioned it previously and it added another strand to the web of coincidence which wrapped itself around this case. Such connectivity was the DNA of Knutsford life. People did not think about it, it was just the way things were. But even Jackson was surprised by this particular link.

Miss Taberer was a niece of Nellie Clayton and had been staying with her and her husband Thomas at their home on the Tatton estate where he was a clerk. On the Sunday she walked along Mere Heath Lane to visit Nellie's mother, Elizabeth Hough, a widow who lived on Heath Side, and she was returning to the Claytons' cottage when she came across Bould's body.

Both the Taberer and the Clayton families had close ties with the Parrotts.

Elizabeth Hough was formerly Elizabeth Taberer, matron of the Knutsford workhouse and wife of the master, William Taberer who died in 1888. Elizabeth's second husband in 1893 was James Hough, a successful grocer and property owner, and an ally of the Parrotts, acting as executor to the wills of both Thomas and James Parrott snr who bequested money for the education of his five grandchildren with a large cash sum for James jnr at the age of 21. Hough, therefore, had a big say in the upbringing of James Crossley Parrott and, as shown later in this book, that upbringing was unusual and deeply marked him. When Hough died in 1898, Elizabeth moved from King Street to one of the houses he owned on Heath Side.

As for the Claytons, Thomas's father was Job Clayton, the town's Collector of Taxes – and an acquaintance of Thomas Parrott, witnessing his will in 1887.

It seemed that Miss Taberer (Mary Ann thought her forename was Matilda) had had tea with Elizabeth Hough and saw Bould's body lying in the verge as she walked back to the Claytons' cottage. Unsure of what had happened to him, she went up to him and lifted his head.

Jackson was non-plussed. While the Taberers were very familiar to him, he did not know this particular lady who, apparently, had walked into a murder mystery and then out of it, unimpeded. Presumably, she did not know Parrott but either for or against she could hold vital evidence. Surely the police knew something of it, but Pierce had said nothing and there was no sign of her name in the witness depositions.

"The Taberers are involved," he told Annie over their lunch. "Nellie's niece. She saw the body and she even touched it. But no-one saw her her. Apparently." He shook his head, disbelievingly.

Pierce was touchy when Jackson tackled him on Monday morning. He had not slept well and was preparing for the inquest on the infant boy. "You've got it wrong. Typical gossip as usual. The Taberer woman was there but *after* the others and she didn't touch him. She had gone by the time I got there. She can't add anything to the evidence." When Jackson related events to Bentley, suggesting they get hold of the new witness, the barrister demurred. "I don't think it's necessary Tom. It might just complicate matters."

Jackson was suspicious but there was nothing to be done. 'Miss Taberer' was the forgotten witness of the Bould murder case. The police accepted she was on the spot, but neither they nor the defence thought it worthwhile using her. Why? Her absence from the process highlighted the naiviety of investigative work in that era.

British police did not have the best of reputations in the Victorian period. For decades they rode a roller coaster of rebuke and praise, lampooned in cartoons and music-hall songs as drunks, womanisers who took advantage of young housemaids, and thieves in uniform, yet admired for courage in the face of armed robbers and street hooligans. 'A policeman's lot is not a happy one,' – the policemen's chorus in Gilbert and Sullivan's The Pirates of Penzance.

They worked long, arduous hours, patrolling their beat on foot. Chief Constables cracked down on them for misdemeanours, particularly drunkenness, they had no guaranteed pension, no trade union – some officers were imprisoned after campaigning for one – and little equipment. Some even had to pay towards a back-up uniform. Those in charge of a station sometimes had to ask their wife to deal with certain duties, especially when a female was arrested. Gradually pay and conditions improved, a union was formed and the 'modern' policeman emerged. By the end of the 19th century the Met had earned the tag of the best force in the world.

But even at Scotland Yard, the HQ of the Metropolitan Police, the art of detection remained basic. They had detectives, or rather plain clothes officers who sometimes dressed up theatrically to go undercover, but only a small percentage of criminals were nabbed by a forensic approach. Police relied heavily on confessions or on the spot witnesses. And even when arrested many villains got off scot free because prosecutions fell down through lack of evidence.

Crime statistics for the period under review are either unavailable or unreliable, but it seems that less than 25 per cent of indictable offences, possibly as low as 20 per cent, ended in convictions. A worrying percentage of those resulted from mistaken identity because witnesses were guided, even goaded, into picking someone out of a line-up, whether or not it was the masked man, wearing a hooped jersey, whom they saw climbing out of a window with a stuffed bag marked 'swag'.

When the author examined his own credentials as a potential eye witness, he failed miserably. The test was to scrutinise a video without a pause or replay facility of a staged scene in which a laptop was stolen from an office, and then to pick the culprit from an identity parade of eight vaguely similar men. My instinct was that the thief was not present – correct. But, because I expected him to be there I picked out someone who resembled him. Wrong.

Parrott might have persevered with his first alibi, that he never even went into Mere Heath Lane, had it not been for the fact that Little Dot knew him well and was adamant that it was him. It seemed that Pierce stupidly tried to make it easier for her at the identity parade by ensuring that Parrott was the only man in the parade with specs. His lawyers cottoned onto this and, for a short while, it offered serious potential for the defence, but they pulled back from applying heavy handed pressure on an 11 years-old girl, the daughter of their friend and clerk.

Arthur Conan Doyle's Sherlock Holmes and a host of other paperback sleuths were far more efficient than most police forces. They poked into tiny crevices in floorboards, spotted minute bloodstains through huge magnifying glasses, and possessed remarkable scientific expertise which helped them to bring criminals to justice. 'Elementary dear Watson,' Holmes would boast to the doctor after solving another multi-faceted crime. Such fictional heroes made the real-life bobbies look like lumbering amateurs. The Cheshire force might have profited from calling on the man thought to have inspired Conan Doyle's Holmes character, but Manchester's

Jerome Caminada, a pioneer of criminal detection, had retired two years earlier and was now reaping the profits from his best selling memoir. And then, as now, county forces had their pride. Colonel Hammersley would not have wanted an outsider on the case, taking the glory from his men.

Jerome Caminada, a pioneer in detective work

No matter how hard they worked, they could do little about the ticking of the clock. Everything was so hurried in the vital early stages. Arrested on April 20, Parrott was due to be committed for trial on May 4, a gap of only two weeks in which all the evidence had to be garnered. Inevitably things were missed or not fully pursued. A less unflappable figure than Pierce would have thrown his hands up and surrendered at the volume of work he encountered at the start of that second week.

But at least Parrott was out of the way, incarcerated in the gaol rather than the police lock-up across the yard. And such was the way of things that for the next 48 hours, Britain's most sensational murder was relegated into third place behind the return of the Cheshire Volunteers and the crowning of Lottie Cragg, Queen of the May.

ADJOURNMENT
(called for by the Author)

As I delved deeper into this story, my regular outbursts of surprise became constrained by a mood of inevitability – that just around every corner, in every nook and cranny, there would be a weird and wonderful connection. It was an affair layered in coincidence.

In many ways Knutsford was no different from thousands of other small towns except how many of those boasted a county court, major prison, police station, parish church, workhouse, town hall, railway station and part of the main street within a quadrangle of 350 yards by 250 yards? Not to mention a murder site less than a mile up the road. Long-established families of traders, officials and professionals had lived and worked together for decades. So much suffocating closeness.

For example:

Tom Jackson's employers (William) Inman and (Edwin) Ashworth Solicitors dealt with the Parrotts' business affairs. Jackson helped to make up the wills of James's father Thomas Parrott and his grandfather James Parrott snr in 1887 and 1888 respectively. The firm managed investments to pay towards the upbringing and education of the Parrott children.

Mary Flood also had close ties. She lived only a few doors from the Parrotts for many years, and was a witness at the wedding of Tom Jackson and Annie Wright at the parish church. She then took on the role of 'auntie' to the Jackson girls.

James Parrott was first placed in a cell just 30 yards from the Jacksons' home, Orchard Cottage, and not much further away fom the prison shed where he would be hanged if convicted. Tom's daughter Dorothy, her 'auntie' Mary and Mary's husband Thompson were witnesses for the Crown, but Jackson's law firm was stoutly defending the prisoner, thanks to the barrister Lance Bentley who, inevitably, lived close to Orchard Cottage and was a friend to all.

All met regularly, whether in the course of their work, or socially, perhaps while shopping in the street, or at church, or at Freemasons' meetings at the Royal George, the latest of which had been on April 9, two days after the murder.

Indeed, among those at a Knutsford Cricket Club AGM were seven players, all directly linked to the Parrott case - Dr Theodre Fennell, the solicitors Inman and Ashworth, Bentley, Jackson, Caldecutt and Murray Speakman - the treasurer.

The club ground was in Mere Heath Lane, and Bould's body was found in the hedge, a few yards away. One of his last views was the close-cut outfield ready for the start of the season.

It was almost as if Knutsford, like Mrs Gaskell's Cranford, breathed in its own world. John Bould had entered it and, for some reason, had been spat out.

Should I have been surprised by all this 'nearness'? Perhaps not.

Even in late 1964 when I first walked through the door of the Guardian newspaper office at 113 King Street, Knutsford was a small town, physically and in outlook. Housing estates had swelled the population but its core remained tightly bound with its cliques of shopkeepers, lawyers, councillors and officials.

The Flatters were still operating as the town's chief removals business, my father worked at the post office where John Bould posted his last letter and where James Parrott's brother John was employed in 1901 as a rural postman. The police station sergeant, a pleasant and diligent bobby, lived close to us, as did the Clerk to the Justices whose first, and sometimes only, piece of conversation was: "How's your mum?"

Almost opposite the Guardian office was the White Lion, run by the council chairman and where on a Friday night the Clerk stood at the bar, quiet and solitary, downing four pints of mild.

Once, having witnessed a drunken incident in King Street, I had to give the police a statement. I went to the station, and, like Parrott, sat down in the kitchen with a cuppa while the sergeant wrote it down. The building was different, a couple of hundred yards from Sergeant Pierce's 1901 HQ, but the routine was strikingly similar. Later I gave evidence for the defence at a magistrates' court hearing in the Sessions House. The Clerk handed me a Bible, and frowned when I said I wished to affirm, but at least he did not embarrass me by asking about my mother's health. A constable who lived opposite us, stood entry by the door, the sergeant, manned the dock and the defendant winked at me. He just happened to be a friend. The public gallery was full of other pals. It all felt so homely. Thanks to my extremely slanted evidence, favouring my friend, the verdict was not guilty. While the 'gang' went to the pub to celebrate, I went to the toilets, feeling sick. For various reasons I had felt it justified, but I had not found it easy.

Looking back at that unsavoury episode helps me to understand the behaviour of certain people in the Bould murder case. Pierce, for example, made mistakes as he took a statement from Parrott while sitting in the kitchen of the police station. Harry Yarwood went to great lengths to protect his friend George Rowe for what he considered were good reasons. There were lies and deceits. And there was concern from lawyers, bobbies and prison warders for Mary Ann Parrott who visited her son daily. "How's your mum?" they asked him solicitously.

CHAPTER 12

'The subject of servants was a standing grievance'
– Elizabeth Gaskell (Cranford)

'Faithful Servants! Cast iron hollow-ware is strong,
clean, quick and economical, the very qualities of the
faithful servant. And like good servants, CAST IRON
utensils keep their places without a murmur for 10,
20, 30, even 50 years...' - magazine advert, 1901

MISS FRANCIS.

The 'faithful servant'.....Mary Jane Francis,
an artist's sketch. © Reach PLC.

'DEAR Miss Frances..' Huh, Mary Jane scoffed silently, can't even spell my name. 'Dear Miss Frances,' she read it over. 'It is high time you told the whole truth about what happened. We know there is a lot more to it. Please remember there is someone in the prison who is innocent and is suffering. You may have something to hide but is it worth a man's life? If you do not speak out now you will never redeem yourself in the eyes of Our Lord.'

She burst into tears momentarily before regaining control. A 'domestic' could not afford undue emotion. But no-one seemed to care that she, too, was a victim. That she, too, was suffering. The police never left her alone. Questions, questions. Mrs Speakman hardly spoke, except to issue curt instructions. Mr Speakman was angry because of Sergeant Pierce questioning him about a revolver. She only left the house upon necessity, imagining the jibes and sneers she might encounter in the streets. Now this letter, opened only after steeling herself.

On the point of tearing it up, she heard a clang and an exclamation from the kitchen, Jane Pickstock dropping something. It pulled Mary Jane up. The hardness came back into her eyes. Pushing the letter into a pocket, she adjusted her pinny, fiddled with her hair, and marched down the stairs. Work to be done.

Often her day started before 6am and ended in mid-evening, unless the Speakmans had people in for dinner when she would crawl into bed close to midnight. It ranged from heavy manual work, on her knees scrubbing away with a bar of soap or a concoction of beeswax and turpentine at the linoleum covered scullery floor, to the delicate touches required of a skilled cocktail waitress. She enjoyed one half day off each week and one full day each month, and could do little without the supervision or express consent of her employer. Her wages were paltry but at least she had bed and board in a large, fashionable house. (The Speakmans were respected for their taste).

Women were slowly breaking free of such drudgery with more job opportunities in stores and offices, although in England and Wales over two million were still harnessed in service, and in London and other cities one in three also doubled up as prostitutes at some time in their lives. Mary Jane's future at the Speakmans' was bleak, a return to her Welshpool origins was inevitable but until then she would carry on as normal. No-one would label Mary Jane Francis a slacker. And she would still have her day in court.

Mary Ann Parrott also had a letter, although it was addressed to 'James C Parrott', sent by a Mr Thomas Welsh, managing director of Welsh and Co, a Liverpool trading company. 'Dear Mr Parrott, We wish to thank you for your new application. Unfortunately, as previously advised, the position has been filled.' Dictated and signed by Welsh, typed by a woman clerk. Men dictated, women typed.

Well, she thought, at least James will not have to explain why he is now unavailable. She almost smiled. He had said something about a new job, a big chance to make something of himself, but he had talked to his brothers about it more than her. Africa, it was. Perhaps she should show it to Tom Jackson, just in case it had some relevance. James had always been a mite fanciful. Sometimes she would say something to him and get no reply. 'Away with the fairies,' – that was it. Or, the other side of him – wild talk about going up the Amazon or down the Nile. The money from his grandfather had made it worse. She put the letter in her wicker basket, asked daughter Mary to look after things and walked up to the solicitor's office.

The streets were busy. Carts, pushed and pulled by thickly muscled men and horses, rumbled by. You had to be careful – the pavements were narrow, the traffic heavy, and the horse droppings plentiful, but the sun was out, and there was a cheerfulness about, a flag here and there, a line of bunting over the Royal George archway, and lots of banging and shouting from the builders in Drury Lane.

In other circumstances Mary Ann would have felt elated. The Volunteers were coming home. Hurrah! She was as patriotic as anyone. But her son was in gaol on a charge of murder. She caught one or two glances and kept her head down. The letter lay on a napkin covering a dish of rabbit pie. She had taken time over it, carefully boning the meat, wrapping it in flour and stewing it with a little beef before applying the pastry top. All the while hoping James would eat a little more today. Sergeant Pierce was another with a letter to think about. Torn and badly creased, as though it had been crunched into a ball, it contained nothing of value to the case – little more than a 'How are you dear brother?' from Teresa Neagle, adding that she would like to visit him over Easter and would he reply promptly as usual. John Bould had scribbled a couple of notes in the margin, difficult to decipher as they were in pencil, but clearly a personal memo on how to frame his response. One line said 'trade is poor', and another 'not quite settled yet', as though he intended putting her off. The coroner's view was that it was irrelevant, but it was where it was found, not its contents, which concerned Pierce.

Fred Copeland, who ran a grocer's a couple of doors away from Parrott's home, saw it lying inside the nursery railings as he walked along Garden Lane several days after the murder. Copeland poked his umbrella through the railings to retrieve it, spotted the name Bould on the envelope and immediately handed it to the police. Why had it not been seen previously? His own men had covered every yard of the nursery looking for the gun. Could they have missed that too? Pierce ordered another search and, again, they ended up empty-handed. But it made him think again about the killer's escape route.

The discovery of the letter indicated that he sprinted down Mere Heath Lane and swerved right onto the path through the nursery leading him onto Garden Lane. The only logical reason for that was to reach the town centre via Manchester Road instead of the busier Tatton Street. But, initially, the police had focused on Tatton Street because, eventually, Parrott had admitted using it. The more Pierce considered it the more he worried. Their case was flimsy enough as it was, he could not afford a new contradiction. He linked up with Constable Davies, explaining: "We need to confirm which way Parrott went. Let's ask around."

They called first at the Feathers. Then at the Flatters' the family of carters who had helped remove Bould's body. Henry invited him into the front sitting room where his daughters Daisy and Louisa sat at the table, reading. No, said Henry, he had seen nor heard anything unusual until Hugh Daniels came banging on the door that night saying a body had been found. Just then Daisy leaned across the table, whispering to her sister. "She says she saw something."

Henry shrugged his shoulders. "Ask her if you like, but...well, to be honest she's a bit younger than her age, if you know what I mean."

Pierce took the hint. Dealing with children was a skill – he was good at it. Carefully removing his shako, he plonked himself on a chair, drew it closer to Daisy and smiled. "Tell me what you saw."

Daisy, nine years-old, was sparrow like in physique and struggling to keep up at school, nevertheless she was a chirpy child with a disconcerting habit of staring straight at you with bright eyes while appearing to be looking at something else in the distance. Waiting for her to speak, Pierce felt slightly uncomfortable. Then, in a high-pitched voice: "I was reading the Easter card our Lou made for me," glancing at her sister. "I saw him go past the window very fast."

Keeping his voice level, Pierce asked: "Was it someone running?"

"Yes, I think so."

"Did you see what he looked like?"

"Hmm," Daisy looked again at Louisa who shook her head. "No..but he had something in his hand. "

Pierce almost blurted out 'Like a gun?' checking himself just in time. "What was it, Daisy?"

"A handkerchief, I think. A white one."

Pierce had to check himself again, from laughing, partly from his first silly thought that it might have been a gun, but also from relief because he knew for certain now that it was Parrott. "It was the handkerchief," he informed Davies on the way back.

Three of the Mere Heath Lane witnesses had seen Parrott holding a white hankie. Two, Thompson Flood and John Parkes reckoned he was sitting on a field gate, waving it above his head, for a while leading the police to wonder whether he was signalling an accomplice, although they quickly put that notion on the back burner. Dorothy Jackson remembered seeing him with the handkerchief wrapped around his wrist, and perhaps it was still like that when he rushed past the Flatters' window.

Daisy's surprise input solved the problem with the letter. A minor matter but still a loose end, which Pierce needed to be knotted. They could continue to concentrate on Tatton

Street rather than Manchester Road if further searches or enquiries were necessary.

Otherwise, the police did not bother too much about the hankie but it remains one of many curios in this case.

Parrott's behaviour in Mere Heath Lane was unusual to say the least. He claimed he stopped near the Knutsford end, close to the murder site, to 'accommodate' himself, meaning to urinate or to defecate – he was never asked which. For privacy, he tried fields on either side of the road without finding anywhere appropriate and even entered a shed, only to find someone else there who told him to 'Clear off!' Various people saw him going through two field gates and Flood and Parkes, from different viewpoints and distances, were adamant they saw him sitting on one of the gates swirling the hankie above his head. Parrott's explanation was that he was merely wiping his brow with it.

Putting the hankie aside, what the heck was Parrott doing? Having trekked 16 miles from Manchester to within half a mile of his home, was he caught short so suddenly that he had to take a leak or whatever immediately? If so, why did he then take so much trouble finding a suitable spot? Parrott also reckoned that he needed a rest after such a long walk. Yet home and the Sword and Sceptre where he claimed he went for a beer were within easy reach.

Much of this might have been a side issue, if not for the timing of events. Again, the police failed to gather vital detail. What might have been useful evidence flapped in the breeze, like Parrott's hankie. There was no formal way of recording witness statements, and police officers had little or no training in how to take them.

Pierce's method, using blue sheets of thin foolscap, a pencil and good manners, was painstakingly slow and counted against delving into the finer points. And no senior officer advised anything different. Another extraordinary aspect was that, despite the presence of the Chief Constable and two superintendents, a sergeant gradually took control of the investigation. Obviously Hammersley, Leah and Okell had great faith in him. Perhaps they saw in Pierce, Cheshire's answer to Jerome Caminada. Their very own Sherlock.

Nailing this high-profile case would be a plume in Pierce's shako. But he knew that Parrott would not crack easily. "Looks no more than a schoolboy – huh!" Pierce was reading with mounting exasperation a newspaper report which highlighted the accused's youthful countenance. He closed the paper, pushed it from him, and fixed his attention on his wife, stirring a pot of stew on the stove. "I've got to meet up with Francis Ashworth and one or two others at the Angel later. They want to hear about the arrangements for tomorrow."

The Volunteers' ship was due to dock at Southampton in the morning and they would then entrain to Chester before dispersing to their hometowns, each of which planned a huge civic welcome, with Ashworth, the council chairman, and other dignatories at the forefront in Knutsford. Pierce had to organise a substantial police presence, both to honour the returning soldiers and to guard against any alcohol fired bother. A lot of ale would be drunk. Pierce grimaced. And 24 hours later, Royal May Day. Annie set down a bowl of stew. "Here – and don't gulp it down. I don't want you suffering from your stomach when you're discussing affairs of state." Pierce grinned.

The meeting at the Angel Hotel went well. Lots of whisky and handshaking. The dark clouds of war and murder hung over their town and only that morning some of them, including Leicester Caldecutt, Pierce and the prison surgeon Doctor Theodore Fennell had been involved in the shocking inquest on the toddler who had been accidentally suffocated while sleeping in a bed with four other children at their home in Market Place. 'Over lying' they called it. Their drunkard father and his subservient wife were slated by Coroner Yates for keeping their family in filthy conditions. Yates refused to accept that, in Knutsford, a large family had to live in two rooms, one a kitchen, the other an all-in living and sleeping area, at a rent of six shillings a week. But, as Caldecutt said to Pierce: "They're not the only ones."

Yates ordered the case to be sent to the National Society for the Prevention of Cruelty to Children for possible prosecution. And Caldecutt was right. Already in the NSPCC dossier was a distressing story of a Knutsford alcoholic, deserted by his wife and left to care for an 18 months old boy. They lived in Swinton Square, neighbours of the Engbersons. The tiny cottage was, according to Fennell, unfit for any type of habitation. It stank so badly that a police constable retched and had to rush outside. In another case, five siblings, sleeping in filth and covered in vermin bites, were extricated from a cottage in Minshull Street after being refused admission to school.

But at The Angel everyone was happy. And why not? No bad smells here. The proprietor John Walton managed a high-class establishment, clean, warm, lavishly furnished, and the only stink was that of Imperial arrogance and hypocrisy which enabled essentially good people to gloss over the harrowing stories of British concentration camps in South Africa. And these *were good* people, hard working, humane. Pierce had slammed the father of the dead infant as 'worthless' – his wife was 'far better' The council, under Francis Ashworth, were trying to improve living conditions in the poor areas. Ashworth himself was involved in many charities, even setting up orphanages in India. And they all loved Knutsford. For the next 48 hours at least they could concentrate on its finer points.

Pierce assured the ensemble that the Volunteers' homecoming would not be marred by unbecoming behaviour. Walton promised to make the official dinner at The Angel an occasion to be talked about for years to come. Walton bowed to a short round of 'Hear Hears'. It promised to be a memorable week for the hotelier. As well as the applause, he could hear the tills ringing. With the Volunteers' event and the May Day, the Angel would be packed to the rafters. And then there was the little matter of the inquest where the jury foreman would be asked to stand and give the verdict. Walton was the foreman.

Midnight beckoned when the meeting broke up. The sky was clear, the moon bright. Fennell nudged Pierce. "Good for the poachers, eh sergeant?" Pierce grunted. He had endured many a late night, most of them fruitless, hunting down the poachers with their nets, sticks, stones and sacks of dead rabbits. A few weeks previously he had nabbed three of them at the smithy on Church Hill, a rare success and they had had the audacity to claim he and his constables had illegally smashed their way into the building, and, worse, that in the past he had tried to bribe them into 'grassing' on other miscreants. Lance Bentley had defended them. Only doing his job, but the accusation still rankled with Pierce, even though the magistrates had dismissed it out of hand.

Poaching thrived on the estates and farms around the town. Outlawed by the Night Poaching Act of 1828 and The Game Act of 1831, it was a serious business with gaol sentences in store for the worst offenders. Sometimes it exploded into violence with clashes between poachers and gamekeepers. In 1873 the son of the gamekeeper at nearby Peover Hall, home of Sir Henry Mainwaring, had been shot and fatally wounded by a poacher's gun. Three men were convicted of manslaughter and given five years penal servitude.

Pierce walked slowly home, down King Street to its junction with Church Hill, taking a peep at the smithy. All quiet and in darkness. A few yards further down the street lay the Parrott's home where, in the kitchen, the smell of rabbit lingered. Pierce momentarily considered paying Mary Ann a visit but it was late and he continued up Church Hill, moving quickly against the cool air, his boots hammering the cobbles..

CHAPTER 13

'When the boys come home,
From across the land,
We'll be happy then again,
And peace will be
In every heart...'
- verse from music-hall song

THOUSANDS waited for the Volunteers, first in Southampton where Baden-Powell, the hero of Mafeking, led the disembarkation, then in Chester, and finally, for a small group of them, in Knutsford. As the train rolled in, the band played, hats and caps were flung into the air, and the cheering reached a crescendo as the carriage doors opened. Five young men wearing khaki uniform and carrying rifles and packs clambered out. Relatives and friends swarmed all over them. Eventually, brigade officers, marshalled by Colonel Mothersill, and police deployed by Sergeant Pierce, cleared a passage, the band set off down Adams Hill and the procession followed.

Sergeant Tom Cash, and Privates Cox, Woodcock, Worrall, and Hankey looked tanned and lean. They were heroes, who had done Britain and Knutsford proud. All five came from working-class homes in the town centre, had spent a year in South Africa and were due to receive the South Africa Medal. At the Angel they were treated to food and all the ale they could manage, the celebrations interspersed with countless toasts and a rendition of The National Anthem, some singing God Save The Queen forgetting that her son was now the monarch. Doctor Fennell made the speech of the night, demanding that all men between the ages of 20-25 should volunteer for active service, for their health and the health of the country. Look at his family. He was Surgeon General of the Knutsford brigade, his sons, a Captain and a Lieutenant commanded it. Every sentence was cheered.

But there was little joy for Private Worrall whose one year-old daughter had just died and was buried in the parish church graveyard. She had been christened Florence Ladysmith Worrall, commemorating the British triumph in relieving the siege of Ladysmith in 1900, just a few weeks after her birth. Her internment was 18 days after that of John Bould and their names are next to each other in the parish register.

But nothing was allowed to spoil the general elation. The drink flowed all over town. Pierce made sure the police were visible, particularly in Market Place and the railway end of King Street. The last thing he needed was his cell block full of drunks on the eve of May Day.

Parrott lay on his plank bed in the prison. Warders had told him of the Volunteers' return. He might have enjoyed a glass or two in the Sword and Sceptre, although it did not worry him unduly. If not for his poor sight he might have been a Volunteer himself. They made allowances for lack of height but not for poor performances on the target range where his defective vision was a major handicap.

There were other reasons for rejecting the army life. He held a jaundiced view of authority, did not mix well, and enjoyed being a loner. If anything, he admired the Boers, the underdogs who were giving the British a hard time with their guerrilla tactics. Parrott might have fancied himself as a guerrilla, well-armed, but lightly clad and with the fitness and endurance to travel long distances on foot. Such soldiers had to be self-sufficient, existing on minimal food. Rabbit pie, perhaps, without the crust.

Parrott had day-dreamed of adventure for most of his life, as had many young Britons fed not only on rabbit but also on stories of courage and chivalry in Boy's Paper and other widely read magazines and books.

The colonisation of exotic lands offered such opportunities. The rush to India had slowed in recent decades following the demise of the East India Co and the re-organisation of the army, but Africa, the 'Dark Continent', loomed large in British aspirations. The south held mouth watering deposits of gold and diamonds – if the Boers could be put in their place.

For some ambitious entrepeneurs the riches of West Africa were even more attractive, especially when the government stepped in and in early 1901 made northern Nigeria a Procterorate. Gold was the primary objective, but tin was also mined and, overall, gross profits exceeded £24million a year. Parrott wanted a slice of it.

Late in 1900 he eyed an advert in the Manchester newspapers. A clerk required by a Liverpool company, trading in West Africa. In January he wrote to Welsh and Co., claiming he had a sound education and some book-keeping experience – an exaggeration. Having worked occasionally as a shop assistant he was accustomed to figuring out small amounts of cash and to filing a few receipts, but nothing more. He did not receive a reply. Apparently Welsh and Co did not want to know. No doubt they received many applications. But, if nothing else, Parrott was persistent. Eventually he won an interview. In late February he met the boss Thomas Welsh at the firm's office and, in his opinion, gave a good account of himself. That night he stayed over with his brother Thomas Holland Parrott at his lodgings in Walton, Liverpool and boasted that he had to make preparations for an overseas trip, adding: "Don't say anything to Mother." Welsh, however, had a different version – Parrott knew full well that the post had been filled but continued to inquire about it, forcing Welsh to send him a formal rejection.

In his cell on April 30 as Knutsford whooped and hurrahed its way through the evening, Parrott re-read the letter which Mary Ann had dropped off and wondered how it had all gone wrong. He cursed John Bould.

If Knutsford suffered a general hangover, the morning of May 1 presented a swift remedy. The day was clear, just a little chilly, perfect for clearing the head. Apart from one or two hostelries which needed a quick tidy-up, everywhere looked spick and span. Bunting and flags hung across the streets which were also decorated with arabesques of coloured sand, a local tradition. The Heath, with its platform, grandstand, fairground stalls and maypole, was ready for the crowning of the Queen and by 9am the first visitors emerged from the railway station. Others were arriving by horse and carriage, pony and trap, and on bicycles.

Angelo Guiseppe, the organ grinder, one of the regular entertainers on show, had a placard mounted above the organ proclaiming: 'I am too old to work.' The lemon drop man barged his way through the crowds offering racing tips with his sweets and the air was battered by the sound of buskers wielding melodeons, banjoes, fiddles and guitars.

A peal of bells from the parish church heralded the start of the procession, which included several bands, the Altrincham Naval Brigade pulling a model of a 4.7 gun, and 700 children made up in character costumes. It all went well. The Lady's Hornpipe brought the grandstand crowd to its feet demanding an encore. Dorothy Jackson and Elsie Cockram obliged. Queen Lottie was duly crowned and her sister, Dorothy linked up neatly with, among others, Norah Jackson and Edith Daniels, swirling around each other in the maypole dance. A wonderful day – 'the only time when the old-fashioned, picturesque village rises to the full height of its stature', according to a condescending report.

Our Knutsford Correspondent walked the procession route, taking notes, laughing off jeers from pals gathered on the steps of the White Lion and itching to get back to the serious business of reporting a murder investigation.

The Parrott family joined in the applause as the procession passed their home. Even Mary Jane Francis had to admit it was 'lovely'. She was enjoying a rare few hours of total freedom, with the police too busy to pester her, and the Speakmans attending a society wedding some miles away. She drifted lonely through the fair, barely noticed.

Emily and Murray were among the distinguished guests at the wedding of Dr Eustace Hatton, fourth son of a deceased Manchester magistrate, and Beatrice Leigh at Lyme Park, on the east side of Cheshire. The Speakmans, renowned for their sophistication and generosity in gifts, attended many weddings, and here they presented the couple with a silver carriage clock.

Although a fine occasion, neither was in the best of spirits. Mary Jane had let them down badly, their home was constantly and embarrassingly visited by the police, Murray had been questioned by a less than respectful sergeant and Emily would have to find a new maid.

What had Mrs Beeton advised about the management of servants? 'Be firm, strict, yet kind and thoughtful for them and they should respect you and carry out your wishes. If they will not do so it is better to part with them rather than have any discomfort in the household.' Emily agreed. Another issue to be decided was that of a character reference for Mary Jane. Until the scandal, she had had nothing but praise for the 'girl' but now....Refusing a 'character' could finish her, certainly no large house would take her on without one.

Whether they treated their employees well or not (in the context of the period), it is difficult not to feel some sympathy for the Speakmans. They had not asked to be dragged into a murder investigation. Mary Jane had lied that Easter Sunday, if not openly then by omission. The understanding was that she was going to church, even if she had not specifically stated it, and Jane Pickstock had aided and abetted her deviousness. As a result, Emily had come to recognise Sergeant Pierce's strident ringing of their bell, followed by a thump on the door. Even the Chief Constable had become familiar, visiting them on three occasions. And, while each time they demanded to see Mary Jane, they also grabbed any opening to quiz her and Murray.

"May I ask you, sir, if you have a revolver or have ever had one?" That was the lowest moment. Murray incensed, Pierce reddening slightly but waiting patiently for his answer. "No, I have not. And I find it impertinent that you even ask. Am I to understand that I am a suspect in this case? If so, I need to speak to my lawyer."

Pierce stayed calm. "Certainly not, sir. But a revolver was used in the murder, to which your maid was a witness."

Speakman could not hide his surprise. "Good God man, you don't believe she did it do you? With a gun from my house? Really Sergeant, you should not listen to tittle tattle."

At Lyme Park, the Speakmans felt safe from the police and the gossip mongers. They did not mind missing Royal May

Day at all.

While they were toasting the bride, Pierce was congratulating himself on a well-run May Day operation. Maybe it was because the locals were in such good humour, but there had been little for his force to do, except act as crowd marshalls. One or two minor incidents in the ale-houses, quickly sorted out, an accident with a bicycle colliding with a cart – should they report the cyclist for furious riding? Pierce thought not. The most worrying issue was a claim of pickpocketing. Someone had lost a silver watch and chain worth two guineas and, as it had not been handed in at the station, Pierce had to consider it stolen. Nabbing the culprit from over 30,000, well, what could he do? The owner's only hope was that the thief tried to sell or pawn it.

In mid-evening Pierce sat down, it seemed for the first time that day, for a bite of supper with his wife. Their three children and his mother-in-law had already eaten. He gripped his cutlery with hands roughened by his teenage years as a brickie. Sometimes, he thought, people forget that bobbies have a private life, but their plates were still half-full when Constable Smith stuck his head around the door, apologised for interrupting but there was a spot of trouble in the Old Market Place. Could he come?

At Orchard Cottage, Dorothy Jackson danced the hornpipe for the family. She would keep the role for the next two years en route to becoming the Royal May Queen herself.

At 23 King Street, Mary Ann Parrott gathered her family around her to discuss ways and means of keeping their black sheep off the scaffold.

CHAPTER 14

'Shoot straight to kill – never be afraid of a tramp!'
- advert for a pocket revolver, 1901

OLD Annie Tweedy was in a cell, sleeping it off. Sergeant Pierce and Constable Smith had had to call for help from passers-by in restraining her, she scratched and bit with what few teeth she had left, she kicked and flailed away with her bony arms. "Drunk as a lord," muttered Smith. They half carried her to the police station, by when she was barely conscious, and laid her out carefully on the cell bunk, face down so that, if she vomited, she would not drown in it. Pierce wearily finished his half-eaten, warmed-up meal, and prepared for bed. What a way for May Day to finish. He could hear Annie snoring from across the yard.

On the morning of May 2 Tweedy found herself in the magistrates' court dock charged with being drunk and disorderly. Through her hangover haze, she wondered why so many people were there. "It's a murder case," the dock officer told her. Annie, thought processes soaked in gin, almost fainted. "I n'er killed anyone – have I?"

"Not you, dear," the officer replied, and pointed to the young man standing next to her in the dock, apparently waiting for his turn.

Tweedy was discharged on condition that she behaved herself in future. She apologised profusely. "It was all the excitement, sir," she told the magistrate, Major Davies. "With the May Day and the Volunteers coming back I got something to drink." She had pleaded for leniency many times in court appearances dating back over decades. In 1899 she had been sent to the workhouse, her face black and blue, after being kicked by her 42 years-old son at their home in the Market Place.

Parrott made way for her as she shuffled out of the dock. She stank. A minute or two later he was remanded for one day, a technicality because a prisoner could not be kept in custody for more than a week at a time. But it allowed the Press to have their fun with stories of a 'decrepit old woman' (aged 64) sharing the dock with an alleged killer.

Tom Jackson patted Mary Ann Parrott's arm as they left the court. "It will be well and good," he said. The strain was showing on her face. She was almost 40, looking older. Annie Tweedy had suffered a hard life, but partly self-inflicted through drinking. Mary Ann, thought Jackson, could not be faulted for the bleak times she had encountered. He would do everything in his power to help.

Next day, the real business got under way. Parrott returned to the Sessions House for a double dose of the British legal system. Firstly, the resumption of the inquest, then a committal hearing in front of a bench of magistrates to determine whether or not there was enough evidence to justify him going before a jury at Chester Assizes, where the judge would have a black cap handy – just in case.

The main inquest witnesses on Friday May 3 were Pierce and James Goodbody, the managing director of the British arm of the Colt's Firearms Manufacturing Co, based in Connecticut, USA, but with a swanky office address in London's Pall Mall. His evidence, in the author's opinion, was off target. With Pierce guilty of an embarrassing lapse and with the coroner in critical mood, it added up to an unsatisfactory conclusion. Another aspect was that the inquest and magistrates' court hearings were running side by side, causing confusion.

Goodbody had helped in other court cases, once having to identify a consignment of stolen Colt's revolvers. A weapons expert, used to steadying himself and controlling his breathing before pulling a trigger - he was well known at the Bisley shooting tournaments – he appeared assured and at ease, looking squarely at the jury. Yet his testimony was loose, perhaps because the questioning was not accurate enough.

Pierce was taken to task when admitting that he did not caution Parrott immediately before taking a written statement on the morning after his arrest, he was then surprisingly interrupted by Parrott over one issue, and he provoked a resigned sigh from the coroner for forgetting to bring the overcoat with him. "We might as well take the opportunity to adjourn for lunch while you go and get it," said H C Yates, sniffily.

More than 300 people were in court, but this time seats were organised for the women with the men ordered to stand behind the iron railings at the back of the room, rather like spectators at a football ground. Teresa Neagle was absent. There was nothing more she could do in Knutsford. John was buried, and other matters would take their course. Father Roche had been understanding - she was obliged to him and other supportive members of the Roman Catholic congregation – and he would keep her informed of events. Now she was back in Burnley praying she and her brother would get justice, although she remained unsure as to Parrott's part.

Mary Jane Francis was there. She had to reprise her evidence, not for the coroner, but for the magistrates when the committal was heard later. It promised to be a long day and she felt unwell, tired and flushed, just as she had on Easter Sunday when she went for her walk along Mere Heath Lane. She listened intently to the proceedings while feeling for the bottle of medicine in her pocket.

Also among those attending the inquest's last rites were Mary Ann Parrott, her daughters, Mary and Edith, and of course, her elder son. Although not on trial, Parrott sat in the dock. Still in his suit, shirt and tie, he again looked 'respectable' but, one report surmised, 'a little worse for wear from his stay in gaol', adding: 'He sat quietly in his chair....Seated as he was in the dock only his head and shoulders could be seen by the public. He had his arms folded and, from time to time, tightened his lips as though labouring under some strong inward feeling, otherwise his appearance was one of carelessness than one of interest. From time to time he rocked slowly on the hind legs of his chair.'

Parrott heard Goodbody tell how Colt's had received a letter from him in March. It read: 'Dear Sir, Please forward to me by next post, as I intend going to West Africa shortly, one of your travellers' new pocket .32 calibre, central fire, double-action revolvers, six shot, 2 ½ inches barrel, price three guineas, extra plating, five shillings, leather case complete £1, one hundred cartridges, six shillings, total £4 14s., and oblige, yours respectfully, address J. C. Parrott, care of Mr W. Marshall, 33a Portland Street, Manchester. Please find enclosed cheque for £4. 14s'.

Goodbody, a stocky figure, told the court that he treated the order in the normal way. The 'extra plating' referred to additional metallic work on the butt of the gun. The weapon and cartridges were packed into a leather case which itself was placed into a box and despatched from his office to be transported by train to Manchester and eventually to the address given, which turned out to be a hairdresser's run by a Mr William Marshall who allowed his shop to be used as an accommodation address. The sale was noted in the firm's order book, the cheque was honoured, and he heard nothing more of the transaction until contacted by the police.

"Would such a gun fit into this?" asked the coroner at which Pierce handed over the leather case discovered at Parrott's home. Goodbody turned it over, then caused gasps of surprise by suddenly reaching into his pocket and producing a small revolver – a Colt .32. It fitted neatly. But a card pasted onto the interior of the case, bearing the original gun's serial number was missing. Spectators craned their necks for a better view as the case and gun were examined by each member of the jury.

Goodbody continued to give details about the weapon chiefly at the inquest, and, a few hours later, at the committal hearing. The author intends to amalgamate this evidence, and to analyse it, in a section of its own later in this chapter. Suffice it for now that it begs questions.

Other witnesses fitted in certain pieces of the jigsaw.

William Marshall, the hairdresser, confirmed that Parrott had paid him a 'small amount' for the package to be delivered to his premises early in March. He did not know Parrott, it was simply a bit of business, and the prisoner, whom he identified, collected the item promptly without any visible sign of excitement. George Day, manager of Parr's Bank, Knutsford, said that Parrott had opened an account with them, at one stage it contained around £60, but it was closed in late March after the cheque to Colt's had been honoured.

Pierce was called and repeated almost ad verbatim his account of the events of April 20-21 only to be interrupted by a protest from the dock. Parrott could hardly be seen but his voice rang out.

Pierce was recounting how on the morning of April 21 he had asked Parrott about the clothes he was wearing on Easter Sunday and whether he had an overcoat on, at which Parrott pushed forward from his chair, pointed an accusatory finger and said: "No, you didn't! You said 'Where's your overcoat?'" The coroner hushed him, saying: "Wait a bit. If there is anything wrong, Mr Bentley will put it right." Lance Bentley nodded and gestured his client to sit down. The sergeant appeared unruffled, refusing to amend his evidence, but Yates was not pleased when he admitted that he had left the overcoat at the station. And, although Parrott's brief intervention did not materially affect the case, it highlighted something of his character. That, while to some he had appeared 'careless', he was, in fact, paying close attention to the detail, and, like Bould, he was unafraid to stand up for himself. One or two considered him in a slightly different vein after that – and they were right to do so.

What with Annie Tweedy's unscheduled appearance, Parrott's interjection and Pierce's forgetfulness, Yates was getting a little fidgety. When a juryman was spotted whispering something to Parrott's solicitor, Edwin Ashworth, he exploded, demanding an explanation. Ashworth angrily retorted: "If someone decides to speak to me, there is nothing I can do about it."

Lunch came at a convenient moment. Afterwards, the overcoat lay on the Clerk's desk, in full view of the jury. Dark brown, of no distinctive style, and obviously much too big for Parrott. But, as nothing else was said about it, they wondered why the coroner had been so keen for Pierce to fetch it. Pierce wondered too and, like Dr Smith, he thought maybe the coroner enjoyed putting people in their place. Yates certainly enjoyed his summing-up, much to the embarrassment of George Rowe. Harry Yarwood also came in for some stick, but his skin was much thicker. Rowe grimaced, Yarwood beamed, leaned back in his chair, and scratched his ear.

For Mary Jane, the coroner's words were vindication, although he did not go so far as to call Rowe and Yarwood liars. In summarising the affair of The Three Horsemen, he asserted: "It all goes to the credibility of Miss Francis, and the surrounding facts are more in favour of her than of Rowe. As for Yarwood, he must have heard the church bells even if he had no other reminder that it was Sunday." He couched his words carefully but no-one missed the scorn in his voice.

Yates warned the jury that, while it was obvious that Bould was murdered, they had to decide whether there was a prima facie case to name Parrott as the killer, or whether they should merely class it as 'wilful murder by person or persons unknown'. The foreman, John Walton, led the jury to their retiring room at 2 30pm and on their return, an hour later, he announced: "Murder by person or persons unknown". Parrott's legal team could barely hide their delight. As the coroner had emphasised, this was not the criminal court, and, in theory, the verdict could not hold sway at the trial. But it was bound to colour atttitudes. Here was a jury who had heard most, if not all, the evidence to be produced at the Assize court and they, in their wisdom, had decreed that it was impossible to condemn Parrott. Colonel Hammersley and Superintendent Okell, sitting next to the coroner, exchanged looks with Pierce. A tough job for the police had become much tougher.

This was Yates's last involvement with the case. He discharged the jury, picked up his silk top hat and cane, and left. Everyone else shifted to the second court at the other end of the Sessions House where two magistrates, the chairman Francis Ashworth and Ernest Leycester were ready for the committal hearing, a completely separate event but, as far as the evidence to be offered, basically an encore of the inquest.

Court Two was smaller, more intimate, with Parrott more

visible in the dock. By then it was almost 4pm, a sense of weariness descended on the proceedings, and, as Saturday had already been reserved, they called it a day just after 6pm, agreeing to return the next morning with Bentley promising, under his breath, 'some fireworks'. By then he had reluctantly stood aside as leading counsel for the defence, the role being taken by the Manchester based Thomas Clarke Pilling Gibbons, who, a week earlier, had suffered much good-humoured abuse as the judge at the annual mock trial staged by the city's law students. Gibbons was good, but Bentley resented being shoved into the secondary role, he was not a man for the shadows.

Others pondered their futures.

Mary Jane was on the brink of leaving Knutsford. The police had taken the malicious letter from her, telling her not to worry. Her father had arrived in the town, travelling up from Welshpool via Chester. "You're coming home," he said. It bolstered her. One last foray into the witness stand and this miserable episode would be over, at least until the trial, and she could get her life back.

William Pierce reckoned certain people were trying to push him around, to provoke him. But behaviour like that only deepened his resolve. The Chief, Okell and Leah had put their faith in him, he had one foot on the promotion ladder and he was going to climb it, no matter what Bentley and co threw at him.

James Crossley Parrott sat straight-backed on the edge of his bunk, trying to figure out when he was happiest. As a youngster, until his father's death, life had had a certain lightness with his parents busy in the shop and his grandfather relating stories about the farm in Holmes Chapel. It dimmed with the family's illness and deaths. It darkened further when he had to go away, but it was there, at that place, where he learned that solitude was not necessarily loneliness, and that a solitary person could be stronger than one in a crowd, although the knowledge was hard-earned. And on his return to Knutsford, it was impossible to settle. He had plans, ambitions which a small town failed to answer. No, the moment of true happiness he could pinpoint to the day when he collected his package from the hairdresser's in the centre of Manchester, clenched it under his arm, and walked to his Aunt Annie's place in Irlam of t' Heights where, occasionally, he stayed. He laid it on his bed, slowly unpacked it, and almost choked with pleasure at the blue gleam of metal which greeted him. With due reverence, he extricated the Colt .32, stroked the short barrel, admired the scrollwork on the butt for which he had paid an extra five shillings, checked the mechanisms, and aimed it at a wall mirror. Light spots reflected off his spectacles but no-one would call him 'Speccy four eyes now', or anything else for that matter. He filled the six chambers with cartridges.

In his cell that Friday evening, Parrott leaned back against the limed wall, savouring the memory, how the revolver slipped so easily into a pocket, its perfect balance in his hand. With so much shilly-shallying court business, he had eaten little since breakfast, but he rarely suffered hunger pangs. Tomorrow was another day in the dock, and, after that, well, either he would be set free to follow his dream, or he would have a few quiet weeks to himself while others battled over his life.

Saturday came brightly, although the makers of 'Warner's Safe Cure' painted some grey clouds over life. 'Today there is light, tomorrow there may be darkness,' their advert warned. Their 2s 9d bottle of 'medicine' would save you from jaundice, gall stones, and one or two other nasty ailments. Mary Jane Francis relied on Dr Appleby's prescription for her problem. She swallowed a teaspoonful, wondering whether it would get her through the day, said 'Cheerio' to Jane Pickstock, picked up her bag, and went out to meet her father, who was boarding nearby. He would be in the public seats while she, again, gave her evidence. Hopefully, she would finish in time for the early afternoon train to Chester, from where they would make their way to Welshpool, and then to the cottage at Llansantffraid. Home. Leicester Caldecutt and Tom Jackson also hoped for an early getaway – Knutsford were playing at Bowdon, one of the hardest matches of the summer, but by late morning it was obvious they would have to forfeit their cricket.

There was little change in the evidence as such, but Parrott's defence team of Gibbons and Bentley harried several witnesses into minor concessions before clawing at Pierce's failure to give the prisoner a full caution when making his revised statement on the morning after his arrest. An entertaining exchange between Mary Jane and Gibbons livened up a tiring, dull day. It stemmed from the barrister's sly attempt to smear her by building on rumours that the murder was a result of a love affair. Gibbons questioned her claim that she had never been in Mere Heath Lane before Easter Sunday and asked sneeringly if she was there to meet a man.

She was resolute. "Never, although the public say that I have." When Gibbons told her: "Never mind what the public say," she retorted: "I don't. I will gain the day yet and I have still got my character to which countesses and earls can speak of." *(Laughter)*.

Gibbons: "You have no sweetheart or anything of that kind?" "Oh yes, an old sweetheart but he is no good. But, never mind, I like him." *(More laughter)*.

And when counsel asked about the incident with Rowe and whether she liked his arm around her, she said: "I did not. I said to him 'Please take it away'." *(Laughter)*

But most of her evidence was in serious tones, mainly a repeat of previous hearings but perhaps more decisive on some points, namely that, when she first saw Parrott in the lane it was about 6 45pm; that the man leaning over the body was actually touching Bould's chest with his hands; that he ran off 'as fast as he could' and that he was definitely wearing a long coat, either an overcoat or a macintosh. Despite that, she still could not swear that this man was Parrott.

Four witnesses from the Sword and Sceptre, the licensee Robert Lee, his wife, a daughter, and a barman who all knew Parrott by sight, told the court that they could not recall him being in the pub on Easter Sunday evening as he claimed. Skilfully cross-examined by Gibbons, all had to accept that they might have missed him or, in the case of Florrie Lee, the daughter, that she might simply have forgotten.

Gibbons then ripped into Pierce who formally cautioned

Parrott shortly before charging him on the Saturday night but not before his second statement the following morning when the sergeant carefully wrote down each question and answer as it happened. Pierce remained steadfast, and the magistrates over-ruled an objection by the defence that Parrott's statement had been illegally procured.

Despite Bentley's earlier optimism, the committal to trial was inevitable and Parrott, looking slightly more anxious than at any time, was again remanded in custody.

Mary Jane and her father arrived at the family cottage late that night. Her time in Knutsford was over. Indeed, her time in service was over, too. No more waiting on countesses and earls and strict mistresses. As for Caldecutt and Jackson, Saturday ended miserably with the news that Knutsford had suffered a humiliating 231 runs defeat at Bowdon.

GUN LAW

AT the turn of the 19th and 20th centuries, many more people legally used and/or owned handguns than of now. Advertised in newspapers and magazines, they were sold on the open market by major firearms manufacturers like Colt's and Smith and Wesson, perhaps the two best known, and also by numerous smaller firms. Second-hand guns exchanged hands in pubs and clubs and sometimes on the street.

The manufacturers dealt in pistols and revolvers, very different in design but equally deadly in the wrong hands. The pistol of 1901 was basically similar to a modern handgun with a magazine of bullets pushed into the butt, capable of firing – so one manufacturer claimed – five shots in a second.

A common revolver of the same year was a smaller, more sophisticated version of that which 'tamed the American Wild West', with the cartridges slotted individually into a revolving chamber. In the case of the Colt .32, this was also automatic in that the user did not have to manually engage the hammer as of old, the mere pull of the trigger discharged one bullet and simultaneously readied another. Colt's, termed it 'double action', and it, too, catered for rapid fire.

So-called pocket revolvers were all the rage with manufacturers targeting travellers and cyclists, particularly women who wanted protection as they pedalled gaily along lonely country roads. Some had been attacked and robbed by vagrants.

'The Cyclist's Friend', trumpeted one advert for a pocket gun, featuring a young lady on a bike with the tag: 'I fear no tramp'. This 'lovely little shooter' was small enough to slip into a watch pocket, cost a meagre 12 shillings and could be bought with 100 cartridges from T W Carryer and Co.,

Ltd, Newcastle, Staffordshire. In the USA, the Iver Johnson Cycle Revolver was 'designed especially for cyclists', although they also made one for women alone at home with a slogan 'Never be afraid of a burglar'. They also focused on the safety element. The gun could not be accidentally fired, and to prove it they circulated a poster showing a little girl in bed with a doll, but playing with one of their revolvers.

Colt's .32 New Model Pocket was something else. Top of the range, bang up to date. So good that Harry Palmer (aka Michael Caine) used one in the spy thriller movie The Ipcress File in 1965! They had started making it in 1893 and, continuing, had constantly improved it. Like most revolvers it was easy to maintain and repair but also tough, reliable and precise, probably the best of its type. Which is why Parrott wanted it. While there is no evidence he had any great knowledge of guns he was happy to spend a total of £4 14s when he could have obtained an inferior one like Carryer's for a lot less. Used guns imported from Europe went for a few shillings. But the cheaper guns were often inaccurate and liable to malfunction.

Parrott's letter to Colt's of London was exact in its detail, copied from their advert. Of several barrel lengths available he opted for the shortest, 2 ½ inches, making the overall length of the gun less than 5 inches. Because of the spherical shape of the chamber, a revolver could not lie flat like a pistol, but it was easily tucked away in a coat pocket, especially a gun as small as Parrott's. It was sometimes labelled as a 'traveller's gun' and, in his letter, Parrott mentioned he was shortly to leave for West Africa. With the Colt came 100 .32 calibre cartridges. These were Colt 'short' cartridges, of a particular dimension to fit the New Model Pocket. One bullet of this type was retrieved from Bould's body.

James Goodbody told the coroner and the magistrates on May 3 and 4 that, unless specifically asked by the customer, Colt's always supplied these cartridges with this revolver. At first this seemed a solid piece of evidence for the prosecution, indicating that a bullet from the type of gun owned by Parrott had killed Bould. But, under cross-examination, Goodbody accepted that the Colt 'short' could be fired by other makes of gun.

In response to Lance Bentley's probing, Goodbody claimed that Colt's made 'thousands' of the New Model Pocket each year, and that they could be found in 'all parts of the country'. Initially he agreed with Bentley that they were stocked at all leading gunsmiths, but he amended that to say 'at least in London', otherwise they had to be purchased by mail order. Bentley then asked him about the cartridges. These were made in Hartford, Connecticut, USA, by the Union Metallic Cartridge Co, and said to be adapted for use by Colt's and, significantly, other revolvers.

"A great number of revolvers use the same, don't they?" Bentley insisted.

"Several do," said Goodbody, adding a few moments later, "About half a dozen."

No wonder Bentley appeared pleased. He had popped another prosecution bubble. Goodbody, the only firearms expert in the case, was agreeing readily with the defence suggestion that a gun other than the type owned by Parrott could have been the murder weapon. And, although definitely a Colt .32 calibre, the bullet recovered from Bould's body could not be traced to the batch sent to Parrott as they bore no specific marking.

What perturbs the author about Goodbody's contribution was the absence of detail. For example, he said 'thousands' of the New Model Pockets were turned out each year, but there was a hint of salesman's jargon in that. In fact Colt's were producing between 2000 and 3000 each year, all at their USA plant, and the great majority were sold in America.

Although top quality and much cherished, the brand met resistance in Britain, simply because they were not British. It had been 45 years since Colt's had closed down their London factory in Pimlico, having failed to counter competition from British companies. The Colt's revolvers were also extremely costly, and not generally available over the counter in Britain other than in top London gunsmiths. With the firm's order book at his fingertips, Goodbody could have told the courts exactly how many had been sold to British customers. Of course, it suited both the defence and Goodbody to imply that they were so popular that the country was flooded with them.

Goodbody's information about cartridges was also flaky. The Colt .32 could be used in 'half a dozen' different types of revolver. But he did not say which, nor was he asked whether his knowledge came from experience, or test reports, or whether he was meekly following the guidance of the manufacturer, the Union Metallic Cartridge Co. This might seem like nit-picking. But the notion that this cartridge was so versatile might have been challenged.

James Goodbody (right) at a firearms exhibition

The author's research reveals that not all .32 cartridges were inter -changeable. A cartridge designed for the .32 Smith and Wesson revolver was a hairs-breadth too wide for its Colt counterpart. Conversely a .32 Colt cartridge would leave a miniscule space in the chamber of a Smith and Wesson and, while it could be fired, the performance might be affected with the risk of damage and/or injury.

Nor was Goodbody asked about the mechanics of actually firing a revolver. For some, including Teresa Neagle, it beggared belief that this was the work of an inexperienced shooter because firing a handgun properly poses problems for a novice, particularly in controlling the recoil which forces the hand and/or arm out of line for the next shot.

Target shooters practise, among other things, body position and breathing methods and for a completely inexperienced marksman to score a 'max' is exceptional, but more likely if the target is at point -blank range, if the gun is well engineered, light and balanced in the hand, like the New Model Colt even though it needed a strong pull on the trigger. It was – and still is - impossible to conclude that the killing gun must have been a Colt, like that owned by Parrott, but the probability was higher than Goodbody suggested. Called by the prosecution, he proved a useful defence witness. Edward Giles, the Chester-based solicitor, acting on behalf of the Crown at the committal, looked out of his depth against Parrott's sharp-shooting barristers. Bentley might well have shouted 'Bulls eye!'

A pocket revolver similar to the one bought by Parrott,
advertised as a 'friend' for travellers and cyclists

CHAPTER 15

'In Knutsford's fair town there are first class hotels
Where they give board and lodging for all the big swells
They've all blinds on the windows and bolts on the doors
And beautiful carpet laid down on the floors
But the grandest of all and now in full swing
Is the fine looking hostel controlled by the king
I was in it myself and am able to tell
There's no digs in Europe to equal Knutsford Hotel
– anon, c1916'

THAT skit on Knutsford Prison, which runs to 10 verses, was written by an un-named Irish rebel, one of over 500 lodged in the gaol after the Easter uprising of 1916. Shipped to Liverpool, they were put on trains at Chester, escorted by Cheshire Regiment soldiers. Generally, the Irish were not treated badly in Knutsford, but they complained bitterly about the food, 'potatoes which were green or black', and one claimed that he licked the lime off the cell wall for extra nutrition.

Parrott had spent only two weeks in a cell by the time his case was sent for trial at Chester Assizes. He was to remain in prison for almost another three months before entrusting his fate to a jury. Gaol regimes had softened a little in recent years – the punishing treadmill and crank handle routines, classed as exercise but really to keep convicts quiet, had disappeared from most prisons and the Silent and/or Separate Systems were under review, but it remained a tough life with strict discipline, hard work, and poor diet.

Knutsford's prison opened in 1820 and 81 years later had not changed a great deal. Capable of accommodating over 500 males and females, including juveniles, the cells were arranged in four main wings over four storeys, the whole in a wonky radial design with a central open yard where convicts were allowed an hour's exercise, walking a circular route in silence and maintaining a 'social distance' from others. Otherwise they were mainly confined to their 10 feet x 6 feet (approx.) whitewashed cells, each furnished bleakly with a plank bed, wash basin, chamber pot, scrubbing brush, and bible.

A cell at Knutsford Prison, sketched by an Irish prisoner who wrote of the Knutsford Hotel and his 'apartment'. That was in 1916 but the cell was unchanged from Parrott's time at the gaol

They were forced to work for their meagre meals. Picking oakum, the re-threading of fraying rope (hence 'money for old rope'), was one of the main activities. Other tasks included sewing mailbags, boot and clothes mending, and bookbinding. Some were employed as cooks, bakers, stokers (the steam-heated prison had around 100 chimneys), washers, and general labourers.

Food was short in quantity and quality, although Knutsford had its own bakery, built by the prisoners in 1879 after moans about the integrity of loaves delivered by a contractor. With the bread, there were potatoes, a little meat (about eight ounces per week), bits of vegetables and fruit when available, soup and gruel, thin rations indeed considering they had to work.

While there had been reform with more on the way, the prime objective of this rigorous and monotonous regime was to stop convicts inter-acting and spreading infectious ideas. In general, to dumb them down. But it was also to punish, and thereby to act as a deterrent. Those guilty of violence within the gaol could be birched, subject to Home Office approval. One, Frank Holland, a 21 years-old Manchester baker doing 16 months hard labour for theft received 16 strokes after one incident at Knutsford.

Three years before Parrott's incarceration, an official inquiry was held into the treatment of a convict named John Graham who died of tuberculosis within a few days of his release from Knutsford. Supported by their doctor, Graham's family in Glasgow claimed the mean diet and medical neglect had led to his death but the GP refused to attend the hearing as it would disrupt his holiday plans. Without his evidence, the tribunal spent little time in exonerating the governor Major Nelson and the surgeon Dr Fennell.

Parrott was viewed in a more sympathetic light than others because he was only on remand, awaiting trial, and therefore to be presumed innocent until found guilty. He had a cell to himself, wore his own clothes, did not have to do 'hard labour', continued to benefit from Mary Ann's cuisine, had some reading material and received occasional visits from lawyers and the chaplain, Reverend Truss. But these luxuries counted little for him. He did not need them. Unknown to most, this spindly, butter would not melt in his mouth, 21 years-old was a stoical battle-hardened veteran.

"He's at it again." warder Alf Hubbard told his colleague Edward Robinson. "Just sitting there, staring at the wall. Been like that for two hours now. Like he's in a trance or summat."

Some concern existed over Parrott's mental stability. The hangman's noose dangled over him, and his behaviour did not follow normal patterns. If guilty as charged, he should have been distressed, sullen, resigned, or even falsely high-spirited. If innocent, would he not have protested against the injustice of it all? Parrott gave nothing away. In his cell, he barely moved for hours. He ate cautiously, as though fearing it was poisoned. In the yard he walked quickly for an hour, following the outer of five concentric white lines painted on the concrete. "Wonder he doesn't go dizzy," grunted Hubbard.

The warders did not know what to make of him. Major Nelson had ordered them to keep a beady eye on him, but observing Parrott was like watching paint dry. And they had enough on their plates. They were short-staffed, as many prisons were, and two of them had been hauled in front of the governor for misconduct. Nelson discussed the situation with Dr Fennell. They agreed that while Parrott was a rare breed, that did not make him insane, or likely to harm himself. Fennell had little sympathy for a young, healthy man who had landed in gaol, rather than on the front line in South Africa. Nothing wrong with him that a spell with the Volunteers would not cure. Nelson decided to relax close supervision – Parrott was deemed sound in mind and body.

"Of course, he is," said Pierce when told the news. "And he's a good actor, to boot."

As others debated his state of mind, the man himself settled down to bed and breakfast a la Knutsford Hotel. Perched on the bunk, he let himself drift. Eyes closed, he pulled in some memories.

His father Tom. "Head stuffed with nonsense," his mother exclaimed. "And where we do we get the money from?" Even as illness and debts gripped him, he still talked of making his fortune. The young Parrott was close to his father. His death left a gap which his mother, despite all her fussing, could not fill. Briefly, his grandfather James snr, offered more of what he needed, but he was gone less than a year later and, from then on, it was all down to Mother. It must have been hard for her. He remembered sitting on the stairs one evening, listening to her talking to the grocer James Hough and Tom Jackson. She sounded unhappy. Not long afterwards she shocked him with the news that he had to go away, to a special school. She was unable to fend for and feed five children on her own. And, anyway, it would be 'good for him'. Oh yes, good for him, thought Parrott, pushing his back against the cell wall. He had never accepted it. If the warders had continued to peek at him they might have seen his face change at that moment, that twitch at the corner of the mouth, a slight reddening in his cheeks, the only signs of emotion that anyone ever saw in him.

The face and the voice of the doctor swam into view – another recollection. "Not much we can do for him. One day people will realise that vaccination is the only way to stop this sort of thing." Parrott was laid low with a severe dose of measles. Mary Ann mopped his brow with a cool cloth and somehow he came through a high fever, but the virus affected his eyes, worsening the weak vision from which he already suffered. Spectacles helped. However his frail frame, short sightedness, and diffident manner made him a soft target for the bully boys. Gradually he learned how to cope, mentally constructing a fortification, first of timber, then, while at school of solid concrete. Nothing could get to him. And from behind his defences he could take imaginery pot shots at his enemies.

Parrott shifted position slightly on the bunk. Although most prisoners worked silently there was a general din about the place which intruded on a man's thoughts, but he had the knack of shutting himself off. Always had. He had read somewhere that to stay sane in prison, particularly in solitary, it was essential to keep the mind 'revolving'.

There was the day when, accompanied by his mother, he travelled to Watford, his belongings neatly stowed in his grandfather's suitcase. He was surprised to see that the special school was a large, imposing complex in more than 30 acres of well-maintained grounds. Over an arched entrance, scrollwork carried the title London Orphan Asylum.

This was an orphanage like no other. The buildings were high and wide, dominating, yet graceful, the general appearance being more of a public school than a refuge for outcast children.

This institution was the brainchild of a Victorian clergyman and philanthropist, Doctor Andrew Reed, who devoted his life to social reform and had a talent for enlisting support and cash from the high and mighty of London society - royalty, aristocracy, bankers, and merchants. The orphanage was first based in magnificent Palladian style buildings in Clapham, south London, but moved in 1871, 10 years after Reed's death, to a purpose-built site close to the London and Northern Railway at Watford Junction. Here the construction changed to Victorian Gothic but the ethos remained consistent, 'to provide relief to destitute orphans, to rescue them from walks of vice and profligacy, to provide them clothing and maintenance, to fix the habits of industry and frugality, and to place them in situations where these principles shall not be endangered and the prospect of an honest livelihood shall be secured'.

Reed had chosen the word 'asylum' with care. It meant 'haven', a place of respite and care for society's unfortunates. The school's definition of an 'orphan' was a child who had lost both parents or was 'fatherless', embracing someone like Parrott, although other criteria also had to be fulfilled. One was that the child's parents had to be married, another that they were 'respectable', ie: professional people, traders, merchants, clerks. It smacked of elitism. The foundation stone at Watford was laid by the Princess of Wales, accompanied by her husband, the future King Edward V11. Lords and Ladies and rich businessmen filled the ranks of sponsors. Fund-raising balls and events were staged at swish hotels. And children could not knock on the front door and plead for B and B. They had to be elected annually by the asylum's subscribers, the votes being counted at a public ceremony in central London.

In June 1890 the election took place at the Canon Street Hotel with 40 places up for grabs, 13 girls and 27 boys. Parrott squeezed in, 609 votes earning him joint last place.

Mary Ann had put his name forward on the basis that his father had died three years earlier, that she had five children and was in financial trouble, and that, of course, her 10 years-old son had been brought up in a respectable manner. But who sponsored him is unknown. Certainly, she would have needed someone of repute. Outside London, there was no better place than Knutsford to find a big name backer with the likes of Tom Jackson or James Hough acting as middle man. Jackson, into everything, knowing everyone, particularly members of de Tabley Lodge; Hough being on the area's Board of Guardians.

As possible sponsors, high-ups in the Lodge such as Egerton of Tatton and Cornwall-Legh of High Legh, come to mind. Another possibility is Viscount Knutsford, former Colonial Secretary in the government who had granted the charter for Cecil Rhodes' British South African Company. His family were the Hollands of Knutsford. Peter Holland, his grandfather, was Elizabeth Gaskell's uncle (during her time in Knutsford, she enjoyed rides on his pony and trap).

One branch of the Hollands' family farmed land at nearby Goostrey, now famous for the Jodrell Bank telescope, and their daughter Mary Holland married a farmer in Holmes Chapel, James Parrott snr. It was why Mary Ann's second son had been christened Thomas Holland Parrott. By chance, the Viscount's country estate, Munden, was only six miles from the orphanage.

Parrott would have known little of all this, just that he was lucky to be enrolling into a prestigious school with facilities beyond compare.

At a cost of £110,000 it was designed with light, air and space as essential themes. Three blocks or squares were overlooked by a 160 feet clock tower and spire, which could be seen from most parts of Watford. In the centre, the offices and huge dining hall; to the left the girls' buildings, to the right, the boys'. Among other resources, the girls had a music room with 10 cubicles, each containing a piano. Their dormitory was split into sections of 50 softly mattressed beds. The boys' dorm had rooms of 25 beds. They had a boot room, where they learned to polish their footwear properly, and while the girls practised calisthenics, the boys' exercise came in the form of daily military routines, a sergeant barking out instructions.

Worship was in a chapel with a hammered roof, sick children were looked after by a matron and a nurse in the infirmary. But perhaps the most surprising asset was a large, lofty swimming pool, which in winter was covered over to provide a gymnasium. The dining hall was fit for a king with a high, timbered ceiling and stained glass windows bearing the arms of past governors.

At mealtimes, the children formed neat lines, marched to their seats at a dozen long tables and, when a gong sounded, sat down. "They behaved like well-drilled soldiers," said one observer. Food was served by a house matron and monitors. It was basic fare, boiled beef hot one day and cold the next, potatoes, suet dumplings, porridge etc, with occasional fruit and a plum pudding as a treat, but servings were generous. Education was anything but basic with music, languages, and science all on the menu.

Hygiene was exceptional. Parrott, brought up in an area of Knutsford which sometimes stank of sewage, was now able to use flush toilets spaced around a giant communal bath. Everywhere was kept spotlessly clean. The managers were determined to avoid a repeat of a typhoid epidemic which had swept though the orphanage's former site in Clapham in the 1860s, one of the factors behind the move to Watford.

The LOA could accommodate around 600. When Parrott registered he was one of 324 boys and 188 girls. Headed by the warden, retired Lt Colonel Henry Coyne and his wife, Julia, there were over 60 full-time staff, including a headmistress, nine governesses, six pupil teachers, a matron, eight house matrons, an infirmary matron and nurse, a cook, two needleworkers, 15 maids, six laundresses, and 10 general servants.

This, then, was to be Parrott's home for four years. Of

thousands of youngsters who passed through its doors, he was one of the very few glad to leave. Probably, he preferred The Knutsford Hotel.

Parrott was a loner. At home in King Street he could retreat to his room and read - stories of derring-do, heroes of British Imperialism performing wild deeds in faraway places - or he could sit cross-legged on the bed he shared with John, imagining himself as one of those heroes, a Gordon in Egypt or a Nicholson in India, going down deep into his world, so deep that once Mary Ann had to shake him by the shoulders to get his attention. Since her husband's death, James had become troublesome in other ways. The chance of a place at the LOA came at the right time. "You'll be alright, lots of other boys to make friends with." That is what he needed, friends. Someone to bring him out of himself.

But perhaps the best equipped and managed orphanage in the country was the wrong place at the wrong time for a dysfunctional 10 years-old.

Psychologists agree that not enough research has been carried out on 'boarding school syndrome', how being forced out of a loving, close environment into one of strict discipline and high expectations can affect the mental health of a child. But there is enough evidence to warrant concern and in 2015 new guidelines were introduced for UK institutions. However, in Victorian times and for much of the 20th century, such issues were either not recognised or contemptuously brushed aside.

Doctor Joy Schaverien, a modern British psychotherapist who has written extensively on the subject claims: "When a child is brought up at home the family adapts to accommodate it...but in an institution the child must adapt to the system. Combined with the sudden and repeated loss of parents, siblings, pets and toys this causes the child to shut itself off from the need for intimacy. This can cause major problems in adulthood – depression, an inability to talk about or understand emotions, an urge to escape from or to destroy intimate relationships."

One significant point is that the deepest psychological effects manifest themselves in later years, not during the actual childhood experience. A Scottish man who was sent to boarding school after the death of his father admitted: "It took me 20 years to complete my adolescence."

Nick Duffell who has also investigated the syndrome explains: "It is an adult problem with its genesis in ruptured childhood attachments, exacerbated by the high expectations from social privilege conferred to boarding institutions."

While the LOA was categorised as an orphanage, it was developed and organised on the lines of an elite boarding school, with superb facilities, and favoured by the nation's wealthiest and most powerful social class. Its young residents were expected to appreciate their luck in being admitted there and to respond appropriately. Most did and went on to make useful contributions to society. Some progressed to university, some made their way up in business and commerce. Many looked back on their time at the asylum with great affection and gratitude and stayed in contact, forming an old boys' association, raising cash and donating prizes at the annual sports and speech days. One former pupil laid out £5000 to build the chapel.

Inevitably, a small minority failed to hit targets. When a fellow pupil of Parrott's, Ernest Nightingale returned home for the Easter holiday in 1891, he complained to his mother that the academic work was difficult and that he wanted to drop a class. Hearing of this, his head teacher treated the matter seriously, as though an affront to the asylum's raison d'etre.

A minute from the Board's report for July that year stated: 'His complaints against his master were groundless – that he was a boy of fair abilities – that his mother was most injudicious and that this desire to enter a lower class so that he might avoid Algebra and Euclid, arose from sheer idleness. The Board ultimately saw the boy and reasoned with him, the Chairman pointing out that while a scholar he must learn what was thought best, and be subject to discipline and he was enjoined to behave himself better in future.'

While that seems a progressive way of dealing with the matter, persuasion rather than force, it also suggests a results based formula which would not have suited some. Parrott, being one. Obedience in general behaviour was also demanded. Indiscipline could warrant corporal punishment, although this was no different to any other school, then and for many decades afterwards.

At holiday time, Parrott returned to Knutsford, receiving a prodigal son's welcome. He had sacrificed himself for the good of the family. One less head to feed enabled Mary Ann to keep hers just above water. The business continued, albeit falteringly, and the Parrotts stayed respectable and optimistic. They owed him. Other than taking long walks he rarely left the confines of the family home. He had no particular friends and preferred to hang out with his siblings. He was closer to his sister Edith than his brothers Thomas Holland and John, who was shooting up fast, and although five years younger, was certain soon to outstrip him in height. His mother fussed over him, trying to make him eat more.

Back at the LOA, Parrott was regarded with suspicion. His poor vision was a massive handicap, not simply because he had to get close up to identify objects and people properly, but also because other people did not understand it, why he was so reserved, why he failed to grasp algebraic formulae chalked on the blackboard some distance from his seat. Spectacles helped but by no means cured his deficiencies. He became isolated, which was exactly what he wanted. Alone with his thoughts, even though surrounded each night by 24 other lads. It made life easier. Parrott developed into a survivor, able to endure.

Over those four years he merited little attention, never earning a mention in the academic reports. All the LOA's children had to leave at the age of 14. In the institution's terminology they were 'discharged'.

Great efforts were made to find them a suitable job, or to further their education. Some were given a new outfit. All were presented with a bible and wished good luck. Parrott was discharged into 'the care of his mother'.

It soon became clear that he was that rare item – an anonymous failure of the London Orphan Asylum, but now a famous resident of The Knutsford Hotel.

CHAPTER 16

*'He is not responsible for his actions.. to an
extent' – Mary Ann Parrott, 1897*

PARROTT walked out of the orphanage for the last
time on a warm, still July morning in 1894, his
clothes again packed into his grandfather's case,
this time with a bible tucked down the side. He was
three months short of his 15th birthday.

Watford Junction station was just a few minutes away
and he strode out cheerfully with a sense of liberation.
Soon he was heading north. At Manchester's London Road
station, he could have switched to a Cheshire Lines train
heading through the city's southern suburbs and Cheshire
countryside to Knutsford where Mary Ann had promised a
grand homecoming, with everyone waiting on the platform.
But the thought of him being hugged and kissed by his
mother and sisters with brothers Tom and John looking
on in amusement was too much to bear. Parrott had other
plans.

Swinging the suitcase, he stepped out of the station into the
grit and grime of Britain's biggest and dirtiest city outside
London. Ignoring a long line of cabs and the siren aroma
of a fish and chips shop next to the Coach and Horses – a
pub where Marx and Engels had occasionally met - he made
his way across Piccadilly, and through the hustle and bustle
of Market Street. His compass pointed to Salford and then
Irlams o' the Height. The Islips, Auntie Annie and Uncle Alf
would have a right turn when they saw him on the doorstep.
Manchester was too busy to notice another pale-faced,
weedy youth – there were thousands of them around -
even though he lugged a posh looking suitcase. Horse-drawn
vehicles, double-decker trams, cabs, traders' carts, private
carriages, brewery drays, threatened to mow down any
unwary pedestrian. The street life shouted at him. Shoppers,
clerks in bowler hats, managers and businessmen in silk
toppers, traders in caps and ragged kids disappearing down
dark alleys. A military brass band marched along Market

Street. Parrott dodged them all.

Further on were huge warehouses, factory chimneys spewing black smoke, workshops, the cathedral, the 250 feet high ventilation tower of Strangeways Jail, and the stinking River Irwell which he crossed via Blackfriars bridge into Salford. An hour later, after a journey of four miles, he turned into Claremont Road, Irlams o' the Height, banged on the door of number 15, smiling at the astonishment of his aunt, while Alf grabbed the case and said: "Young James. What a turn-up for the book."

Parrott knew his Knutsford family would be disappointed at his non -appearance, but he needed a few days grace and Aunt Annie's was a haven. She pandered to him but, unlike his mother, knew when to leave him alone. And Uncle Alf treated him in a manly fashion, sharing confidences, joking quietly about women who fussed.

The Parrotts and the Islips were entwined. Mary Ann and her younger sister Annie came from a Huddersfield family and James Crossley Parrott was named in honour of their brother, Crossley, a book-keeper who died at the age of 18, as well as his grandfather, James snr.

Before meeting and marrying Alf Islip, Aunt Annie had lived with the Parrotts in Knutsford for a while although she and Alf settled down in the Gorton district of Manchester where they once saw Emmeline Pankhurst deliver an address to an open air meeting of over 10,000 and where William Gaskell, husband of Elizabeth, had fought unsuccessfully for a seat in Parliament. They loved Knutsford and one of their many visits to the town was in 1884 when they and the Parrotts were in a crowd of thousands who witnessed William Gaskell's funeral, his coffin arriving from Manchester at the station and being carried over the road to the Brook Street Chapel graveyard where he was laid to rest with Elizabeth. Parrott preferred Irlams o' the Height. Lacking real friends, dislocated from the Knutsford environment by his four years in Watford, he reckoned his future lay there, on the edge of a big city which offered plenty of opportunity, without making demands, and without poking into his privacy. But, after two postcards had arrived from home, his aunt said he had to go, his mother was getting anxious, and he waved goodbye. Thankfully, no-one was waiting for him at Knutsford station and when he arrived at the house, only John had something to say. "Where've you been?" Mary Ann had hoped that, as well as saving money, his time at Watford would have matured him, stop some of his 'silliness'. The dual blow of losing his father and grandfather had affected him, she accepted that, and ameliorated her reactions accordingly, but she suspected other causes and feared for his future. While she wanted so much to help him, she had four others to think about and a business to maintain. Her position was parlous. Widows received no financial help from the state. Debtors could be sent to gaol, whole families could end up in the workhouse. She urged him to find work.

Fellow traders helped with brief stints behind various counters, but he was unable to settle and by the middle of 1895 he was drifting from one shop job to another, staying sometimes at Irlams o' the Height. It was then that he first came to the notice of the police and it was then that Mary Ann knew for certain that the boy she loved but had always regarded as troublesome was heading towards disaster. "I'm at my wits' end," she confided to her daughter Mary. "I just can't get through to him."

Parrott, short of cash, stole a bunch of ties from a Manchester store hoping to sell them. He was seen, identified, quickly arrested and spent a few hours in a cell. Next day, September 25, 1895, he appeared at the Manchester Petty Sessions and was discharged without penalty, the magistrates taking into account his age, his plea of guilty, although the theft was so blatant he could hardly deny it, and the fact that it was his first conviction. But he was given a severe warning that if he offended again he could go to prison. He nodded and walked out, branded as a petty thief, the seed of resentment which had niggled him for so long now beginning to swell in the pit of his stomach. Fortunately for his family the case was not covered in the local Press.

For the most part, Parrott lived in the Manchester region, either at Irlams o' the Height or in cheap digs, depending on where he obtained work. Usually he described himself as a grocer's assistant, but sometimes promoted himself to 'grocer'. Gambling excited him. He played cards and pitch and toss and began to study the horse-racing odds published in the Manchester Evening News and Manchester Courier. He bought some clothes, took up smoking, drank beer but not to excess, and started to shave, leaving a whisper of a moustache. And when he was next dragged before the city's Bench he looked quite the young man about town. This time, however, the crime was much more serious and there was no second chance – the magistrates packed him off to Strangeways for a month's hard labour.

This second appearance occurred on June 15, for stealing £11 10s, worth almost two months in wages to a young shop assistant like him. From where and from whom he stole it is not clear. However, it was cash, not goods, and he was not charged with breaking into someone's property or using threats or violence. It might have been a purely opportunist theft from a shop till, but the magistrates had little option but to jail him. It was a large amount, he had already been warned about his conduct, and, at 16, he was regarded as an adult offender. Short sentences usually meant 'hard labour', and the shorter the term, the harder it got, the aim being to deter comparatively minor offenders from developing into career criminals - 'a short, sharp shock' often ascribed to the juvenile detention centres of the 20th century. As the Manchester Bench sat in a courtroom adjacent to the Srangeways prison, Parrott was soon in a cell and over the next four weeks, while his mother fretted in Knutsford, he bemused warders with his capacity to 'do a shift'.

The isolation of the separate system, the tiring manual graft, and the dreadful food appeared not to concern him at all. With no remission for good behaviour, Parrott served the full term, being released in the middle of July. Aunt Annie was waiting for him. By then Mary Ann and the family were in Knutsford's Princess Street, and when he returned home it was to live a few yards from several worthies, including Leicester Caldecutt and the doctors, Smith and Fennell, and to work on and off for various shopkeepers.

He missed the buzz of Salford and Manchester, where he could lay a bet on almost any corner, but that did not stop his gambling. Even sedate Knutsford had its shadowy nooks and crannies where street bookies lurked. One, arrested by Sergeant Pierce after monitoring his movements over two days, had more than £5 in coin in his bag after taking bets for a major race at Chester. And it was easy anywhere in the north-west of England to locate a pitch and toss ring, where two coins were flicked into the air. If both landed heads up, the punter won. One head and one tail resulted in a dead rubber, the coins being tossed up again. Two tails and the banker, usually a bookie, pocketed the loot. It was a simple, popular game of chance, noisy and exciting with large groups of men shouting out their bets. The adrenaline flowed and Parrott came alive. Horse racing attracted the more analytical side of his nature, weighing up form, course conditions and odds and with the main-line Press only summarising the information, he began to buy The Sporting Life which provided more detail. Gambling in many forms was sweeping through Britain. Parrott was caught up in it, as were millions of others who, according to the Anti-Gambling League and other social reformers, needed protection from their own folly. A salutary poem published in the League's newsletter, The Bulletin, carried the lines: 'He saw a ragged breeked urchin run; A'shouting 'All the winners!'; And The Devil smiled as he sniggered 'What fun'; What a bait for the greed fired sinners.'

And so it is a fair bet that he lost money, giving him a reason to steal. Or he might simply have had a dishonest streak and could not resist temptation. Again the local Press missed the story, saving the family from embarrassment and, for a while, Mary Ann was able to contain him. But this spindly,

'would not say boo to a goose' youth was to spend his 18th birthday in another cell with questions growing over his mental capacity. And this time the whole of Knutsford knew about it.

Parrott was working in the town of Altrincham when he climbed another step on the criminal ladder, breaking into licensed premises and stealing two pounds of sweets, chocolates and caramels. The type, quantity and value of the goods was immaterial, this was burglary and an escalation in Parrott's record. He now had three convictions for dishonesty in the space of two years, he had to be treated as a habitual offender and, as such, the Petty Sessional magistrates in Altrincham did not have the power to deal with him. They sent him for sentence to the higher court, the Cheshire Quarter Sessions, where he faced anything up to 12 months imprisonment, depending on any mitigating factors he produced and on whether the judge had enjoyed his breakfast or lunch.

Parrott was remanded in custody, handcuffed and taken to Altrincham railway station for the 20 minutes ride to Knutsford, where he found himself in a cell close to the one he was to inhabit four years later. He stayed in that cell for 10 weeks before his case was brought before the Quarter Sessions. As a convict – only his sentence had to be determined – it was 10 weeks of hard labour. His mother sought out Tom Jackson for advice. He asked her: "Are you prepared to go into the witness box as a character witness?" She agreed. Jackson persisted: "The thing is -you might have to talk about his problems, and the Press will be there."

Mary Ann hesitated. "Will it save him? I don't want him to be in prison for any longer than necessary."

Jackson also hesitated. "All we can hope is that it will help."

Neighbours and friends sympathised, as they had always done with issues over James, but opinions varied. Some doubted the wisdom of pleading for her son, others gave support. On October 18, 1897, Mary Ann and Edith put on grey skirts and coats and walked to the courts. Jackson was already there, chatting with a group of solicitors and clerks in the tea room. "He'll be one of the first up," he told her, having already had a word with the Clerk, Caldecutt. Parrott was with a number of other offenders in the holding area. One, a clerk from Ashton under Lyne, was taken up into the dock and returned just a few minutes later, shaken by a 12 months sentence for a minor fraud. Britain frowned on financial cheats.

Parrott went up, observing his mother and Edith, Jackson on the corner of the solicitors' bench below him, Caldecutt at the Clerk's desk, and a stern looking man straight in front of him, in the centre of a row of magistrates. Parrott and Horatio Campbell Yates were meeting for the first time, 'H C' acting in his other role as Chairman of the Quarter Sessions.

The court heard a summary of the offence. It did not take long, a forced entry at the premises of a Mr Potter, two jars of sweets taken, the burglar disturbed and arrested shortly afterwards. A police officer read out Parrott's antecedents and Yates's brow furrowed.

"This is a very serious case," he said. "Is this prisoner represented by counsel?"

"No," said Caldecutt. "However we understand that he comes from a decent family and that his mother wishes to give evidence on his behalf."

"Does she, indeed? Well, call her."

Mary Ann went into the witness box. She glanced at Parrott. He did not acknowledge. Jackson, however, gave her a nod of encouragement and Caldecutt spoke kindly as he handed her the bible and card. "Please take the oath on the card and give your name and relationship to the defendant." Mary Ann did so. There was a pause while people looked at her, then at Parrott. "Well, Mrs Parrott," said Yates. "This is a pretty affair, isn't it? A thief and a shopbreaker hoping his mother can rescue him from the punishment he so richly deserves."

She recognised most everyone in the courtroom. Caldecutt, Jackson, the police officers, one or two neighbours who had turned up and were in the public gallery with Edith and, of course, the sallow-cheeked boy who hated being fussed over. And she had been in this very witness box before, giving evidence against the scoundrel who stole her father-in-law's belongings. Despite all that familiarity, she felt a strange loneliness.

Caldecutt coaxed her to give some general detail of Parrott's life, the deaths of his father and grandfather, his time away from home caused by financial pressures, how she had tried to bring him up proper and how he had always seemed a little different from his siblings. It had been difficult.

"He is not responsible for his actions," she said.

It burst out louder than she intended, and realising the effect this had caused, adding "to some extent." Her right hand rested on the bible. She blinked a tear, and stared down, not daring to look at her son. After conferring with his colleagues Yates ordered Parrott to stand.

"You have admitted a most serious crime for which a 12 months sentence would, in many eyes, be wholly appropriate. However we have considered mitigating factors. You have pleaded guilty, you have already spent over two months in custody, and your mother has had the courage to stand up for you in court. It is to your shame that you have brought her to this and we can only hope that you honour her and mend your ways."

Parrott received one month's hard labour, an extremely light sentence for a shopbreaker with a record. Jackson mouthed a 'Well done' at Mary Ann but a wave of nausea gripped her and he had to take her elbow as she came down the steps. She hoped she would never have to go through an experience like that again.   In the Home Office's list of prisoners for 1897, Parrott was registered thus: *3419: James Parrott, Knutsford, b 1880, ht 5 3 1/4, complexion fr, hair lt bn, eyes bl, near sighted, scar neck and 1 wrist.*

He was one of around 148000 criminals locked up in Britain, along with 4000 soldiers and sailors after courts-martial, over 12000 debtors, and 1500 who had defaulted on sureties. Knutsford housed more than 500. Some reform on the treatment of convicts was taking place after the Prison Act of 1898, particularly in regard to juvenile offenders and corporal punishment, but not to alleviate the pain for people like Parrott. The Knutsford governor, Major James Osmonde Nelson campaigned for the stepped system in which habitual criminals suffered longer sentences for each offence, no matter how serious. Parrott was lucky. As it was he spent his

18th birthday, November 10, sewing mailbags.By the time of his release on November 18 he had spent almost 15 weeks in gaol on the shopbreaking charge, and a total of almost 5 months out of 18 months, June 1896-November 1897, all with hard labour and for offences of increasing gravity.

There seems little doubt that Parrott needed help but, outside his family, little was forthcoming. The Discharged Prisoners' Society of Cheshire offered some support but it was to his mother he turned. Mary Ann's comment that he 'was not responsible for his actions – to some extent' was met with resigned sighs by those in court, and by those acquainted with the family. It had been suspected for a long time that there was something not quite right with young James, and this was a public admission of it from the person who knew him best.

On his release date, she was waiting for him at the prison gates. Their family home, now in Princess Street, was a couple of hundred yards away. Edith made a pot of tea. She smiled encouragingly. "You're the man of the house now James." At Mary Ann's behest, Jackson had a 'man to man' chat with him, to remind him of his 'responsibilities'. At the end of 10 minutes, knowing he was making little impact, Jackson said: "And, of course, there's your inheritance." Parrott perked up so Jackson added: "You won't be able to use it if you're doing time. Will you?"

For the next three and a half years, Parrott stayed out of trouble. If he committed crime he was not caught. The family moved back to their former premises in King Street but the house held unhappy memories for him, and he could not settle. One brother Thomas Holland found a job and boarding in Liverpool, and the other, John, had outstripped James in physique and maturity and tended to dominate proceedings. Mary Ann tried to keep him under wraps, but he found it impossible to stick to one job and moved around the North-West, always searching for something better. In Manchester and nearby towns like Altrincham and Ashton-under-Lyne, he worked in shops, back in Knutsford he was a labourer for the Joseph Gidman mineral water bottling plant but quit after a dispute between staff and managment. He switched back and forth from Knutsford to Irlams o' the Height and to various lodging houses, depending on where the work was.

It was unusual for someone to rack up three convictions and two gaol sentences before the age of 18, and then suddenly transfer to the straight and narrow. What made the difference for Parrott? Religion? Abstinence from drink and gambling? Peer pressure? Romance? The deterrent of another term in gaol? Judged by his behaviour at that stage, and by what happened later, none of those seem likely. If anything focused his mind on staying clean, it was the prospect of banking a sizeable sum of money at the age of 21 and being free to spend it. But gradually another factor came into play, Parrott's dreams of fame and fortune, to follow in the footsteps of so many Imperial heroes, perhaps even to carve out new trails. It gave him a clear objective for the first time in his life.

CHAPTER 17

*'When first interviewed by the police Miss Francis was
naturally labouring under considerable excitement and
her account of what happened was of a more or less
unsatisfactory nature...' - Manchester Courier, July 1901*

*'....when life fails, What's the good of
going to Wales?' - W H Auden*

SERGEANT Pierce had checked Parrott's record shortly
after arresting him but neither he, nor anyone involved
in the investigation, could talk publicly about it,
or even think of using it against him for fear of prejudicing
the jury. If convicted, it would not matter – there was only
one outcome, whether or not he had 'previous'. If cleared, no-
one would give a hoot about it.

Although he ached to reveal all, Pierce had to grin and
bear the constant portrayal of Parrott as a boyish innocent,
unfortunately trapped in the wrong place at the wrong time.
Pierce had the gut feeling he was guilty and, although the
evidence looked scanty, there was an issue which could be
exploited - Parrott wisely had hidden or disposed of the Colt
revolver but stupidly he had retained the purse wrenched
from his victim's right hand pocket.

Despite Lance Bentley's tricky intervention, the purse and its
contents, a farthing and the coin similar to a half farthing
but which had been ascertained as a commemorative token
from Queen Victoria's Diamond Jubilee, were now central to
the prosecution. Parrott insisted they were his. But Bould
had owned an identical one and, since the murder, both his
purse and coins were missing. Bentley had demonstrated
that yellow pigskin purses were sold by their thousands but
that dented only part of the police case. The coins continued
to jingle. Two men, neighbours but apparently strangers to
each other, owning similar purses, each containing nothing
else but a farthing and a half farthing look-alike. Pierce
sniffed haughtily at the defence claim of coincidence.

Parrott's lawyers were certainly worried, particularly when they noticed an article in the Press claiming the police had 'startling' new evidence causing Edwin Ashworth to send his clerk Tom Jackson on a special mission. Jackson formally asked the prison governor Major Nelson for permission to interview Parrott and spent an hour or so with him, pushing a packet of cigarettes across the table, and patiently scraping out bits of information.

A few days later Jackson set off for Liverpool. Getting out at Lime Street station he asked a porter for directions to Renshaw Street, and was there in five minutes only to be disappointed. Number 23 was partly demolished. Turning away, wondering what next to do, he spotted a curled notice stuck to the shattered remains of a dusty ground floor window. 'E Bowker, now trading at 27 Pembroke Place.' Jackson asked around, learned that he had to retrace his steps past the station and along Copperas Hill and 10 minutes later was standing outside a small, dark shop with net curtains and a white painted sign above the door 'Books and Fine Arts'.

Edward Bowker was 48 and had grown up surrounded by books. His father Adam ran the business for many years and, on his death, Edward took it over. Recently the Renshaw Street premises had been knocked down, hence the move to Pembroke Place, living with his wife and two adult daughters in two rooms above the shop. Most of his trade was mail order, emanating from small adverts under the 'Miscellaneous' columns in newspapers all over the country. His 'The Complete Works of Aristotle', 'Dream Book and Fortune Teller', 'Gay Paris', 'Ovid's Art of Love' and 'Phrenological Self Instructor' competed with the offerings of quacks ('D'Asmail's Celebrated Female Mixture') and fakes like the Brighton trader who sold 'self treatment' advice for men suffering from nervous debility.

Bowker's was musty and dim, the shelves lined with volumes of all types and sizes but Jackson was not searching for a book. Ringing the counter bell he waited while Bowker clumped down the stairs and asked him innocuously: "Do you sell coins by any chance?"

On his return to Knutsford Jackson reported in at the office, slapped a small leather pouch and a receipt on the desk and told Ashworth: "We've got a new witness."

That same day, July 1, a ceremony at Scotland Yard, the headquarters of the Metropolitan Police, launched Britain's first fingerprint bureau, brainchild of a leading civil servant Edward Henry, former Inspector General of Police in India's Bengal Presidency. Henry had developed it successfully in Bengal after early work by Dr William Herschel, a top administrative officer in Calcutta. Initially, it was used to identify itinerants and convicts, rather than as an investigative device. However that changed in the late 1890s under the India Evidence Act, a major advance.

Dactyloscopy, as the scientists called it, was well established, dating back to the second century BC when prints were used in Babylon as signatures to contracts. In 1880 Dr Henry Faulds, a Scot in charge of a hospital in Tokyo, devised a classification system which enabled prints to be more easily compared. He sent it to Charles Darwin's cousin, Francis Galton, who, some years later, published a book well received in scientific circles, and he also offered it to the Metropolitan Police. They politely declined.

By then some police forces were using the Bertillon System of identification, formulated by a police clerk in Paris, which relied on exact measurements of the body, allied to photographs – 'mugshots'. Mark Twain described a court case involving fingerprints in his novel Pudd'n Head Wilson, and in 1892, fingerprinting was adopted by police in Argentina. While the Met were resistant, the British led police in Bengal continued to develop the technique, with Henry supported by two Indian officials in his department, Azizul Haque and Hem Chandra Bose. After cataloguing 19000 samples from Indian convicts, he divided prints into loops, whorls, and arches and, in 1901, after taking over as chief of the Met's CID, he introduced his ground-breaking system into Britain.

Not everyone welcomed it. A letter signed 'A Disappointed Magistrate' appeared in The Times, saying: 'Scotland Yard, once known as the world's finest police organisation will be the laughing stock of Europe if it insists on trying to trace criminals by odd ridges on their skins.'

Rolling out the equipment and training took some time and the first conviction directly attributable came in December 1902 when a labourer Henry Jackson left a partial thumb print on a freshly painted window sill after breaking into a house in Denmark Hill, London, to steal some billiard balls. It cost him seven years in gaol. In 1905 two brothers, Alfred and Albert Stratton were hanged for the murder of a shopkeeper and his wife after a print was located on a cash box. Gradually, astute criminals realised that gloves were essential.

In the summer of 1901 Pierce read about the new fingerprint bureau in the Police Gazette and wondered whether Parrott had left prints on Bould's clothing, or maybe on the penknife, watch and tobacco pipe found in his waistcoat pockets. Too late, of course. The trial was set for July 26 at Chester, all the evidence had been sorted with depositions handed to the defence. Had he done enough? Perhaps one last thing. A day trip to Welshpool and a quiet chat with Mary Jane Francis.

Risky? Of course. But all he wanted to do was to remind of her original statement to him, that the man leaning over Bould's body was the same person she had seen a few minutes earlier at the field gate, ie: James Parrott. Since then she had become uncertain.

Pierce knew full well that, because of the rules of evidence, anything she told him now in a private meeting could not be used at the trial. But he had to satisfy himself that he was not pushing an innocent man, a young one at that, towards the gallows. Mary Jane could help him. The railway timetable showed it was possible to do it in a day. Knutsford to Chester by the earliest train, then to Welshpool, arrive at the Francis's cottage before lunch, leave by 3pm and be home for a late supper. He wrote a brief, polite note to Mary Jane requesting her to make herself available.

Keeping it under wraps raised problems. Eventually, after considering and rejecting various excuses to be out of the office all day, he simply told everyone he was going to Chester on Parrott business. Leaving the police station at 8am, he alighted at Welshpool just before noon and was soon knocking on the door of a cottage, a few miles to the north.

Mary Jane looked different. Older, and she had put on weight. Previously he had only seen her in the Sunday best she wore in court, or in her spruce waitress's uniform at the Speakmans'. Now her clothes were more old-fashioned and homely, a long, billowing frock, the sleeves rolled up, and a frayed pinny. He liked her more like that. Equally, Pierce looked different to her. He was in civvies, a heavy tweed suit and bowler hat which he removed, placing it on his knee when she offered him a chair. She took another, at an angle. A pan on the stove simmered and he eyed a large teapot. But Mary Jane eschewed polite offerings. The sergeant was not a welcome visitor.

They were by themselves and the conversation was stilted. Pierce asked again, trying to sound as apologetic as possible, if she could think back to that moment when she saw the man leaning over Bould's body. Could she describe him? There was silence. He thought she was going to refuse him.

"It is so difficult," she said. "You have to understand I was frightened. It was dark and it all happened so quickly. That man tried to have his way with me and.."

Pierce broke in. "But the man by the body...you said at the inquest he had his hand on the other man's chest. Bould's chest."

"Yes." She breathed in hard. "I couldn't see his face properly. He ran off as fast as his legs would carry him. He nearly tripped over his coat, it was that long on him."

Pierce grunted. He tried another tack. "One of the other witnesses, Daniels, said you told him at the time that the man was wearing spectacles."

"Did I? I might have done. It was so quick and it's three months ago now."

He was getting nowhere. "Miss Francis. No-one is trying to put words in your mouth, we just want to be as certain about things as we can be. Look, there's only the two of us here, and I'm not going to make a note, it's just a chat between us so that I'm clear in my head about it. It won't go any further than this room. Alright?"

She nodded.

"Forgetting about the spectacles, did the man by the body look similar to the man you saw earlier at the gate?"

"Similar, yes."

"Could you go so far as to say it was the same man?"

Mary Jane looked away from him, then back. Sweat decorated his forehead and while it was a warm day, and his jacket and waistcoat were coarse and thick, the cottage was cool, if you were just sat talking instead of getting on with things. Her trust in him was nowhere as deep as Pierce imagined. In fact, her trust in mankind was pretty low. She had read in one early editorial referring to her story – 'Young women of course can be delusional' (Liverpool Weekly Courier April 12 1901). Yet there was an intensity about him which drew her in.

"This is between you and me for the moment?"

He leaned towards her. "I have given you my word." She liked that. Personal, that was, between two people, better than an oath in a crowded courtroom where no-one gave a damn about you.

"I thought straight away that it was him. Yes, that was my impression. But then all sorts of people were asking so many questions. You can get a mite confused and doubt your own self. Now I couldn't swear to it."

Pierce took it no further. She stood at the front door, hand shielding her eyes from the sun as he walked away. A breeze tugged at her frock, she calmed it with her other hand, and already she was regretting her words. Was her memory playing tricks? For his part the sergeant felt the journey worthwhile. Whether Mary Jane came up trumps at the trial, they would have to wait and see, but, in that very private and intimate moment, she had confirmed that he was right, that he, Pierce, had nabbed a murderer. What the lawyers and jury made of it was out of his control. Taking a cab back to the railway station he touched the brim of his hat to some ladies, thinking that there was something about working in plain clothes – even his old suit. Back in Knutsford in mid-evening, the sky was still light, and the town quiet. He walked along Love Lane and skirted the gaol, wondering what Annie had prepared for his supper and whether Parrott, little more than an arm's length away, fully understood the peril he was in.

Whether Parrott lived or died was to be decided in a courtroom battle which highlighted all that was good and bad about the British justice system of that time. The Chester Assizes were to start on July 25 with Parrott's trial fixed for July 26, a Friday, on the understanding that it could run over to the Saturday because of the number of witnesses. Other serious crimes would also be dealt with but Parrott's trial was easily the pick of the bunch. 'The nation awaits the fate of this young man with bated breath,' reported one newspaper. Generally, however, coverage of the case had diminished. There was little to do but wait for the climax.

Parrott's defence at the Assizes was to be prepared by Gibbons and Bentley, although the brief would be handed over to a Welsh barrister, Ellis Jones Griffiths for the actual trial. At a meeting at Edwin Ashworth's office they decided on an all-out attack on the police, particularly Pierce. Gibbons formulated a strenuous objection to the way the sergeant interviewed Parrott, and Bentley promised that he could nullify the purse and coins evidence. As for the girl Francis, they could show she had been placed under immense pressure and was not reliable. One snag – Parrott himself. If ever a man was determined to get himself hung by the neck until dead, it was James Crossley Parrott.

"His appearance is deceptive," said Bentley. "He looks inoffensive. Until he speaks, which is not often, but when he does, it shows a slightly different character."

"Meaning exactly?" Gibbons, stretched back, his hands behind his head.

"He can be a little diffident, off-hand, isn't that right, Tom?"

Jackson, taking notes, frowned. "He can be difficult. Liable to take issue."

Gibbons failed to see what was troubling them. "But all he has to do is say 'Not guilty' and we'll do the rest. He doesn't have to utter another word."

Until recently, alleged murderers had been barred from

giving evidence on their own behalf for fear of needlesly incriminating themselves. But the rules had changed.

Bentley exchanged looks with Jackson. "I'm afraid, that is the problem. He is determined to have his say and it doesn't bode well because, as we all know, his account lacks a certain clarity. If he goes into the witness box it gives the prosecution the chance to push him into a corner and then I'm not sure how he will come over to the jury."

Ashworth was entrusted with the job of persuading Parrott to keep his mouth shout. He delegated it to Jackson.

At Chester, the office of the High Sheriff had instructed two dozen of the county's property owners to report for jury service. Some regarded it as an inconvenience, others were excited, one or two took pride in being elected for such an important role. All were men. Women were not allowed until 1919, but that was not the only discrimination. Many of the country's population were debarred from jury service simply because they did not own or lease property of a certain value. Yet, while the perceived affluence or social standing of a juror weighed heavily, there was no test as to his intellect or general fitness to deliberate on someone's fate. He could be an extremist, an eccentric, a campaigner against capital punishment, even a gun toting gangster. Once chosen, the only way to keep him out was for counsel to formally challenge him as he came to be sworn.

Another problem was the demand for a unanimous decision which sustained until 1967 and was one of the many paradoxes of justice in a democracy which relied on the majority rule in all other voting procedures. It placed enormous pressure on jurors, and too many verdicts were attained simply because some voices in the jury room were stronger than the evidence. A juror was 'answerable only to his own conscience' yet too often he was answerable only to a forceful foreman.

Until 1870, the jury was told that they would not receive 'meat, drink, fire or candle' until they had reached their verdict. Hunger, thirst and sheer expediency might then have taken over from conscience, as in: "I'm starvin' – let's make it guilty." By 1901 that had changed. However a juror was still sometimes made to suffer. There were no 'convenience' breaks, they were kept together in a pack and segregated at all times from anyone else other than court officials, and, most of all, they had to sit patiently and listen to hours of evidence, perhaps complicated and without documentary back-up, then to impassioned final speeches by counsel, then to the judge's summing-up. All to be sifted and debated without so much as a cuppa.

A tired, fed-up jury was dangerous. Even with deep divisions as to the evidence, it could swing one way or the other just to get the thing finished. If the more insistent faction voted for 'guilty' and pushed the doubters into agreeing, then at least the defendant could appeal on the grounds of wrongful conviction. But, if the obverse occurred, leading to an acquittal, that was it. Thanks to the ancient double jeopardy law a person found not guilty could not be tried a second time for the same offence. For 800 years it was an essential element of British justice, but while it protected the innocent from further hassle, it also allowed some to get away with murder, like Donald Hume who killed his business associate Stanley Setty. Acquitted by a jury, Hulme was jailed for 12 years for being an accessory but on release confessed to the killing in a number of lurid newspaper articles, knowing he was untouchable. The law was changed in 2006 after a lengthy campaign by Ann Ming to get justice for her murdered daughter.

An important aspect of trial by jury was impression – how a witness appeared and behaved while giving evidence. Did they look decent, clean and respectably dressed, were they forthright but courteous when answering questions, did they stand upright and make eye contact? Could they be trusted?

Against this background, Parrott's lawyers walked a tightrope. Muted, sitting forlornly in the dock, he looked more a victim than a perpetrator. This was the silent movie Bentley and co wanted to show the jury. Instead he wanted to exercise his right and put on a potentially destructive 'talkie'. Jackson went to see him for one last chat.

CHAPTER 18

'If I were hanged on the highest hill
Mother o' mine, O mother o' mine!
I know whose love would follow me still,
Mother o' mine, O mother o' mine!' - Rudyard Kipling, 1892

IN mid-July temperatures soared over 90 degrees in Manchester and other cities. People collapsed and died. Farmers and estate managers muttered darkly about parched fields. A glut of strawberries depressed prices so much that growers left them to rot. Brewers, though, had plenty to smile about – hops were the only crop to be doing well, and the consumption of ale had soared.

A certain police sergeant was feeling the heat both from the weather and from his superiors. Plodding the highways and byways of Knutsford in such weather was exhausting, but the 'beat' had to be maintained. While he led a complex murder investigation Pierce still had to deal with all the nuts and bolts of keeping the peace in a busy little town. Only the other week he had biked almost six miles to the outlying village of Ashley, pedalling hard around the perimeter of the Tatton estate, to collar a thief who had grabbed the collection box from a church. Each day he returned to their kitchen, slumped into a chair, almost too tired to eat the mound of food Annie placed in front of him. "You've got to eat to keep your strength up," she said. There were hunks of fatty meat, potatoes and gravy and suet puddings. And Chester HQ was suddenly pumping up the pressure. "I hope we haven't missed anything," Colonel Hammersley said. He sounded unusually anxious for a man renowned for a quiet confidence.

This was the county's highest profile case since the Davies brothers 15 years ago and just as sensitive. The police were in a no-win situation. Hammersley could imagine the blast of criticism which would follow an acquittal, but they would also be in the eye of a storm if Parrott was sentenced to hang with, no doubt, nation-wide petitions for a reprieve. Poor

Pierce, the local bobby, would get it in the neck whichever way it went. Hammersley had come to like the sergeant and to admire his persistence but he had also let it be known that Pierce was in complete charge of operations, and therefore responsible for any cock-up.

The heat was oppressive. Mary Ann, walking up the hill towards the prison, had to stop for a rest by the church gate. She took a few seconds, setting down her basket and adjusting her hairpin. How many times had she done this? She reckoned up quickly, every day since April 21 and it was now July 19. Three months, almost 100 times by the time the trial was due to start. And a few more if he was found guilty. She banished the dread thought and brushed a fly off the tea towel protecting her son's food. Some cold baked ham, more appropriate for this weather, but she was fast running out of ideas for him. His appetite was lower than ever. She dropped off the food at the gate each day, regular as clockwork, but on the few occasions that prison regulations allowed her to see him he appeared to be getting thinner and thinner.

"I'm fine Mother," he assured her at their last meeting. "Please don't worry yourself. When I come out you can cook me as much food as you like."

Parrott did not talk much during these visits except to answer her questions. Were the warders still treating him properly – if not she would have a word with Tom Jackson – did he need anything, was he getting enough sleep? Sometimes he responded with that half smile of his. Only once did he initiate a conversation, asking whether she had spoken to his solicitor about the purse. She had. "It is important," he said. Usually, she could see his mind wandering to other places and all she wanted was to put her arms around him and she could not, and, even if she could, he would draw back. It had always been so.

Mary Ann was sweating profusely by the time she knocked on the gate. The warder took the dish, said: "That smells good Mrs Parrott."

"Yes, and make sure my son gets all of it." She laughed and scolded herself. How could she jest when only a few yards away stood a shed where her son might be hanged? Why does he have to be locked up? She questioned solicitors, friends, family. No-one could give her a satisfactory reason. He could live with her at King Street, it would save her traipsing all the way to the gaol each day. It's not as though he would scarper. All this talk of Africa was so much nonsense.

Parrott poked at the meat, ate a couple of forkfuls and pushed it away. The sun was high in the sky over Knutsford. For a week or so now he had heard warders moaning about the heat. But the cell walls were deep, and kept it cool, so much so that Parrott stayed fully dressed in his suit and felt entirely comfortable. In one way, living here was an improvement on life outside. His own room, instead of sharing either with his brother John at home or with a workmate in some lodging house. Here, he could sit and free his mind if not his body. There was frustration, of course, but it would soon come to an end, one way or the other. Only the limitation of physical movement seriously bothered him. He longed to stride out for a few miles – that would be the first thing he would do on release, if...

Jackson had come to see him a few days earlier. "We've got nothing to worry about, James," he said, reassuringly. "Nothing if we can settle the matter with the purse. And that will depend a lot on your mother. The other thing is, we must strongly advise you not to give evidence, to stay silent. It's your right."

But Jackson recognised Parrott's stubborn look. "He said he would think about it but I'm afraid he won't have it," he told Edwin Ashworth later.

"Well," came the grim reply. "Give someone enough rope and they'll hang themselves. At least we have the purse and coins all sorted out. That was good work, Tom."

Parrott was not the only one determined to make an impact at the trial. Mary Jane Francis saw it as another opportunity to put George Rowe on the rack, to tell the world that, as well as being a highly regarded inventor and businessman, he was also a cad, a rogue who had assaulted her. She had not pressed charges because, as she had been reminded more than once, she was a 'domestic', an unmarried girl from the Welsh borderlands, and a bit scatty at that – Pierce and the Chief Constable did not say it but she could read their thoughts. Rowe was a member, by marriage, of one of Manchester's Imperial families, headed by an alderman whose four sons were all doctors, one of whom was bravely serving his country in South Africa at that very moment. Hammersley told her: "Mr Rowe has already suffered immeasurable harm from the allegations in the Press. And, anyway, I'm afraid it's your word against his and Harry Yarwood's."

Mary Jane appreciated the police stance. Bringing a case against Rowe would be time consuming, very costly as it would require a trial, and eventually fruitless. They had told her: "We are not saying you've made the story up, but there were no witnesses to support you. It's a question of practicalities."

Women all over the world have heard the same dismissive line throughout history. Man's abuse of them is the greatest stain on civilisation. Mary Jane Francis was just another silly girl, fair game for a bit of horseplay and if the 'gentleman' went too far, well, she would get over it in time, while he might suffer permanent damage to his social status if charged. Mary Jane had not got over it yet and maybe never would but to continue Rowe's public humiliation by persisting with her accusations would offer some consolation. She was brave.

Because they only refer to reported cases, official crime statistics of the period do not, by any means, display the full picture of sex offences which had risen sharply since the age of consent being lifted from 13 to 16 in 1875. Many girls and young women, often in domestic service, were discouraged by gentle persuasion, or by threat of dismissal, from taking their complaints to the courts. One such preventative measure was to warn them of the embarrassment of giving intimate detail in an open court, populated mostly by men, that their virtue would be questioned, and that they would be accused of fantasising.

A timely reminder of Mary Jane's unenviable position was a court case in Chester that very month, shortly before the trial, in which a young housemaid claimed libel damages against her former employer, owner of a hall and estate in Cheshire, who alleged in a letter that she had behaved 'improperly' with another servant, a footman. She was awarded £5 – but only after undergoing an intrusive medical examination.

Mary Jane was no pioneer of women's rights. She simply wanted justice for herself, so much that although she had been challenged and even laughed at in the coroner's court, although the police regarded the assault as a sideshow, and although some local folk had called her names, she was determined to have another go.

Rowe's life had already changed, there was no doubt of that. Publicly the Pritchards accepted his version of events but privately they seethed at being dragged into a sordid case, and Gertrude had descended into sullenness. Immersing himelf into his boot polish business, he spent more and more time at the Altrincham factory. Rowe dreaded the prospect of hearing Mary Jane repeat her story at the trial. The Press would make a meal of it again. Another headache for him was that if Parrott were found not guilty, it would fuel speculation that someone else must be the murderer, placing him and Yarwood back in the frame, in the opinion of the rumour merchants if not the police. As though that was not enough, Rowe had business problems. Investment was needed to fund expansion but, due to the adverse publicity, offers had dried up.

As the heat bore down on Knutsford tempers flared. Three women were arrested for disorderly behaviour and obscene language after a drunken row in the Market Place. One, a habitual offender, was described in court as a 'virago'. Complaints about the smell of sewage and rubbish from the Moor blended with angry shouts from some bystanders when an Irish labourer was brought to the police station for allegedly assaulting a schoolgirl in a country lane. Two Irish hawkers further inflamed anti Irish feelings, which were constantly simmering, when they sparked off a scrap in the Golden Lion, needing Pierce and two constables to restrain them. A local youth whizzed past Constable Turner on his bike to be called back and booked for furious riding, or 'scorching'. Farmers and nurserymen prayed for rain.

But the sun also shone on the very essence of Englishness with summer fetes, flower shows and sports days, toasts to the new king now that the six months official mourning period for Queen Victoria was over and tributes to the Volunteer heroes. At weekends thousands of cyclists pedalled out of the suburbs of Manchester and Liverpool, following countryside routes. They stopped at roadside tearooms for ice creams, tea and lemonade. 'Partly made in Italy', boasted one brand, bemusingly branded 'Eiffel Tower Lemonade'. Blackpool's own Tower pulled in the holiday makers and in Tatton Park hundreds of Freemasons enjoyed their annual county fete, followed by a banquet. Church attendances were badly hit. Archdeacon Madden of Liverpool spoke out fiercely, claimed that Britain's new 'Pleasure Dome' was rapidly attracting more young men than the Sunday services, partly through controversy within the Anglican church over the South African War, but mainly because a dam of Victorian rectitude had burst wide open. "Young men are turning Sunday into pleasure seeking," he complained. "Railways and steamboats are crowded with men on pleasure bent and the roads are almost impassable with bicycle riders off for the day."

For cricketers it was a golden spell. The Knutsford team's ground was pleasantly situated on Mere Heath Lane, close to the nurseries and the murder spot. Now that the case had moved out of his hands, Caldecutt could pick up a cricket bat instead and he starred in the game against Boughton Hall, a club from the Chester area, scoring 56. Jackson also played along with two of Dr Fennell's sons and Tom Speakman, the nephew of Murray and Emily. Not surprisingly, the cricket club was tightly controlled by and for the benefit of a close circle of businessmen and professionals and yet the game in general held the whole of England in thrall. Nine thousand fans watched a club fixture at Church in East Lancashire. County and international players, like W G Grace and C B Fry were revered.

Parrott preferred horse racing and football. The notebook that Pierce had found at his home contained lists of his bets, most of them losers, and Constable Turner had mentioned that on Easter Monday, the day after the murder, he had seen Parrott at the town club's football match and had talked to him about the shooting. The details at that stage were sparse, but Turner recalled mentioning the approximate time and place and that Parrott said nothing about being there. Yet, after his arrest, Parrott denied that Turner had even spoken about it. It was another example of evidence which could not be proved and was left to gather dust.

July burned on. The second quarterly sessions of the year were staged at Chester, dealing with a variety of offences, one so upsetting that it moved some court officers to tears. Two young women, badly abused at home, decided to commit suicide by taking poison and then throwing themelves into the river Mersey. One succeeded and drowned. The other was rescued and revived by a policeman, only to be arrested and charged with attempted suicide, then a serious offence. A 43 years-old labourer indicted for 'disgusting offences' was sentenced to a year in gaol and 20 lashes of the cat.

As well as dealing with specific crimes, the Quarter Sessions' magistrates also had the power to take up issues affecting the justice system (although this influence was being gradually eroded), one of which was prisoners being chained together when escorted between Knutsford prison and the railway station less than 200 yards away. The chain gang, sometimes comprising 20 men, had to shuffle along in broad daylight, under the gaze of passers-by. One commentator remarked: "It stamps them all as 'gaol' irrespective of their degree of criminality. The even more reprehensible practice of treating unconvicted prisoners in similar manner has been discontinued but it required considerable pressure of public sentiment to obtain that reform."

At the Chester hearings, Frank Merriman, one of the Knutsford bigwigs, elected to the Bench six months earlier, proffered the idea that prisoners could board a train at the sidings, just a few yards across the road from the gaol's side gate, rather than from the station platform. No chains would be needed and they would be on public view for only a few seconds. The proposal needed the co-operation of the Cheshire Lines railway company and Home Office approval. Most of the magistrates voted for it but Horace Trelawney protested: "There is a lot of sentimental nonsense prevailing."

Merriman, who lived in Church House, opposite the prison, reported the argument to Parrott's lawyers. Edwin Ashworth contacted Major Nelson. The governor re-assured him. Parrott would not be part of a chain gang – at least when going to his trial. If convicted he might well be on his return. "That would be the last straw for his mother." Jackson looked glum.

"No," said Ashworth. "The last straw will be the rope. But it won't go that far, will it?"

Jackson pulled a face.

Mary Ann was constantly at him. James was innocent. He was not the type. How could he come home and sleep in the same bed as his brother a few hours after killing someone? It was incomprehensible. Everyone else in town thought the same. Jackson, whose nose was so close to the ground that he could smell the grass growing, agreed with her on the last two points. Of course, it did not make sense, and yes, Knutsford believed in James Parrott. From the outset the town had cast doubt on the possibility that an ogre had sprung from its own loins. It bred justice, bedrock respectability, and maypole dancers, not mad murderers. It was a loyal town, loyal to its monarch, to its Imperial government, and to itself. Parrott, no matter how troublesome, was one of theirs. Bould had been an outsider. For some weeks Jackson had felt the tide rising high in Parrott's favour. He overheard one of the cricket club members criticising the police. A shopkeeper told him: "Tell young Parrott he can have a job here when he gets out."

But 'innocent', 'not the type'? This was the great uncertainty. All the defence unit's work could be shattered if Parrott went into the box, because he was not the same as others – even Mary Ann had suspected it for a long time. He pictured

Parrott, under intense cross-examination, suddenly losing his self-control and then what would the jury make of the 'could not hurt a fly' young man? Parrott had resolutely resisted all efforts to dissuade him from giving evidence and, as a result, no matter how many question marks over the evidence, the shadow of the noose still hung over him.

Caldecutt buttonholed Jackson during a practice session at the cricket ground one evening. "I see the trial is marked down for the Friday so you could be free for the Saturday. We're playing at Kersal." He was in light-hearted mood following his performance against Boughton Hall – a 'rattling good innings', reported Our Knutsford Correspondent in the Manchester Evening News cricket page.

Jackson was non-commital. "There are over 30 witnesses. I can't see it being finished in the one day."

Sheer weight of evidence threatened to cause havoc. If Parrott went into the box, a two days hearing was inevitable and even that might not be enough. Yet trailing it over to the Monday was unthinkable. Other work would be delayed, and even cancelled. The jury would have to be accommodated for a further two nights, costs would rise, all going against the principle that a quick trial was a good one.

"Will depend on the judge," said Caldecutt. "And Grantham won't stand for any nonsense. Come on, let's go and have a look at the wicket. Fennell says it's like a dust bowl."

CHAPTER 19

*'Attired in a suit of grey tweed he seated himself at
the back of the dock with his hands in his pockets and
surveyed all around with an air of easy unconcern'
– Liverpool Weekly Courier, August 1901*

MR Justice (Sir William) Grantham of 100 Eaton Square, London, a former MP, was the senior judge on the Wales and Northern Circuit. On his tour of duty that summer he presided over cases in Monmouth, Caernarvon, Ruthin and Chester where Parrott's trial awaited. Experienced, busy, and generally thought to be fair, he did not tolerate unnecessary delays. If anyone could complete the trial in a reasonable time, it was he. Grantham was also outspoken, as his row with the Dean of Durham Cathedral showed.

Dean Kitchin had hit out over the drunken send-off parties for volunteer soldiers heading to South Africa. 'Bacchanalian orgies' was perhaps going too far, but the main thrust of his controversial sermon was to make people think a little more deeply about the conflict. He referred to an incident when, on the eve of their departure, a group of volunteers carried drunken colleagues to their ship after a brewery had allowed them to booze all night for free.

"With what spirit do we send out our fighting men – with drunken revels, with the excitement of the gin palaces, as if the bottle is the best prelude to battle?"

Grantham, an arch Conservative, was incensed. Sitting in Lancaster shortly afterwards, he used his address to the Grand Jury as a Defence of the Realm diatribe and a public attack on the Dean.

"One is proud to see the spirit of patriotism that has fired the heart of the nation," he roared. "And how our young men have been volunteering in their thousands. The voice of the drunkard has almost hushed, and the sound of crime almost still, yet and in the face of these facts, the Dean of Durham has chosen to slander our nation and throw foul aspersions on these men who in the true spirit of Christianity are ready to shed their blood and, if need be, their lives on behalf of our country."

It exploded into a national controversy with complaints in the House of Commons that a judge had made an overtly political speech – in a court of law at that – and that he had attacked a highly respected man of the cloth whose criticism was not so much of the volunteers themselves but of the widespread lack of gravity and understanding for the realities of war. That the young drunk being carried onto his ship might never return. Yet Grantham was seen as a hero by many, a defender of the faith, certainly where volunteers were being trained, like Knutsford. Parrott himself might well have joined in the applause.

Grantham shrugged off any criticism. As a senior judge he was more powerful than most MPs. The dispute rumbled on, but in the July heat he was more bothered about trying to stay comfortable in his heavy official dress of scarlet robe, stole and wig. Even so, better than the damp and cold of February which had laid him low with a bout of bronchitis. Grantham had retreated to his country residence at Lewes, Sussex, where he spent a few days writing lengthy letters to The Times about the source of his illness – the smog of London, caused he said by factory chimneys belching foul smoke. Later he went to the Mediterranean, Cannes and Venice and, in March, returned to duty.

Bronchitis did not muffle a sharp tongue. Opening the Assizes at Montgomery he noted that the county's crime rate had dropped and tried a joke: "When I was a child I was taught the old adage 'Taffy was a Welshman, Taffy was a thief', but now it should be altered to 'Taffy is a Welshman, Taffy is a good fellow.'" It did not go down well with the locals. Other areas had mixed opinions of him. He divided the community at Bethesda, praising a jury for following the law in a dispute at a quarry works, but then hitting out at the actions of the strikers they had freed, comparing their 'poor heroism' with the 'true gallantry' of 18 Welshmen who had fought off a Boer force attempting to raze a small town in Natal. Over in Leeds where the Corporation delivered two huge bouquets each day to the judge's lodgings, Grantham would pass them to children in the street.

The judge avidly supported the Volunteer movement. While in Caernavon, he allowed his London house to be used for a meeting of brigade commanders. But he campaigned just as strenuously against the open, unlicensed traffic of guns.

One case in Yorkshire highlighted his approach. Edgar Bentley, aged 20, shot dead his friend as they strolled along a road close to their homes. The killer was mentally unstable and Grantham ordered him to be detained at His Majesty's pleasure, having heard of his 'peculiarities' from a doctor, friends and family. The weapon, a cheap German pistol, had been bought from a local shop, no questions asked, and Grantham expressed disgust and anger that a youth with mental issues could legally walk around with a gun in his pocket. He chided the shopkeeper: "It is because you sell them that these murders take place." Bentley had purchased the gun for 10 shillings on the same day that Parrott's order for a revolver landed on the desk of James Goodbody at Colt's.

From Caernavon, Grantham travelled to Ruthin for the Denbighshire Assizes and then onto Chester, where on Thursday July 25 he, his fellow judge Mr Justice Channell who would look after the civil cases, and the High Sheriff, Thomas Brocklebank, rolled up in a horse-drawn, highly polished black carriage to the main entrance of the Shire Hall, designed by the Neo-classical architect Thomas Harrison, and, when completed in 1801, described as a 'magnificent hall of justice'.

The judges and sheriff were driven by a coachman, accompanied by two postilions and a footman. All wore ceremonial garb, the judges in their robes, the High Sheriff in a black velvet rig, under a cocked hat, with his badge of crossed swords, one 'Justice' and the other, with the sword tips cut off, 'Mercy'. A real sword hung from his belt. Their arrival signalled the start of the Assizes. The temperature had dropped, rain threatened, but it remained uncomfortably warm and humid. Making their way through the massive colonnade of smooth, stone pillars they mounted the stairs to the Grand Jury room where a group of distinguished gentlemen waited.

Distinct from the common jury which would try Parrott and others, the Grand Jury was to vet the criminal indictments, to listen to witnesses if necessary and to Grantham's comments, and then to decide which cases merited a trial – a 'true bill' - and which could be immediately thrown out for insufficient evidence.

Common juries were then formed to hear those cases which progressed. Foreman of the Grand Jury that month was a certain Horace Trelawney, of Shotwick Park, who, a couple of weeks earlier, had clashed with Frank Merriman over the chain gang issue. With him were a few other landowners, two more members of the Brocklebank family, three colonels, one the chairman of the county council, an army captain, a church minister etc. - a deeply conservative, patriotic line-up.

The following week some would attend a welcome home reception for the troops of the 29th Company at the Grosvenor Hotel where the 'Pro Boers', campaigning to end the war in South Africa, were blasted in a rousing speech by Colonel Cornwallis-West who signed off with: "There are Englishmen doing what they can to rouse the spirit of the enemy – they should shake the dust of England from their boots and settle in Amsterdam," referring to the Boers' Dutch roots.

Not one of the Grand Jury was a qualified lawyer. And their make-up accentuated the notion that the people who judged came from one class, those who were judged came from another lower down the social scale. However, generally these people were well educated, experienced, and imbued with a sense of English fair play. Parrott could expect a decent crack of the whip.

The official business was conducted in the semi-domed courtroom ringed by Doric pillars. Harrison's design was inspired by the Ecole de Medicine, Paris, with a nod to Rome's

Pantheon, and Grantham sat majestically above everyone. In his opening address he was able to speak unfettered, as the Dean of Durham was painfully aware, although the central element was to sum up the cases before him, and to ask the Grand Jury for their True Bill verdicts. He began with another tongue in cheek dig at the Welsh, quickly salving that cut by comparing their dropping crime rate to the 'shameful' number of prisoners on the English side of the border. His list was a lengthy one, including a sexual assault, fraud, attempted suicide, robbery and a railway employee who had tried to derail a train by hauling a one hundredweight wooden sleeper onto the tracks. And then, he said, was the 'most extraordinary case I have seen in many years'. As, only that year, he had already dealt with a barmaid who had shot her lover, and an army quartermaster who had gunned down all his four children and had laughed about it, the case of James Parrott promised to be something special.

Grantham quickly ran through the main facts of the murder, emphasising at once that the prosecution evidence was not the strongest, although he added that there were 'small pieces pointing to one thing.' The Grand Jury delivered a True Bill, and the trial was set in place.

Next day a crowded train left Knutsford. Parrott's defence team of Edwin Ashworth, Lance Bentley and Tom Jackson stepped into one compartment, Pierce and Dr Smith into another. Also embarking were the Parrott family, minus Thomas Holland Parrott who was travelling to Chester from Liverpool, and the bulk of the witnesses in the case including: Dorothy Jackson, accompanied by her mother, Thompson and Mary Flood, John Parkes, Hugh Daniels, Bernard and Charlotte Engberson, Fred Copeland, Robert Lee, the licensee of the Sword and Sceptre with his wife Annie, daughter Florrie, and the barman John Webb. George Rowe and Harry Yarwood were already on board. The Manchester based Press was heavily represented and Our Knutsford Correspondent joined them. When the last door banged shut, the guardsman waved a green flag, blew a whistle and the The Murder Express steamed out of town heading west.

Parrott had travelled the same route two days earlier, not chained, but guarded by two warders. Quiet as usual, he gazed out of the window at fields which still suffered from sunburn despite recent rain. He had taken time getting ready, washing, shaving, smoothing some of the creases out of the suit he had lived in for several months, adjusting the collar and black tie. All through May and June he had thought about how he would present himself, how he would react to the pressure. Everything would be fine. West Africa would wait for him.

Mary Ann also stared out of the window, contemplating. The stations went by as they crossed the Cheshire Plain. Plumbley (now Plumley) had a nice little garden, and once through the bustle of Northwich and its freight sidings, there was little but fields, shallow brooks, and woodland. She had never been this way before, usually they went in the opposite direction towards Manchester. Such a pleasant trip to see your son condemned. She had to stop thinking like that. James was innocent. If anyone was guilty it was...she had to stop thinking like that, too. She had done her best and she would not let him down now.

The train ride took under an hour. At Chester some took cabs, others walked. With more than an hour to spare before the start, Bentley and Ashworth joined forces with the defence lead, Ellis Griffith, the MP for Anglesey who would serve as an Under Secretary of State in Asquith's government 10 years later. Another Welsh based MP, Abel Thomas headed the prosecution with Ralph Bankes as his second. It sounds like a boxing match set-up, which, basically, it was. Trials were adversarial, the barristers pugilists in wigs, aiming to score blows, under the belt if necessary. Some, like Thomas, relied on an accurate jab, gradually wearing a witness down. Others, like Bentley, went for a knock-out shot, risky but spectacular when it landed, as his uppercut at the inquest with the purse.

But the make or break man was the judge. Both physically and figuratively, everyone in the trial looked up to him.

He had absolute power. Theoretically impartial, he was also a human being, painted, like anyone else, in a myriad of shades, and swayed by countless distractions, a poor night's sleep, indigestion after too many oysters at lunch, the treachery of a diocesan dean. He could forget things, make mistakes, give too much room to his prejudices. A judge's summing up of the evidence to the jury was crucial for, while he had to stress that 'it was for the jury to decide' he could more than hint at his own opinion. As for the barristers, he could encourage those he liked, crack down on those who crossed him. A good judge overcame all, or most, of the obstacles, in conducting a fair trial. But, no matter how inefficient, a judge remained a judge. They were never sacked.

Mr Justice Grantham had enjoyed Chester after travelling through the 'wilds of Wales' (as he put it to the Grand Jury). Its Roman history, cathedral, and river excursions on the Dee were drawing in more tourists – he had heard some American voices – but it had retained a sense of dignity and respect, at the heart of which was the Shire Hall. His rooms were comfortable, the food wholesome. Stories of pig farms being decimated with swine fever and milk contaminated by tuberculosis failed to stem his appetite. But, despite the feel good environment, he was distinctly unsettled. He professed openly that he had never come across a murder case like it.

When he swept into the court at 10 30 that Friday morning he found it bursting at the seams. Barristers, solicitors, police, clerks, and court officials filled the well of the court. Along one side was a panel of two dozen jurors from which the trial jury would be selected, and opposite was a packed Press bench. In the centre was the dock, manned by prison and police officers, most of the public gallery seats were filled and officials had to push their way through the crowds milling around the doors. Witnesses gathered outside, many having to stand. Grantham took it all in with a glance, before easing into his thickly cushioned chair, leaving a clerk to arrange his documents and books on the bench in front of him. The Clerk of Arraigns David Crompton told the dock officers to 'bring the prisoner up' and a few seconds later

Parrott emerged from below.

One reporter noted: 'He is little more than a boy, of slight build with fair hair, pale and sharp features and he wears glasses which impart a somewhat studious aspect to his countenance, suggesting sharpness and intelligence. Attired in a suit of grey tweed he seated himself at the back of the dock with his hands in his pockets and surveyed all around with an air of easy unconcern.

'It was when brought forward to answer the charge read by the Clerk that he betrayed any sign of anxiety or sign of consciousness of the terrible charge hanging over him. Even then the only change observable was a slight increase in his natural pallor and a perceptible falter in his voice as he replied Not Guilty.'

Parrott's demeanour was described in the Manchester Evening News as 'cheerful'. Others in the Press Box thought he looked a little more care-worn after three months in captivity. His clothes had not changed. Neither, apparently, had his self-assurance for while his voice may have faltered it was crystal clear. He stood straight and continued to stand, despite being invited to sit, while the jury of 12 was picked from the panel, the Clerk selecting their name cards at random. One, a Mr Lindop, failed to respond, even when his name was called a second time. "I have some difficulty with hearing," he admitted and was replaced. When after 20 minutes the jury was in place, Parrott sat down, a dock officer either side of him. He seemed calm and composed.

Note: The arrangements in court had not changed essentially between 1901 and 1965 when the author first sat in the Press Box of the Cheshire Quarter Sessions at Knutsford although it seems one of the most important figures during my times was absent in 1901 – the shorthand writer, who sat below the Bench next to the Clerk's desk. Like me, they used Pitman's shorthand and their script was immaculate, thanks to their training and to a pen with a special nib designed for thin and thick strokes. The shorthand writer had to get everything down, providing an almost instant fact-checker for the judge and barristers, who could pull each other up if they believed evidence was being twisted or misinterpreted. As it turned out, a shorthand writer would have been a useful addition at Parrott's trial but while they had been employed for many years at the Old Bailey in London, they were not regularly used in the rest of the country and I have found no sign of one in this case.

At 11am as Abel Thomas rose to open the case for the prosecution, there was a stir at the back of the court with the appearance of the Parrott family, who had stayed back from the early rush for seats. Mary Ann had Mary and Edith at each side with Thomas Holland and John behind their sisters. They engaged the court's attention for a few seconds until Thomas turned to the jury and told them: "Heaven knows the prosecution do not want the conviction of an innocent man. It is up to you, as sensible men, to say whether you can come to any other conclusion than that the prisoner murdered John Bould for the sake of robbery."

And so, suddenly, according to the prosecution, what had often been termed a 'motiveless' murder had a motive. A 'senseless' crime apparently made sense. Bould, one of the poorest of working men, a man of no property other than a few clothes, a watch and chain, a pipe, some 'baccy, a penknife, and a purse containing a farthing and a token, had been done to death for material gain. Actually, it did not make sense. Agreed, Bould had been robbed, his sister's letter had been taken, his purse and coins were missing and, perhaps, the other items in his pockets would have gone too, but for Mary Jane Francis suddenly appearing on the scene. But the overall value was minimal and the prosecution had opted for robbery as a motive, simply because they could find no other. Thomas erred in placing it so quickly and with such emphasis before the jury in his opening address. It immediately raised eyebrows. This robbery, as he defined it, was premeditated and needed the victim dead. But, surely, no-one with any intelligence fired five bullets into a stranger, a working-class man, so that they could rifle through his pockets to see if he had anything worth stealing.

As Thomas continued, Griffith turned in his seat to find Bentley smiling. The case was only few minutes old but the prosecution had made things harder for themselves. Later, though, Griffith was to make an even bigger mistake.

Much of the prosecution evidence was a repeat of that given at the inquest and committal hearings. Thomas informed the jury that, while circumstantial, the evidence contained too many elements to be discarded as chance.

1: Parrott was in the section of Mere Heath Lane at about the time Bould was shot;

2: he had recently bought a revolver which was engineered to fire the type of bullet which killed Bould and his story of selling it to an un-named sailor was absurd;

3: he was in possession of a purse and coins similar to that owned by Bould and which had gone missing from the time of the murder;

4: he had initially lied to the police about his movements leading up to the shooting, and his behaviour afterwards was not that of an innocent man.

Basically, Thomas was asking the jury a loaded question. 'John Bould was murdered and, of all the people it might have been, is not James Parrott the hot odds-on favourite?' He called the evidence.

Pierce did his best. Under fierce cross-examination from Griffith he refused to alter his account of Parrott's arrest, nor would he admit to anything suspect about the way he had interviewed him on the Saturday night in his kitchen, or the following morning when the prisoner changed his story so dramatically. And when Griffith asked why Parrott was the only one wearing spectacles on the identity parade, Pierce retorted: "Because he insisted on it." Griffith, taken aback, glanced over to Parrott who offered nothing in return.

Griffith followed up with an intriguing series of questions, totally unrelated to the evidence and treating the policeman almost like a character witness for the defendant, beginning with the extraordinary: "Was the prisoner not eccentric?"

Pierce replied: "He was very quiet."

"He didn't mix with other people?" Griffith continued, gesturing around the room with his arm.

Pierce: "He never made many friends."

Griffith was determined to underline the point. "He used to be by himself a great deal."

"He took quiet walks," said Pierce.

Neither Thomas not the judge interjected. Should they have done? Certainly. Griffith's cross-examination should have referred strictly to Pierce's evidence in chief – and there was nothing in that referring to Parrott's character. Nor should there have been. Pierce was a station sergeant who did not know him that well. Anything of Parrott's general behaviour, his way of life, he must have learned from someone else and was 'hearsay'. Yet Griffith was able to use a prosecution witness to enhance the picture of Parrott as a lonesome, in need of understanding youth. But counsel for the defence was not finished.

"You have practically had the preparation of the entire case for the prosecution?"

Pierce had expected something like this. He tried to sound off-hand. "To a great extent, yes."

"You have seen some of the witnesses several times?" Griffith's habit of turning statements into questions might well have been subject to objection by Thomas, but the prosecutor let him continue.

When Pierce agreed, Griffith quickly lunged in with: "How many times have you seen Miss Francis. Did you see her several times during the proceedings?"

Pierce shifted a little. He was on dangerous ground. "Yes, several times for the purpose of eliciting a description of the person she had seen."

That was all Griffith needed. He sat down, content.

'There was a buzz of excitement when Mary Jane Francis entered the arena' reported the Sheffield Daily Telegraph. Here was the 'girl' who had captured the nation's attention, outraging and delighting in equal proportions, a 'comely young woman' who had wrecked the reputation of a well-known businessman and who could yet send a harmless looking youth to the gallows. A sex scandal lining a murder case. Reporters were at the ready, licking pencil points. Seats creaked and clothes rustled in the gallery as onlookers strained to get a better view.

Mary Jane, dressed all in black, had come up from Welshpool that morning. She did not feel at her best. The atmosphere in this huge room was far more intimidating than in the Sessions House at Knutsford but she stuck grimly to her story that Rowe had grabbed her, kissed her roughly and had then tried to take 'further liberties'. It 'seemed' as though 10 minutes passed, she said, when she heard two shots and screamed as loud as she could. Rowe and Yarwood then rode off, she turned back towards Knutsford and saw a man lying in the hedge with another man leaning over him with his hands on his chest. All this was a repeat of her evidence at the inquest and committal but she produced a major surprise when Thomas asked if the man near Bould's body was the same as the one she had seen earlier at the gate, later identified as Parrott. "I could not swear to it," she said. No-one, except possibly Pierce, could have anticipated anything different as it was exactly what she had said previously and Thomas had his next question on the tip of his tongue when, lowering her voice, she added: "Although I believe he was the same."

Thomas encouraged her to repeat her answer and to speak up so that the jury could hear. "I believe he was the same – to an extent." Stifled gasps were followed by a few seconds of silence while everyone took this in. Griffith slapped his knee in disgust. Thomas had the chance there to push home an unexpected bonus. Although she had said something similar to Pierce shortly after the murder and at their private tete-a-tete at the cottage, she had told the coroner and the Knutsford magistrates that she was not certain. Now she had gone almost full circle. Something stopped Thomas, probably the realisation that Mary Jane was fragile. 'To an extent' she had added. It suggested that she might buckle under further pressure. He stayed his hand asking only: "What happened then?"

"He ran off as fast as life would take him."

Griffith could hardly wait to get to his feet to remind her of her depositions at the Knutsford hearings 'which you gave on oath'.

"You agreed at the inquest that the two men were not alike, and also that their coats were not alike. Is that correct?"

Her head dropped. "Yes."

Griffith grabbed his chance and attacked. "How often have the police seen you?"

"A great many times. Innumerable."

"Did the Chief Constable see you?"

"Yes, but he didn't trouble me too much." Someone sniggered. The Clerk ordered: "Silence."

"Sergeant Pierce saw you a great many times, didn't he?"

"Oh, yes."

And, with that, the identification of Parrott as the man leaning over the body withered like the wheat in the sun-burned fields. Griffith looked meaningfully at the jury. He had shown Mary Jane to be unreliable and possibly overly influenced by the police. She left the witness box, head bowed and dispirited. As she made for the door she had to pass Pierce. He stared straight ahead.

Griffith continued to have the upper hand on the first day, damming the trickle of prosecution evidence with the bricks and mortar of solid cross examination, or simply letting it dribble away, not worthy of him dabbling a toe in it. Basically, it was an encore of the inquest where the verdict was 'Murder by a person or persons unknown'. Griffith was more than happy with the way it was proceeding.

As a courtroom drama, this Act One lacked the impact of the inquest. Mary Jane's downcast exit left it without personality despite brief cameos from Teresa Neagle and the 'beautifully dressed' Dorothy Jackson. Much of the evidence was familiar, the judge had to intervene only a couple of times, and Parrott remained seated, barely moving or showing any sign of emotion.

Yet there were significant passages.

Rowe waved aside Mary Jane's allegations and Thomas's suggestion that after 'tea' at the Royal George he was 'the worse the wear for drink'. He had owned a service revolver, he said, but had given it to his brother-in-law some weeks before the murder. Upon hearing about the murder, he asked a gunsmith to examine the revolver so as to prove that it had not been recently fired. None of the Three Horsemen were carrying a gun that day.

Neither Thomas nor Griffith pressed him too closely, but when he stomped out of court Rowe knew his troubles were far from over. By the time he returned home, Gertie would have the evening editions spread over the dining room table, telling all and sundry for the umpteenth time of his grubby manhandling of a helpless housemaid.

Yarwood, who saw 'nothing wrong' between Mary Jane and Rowe, was as bumptious as ever, asserting that the 'four, five shots' he heard came from 300-400 yards away in the direction of Knutsford. "I am a Yeoman myself," he bragged. "I ought to be capable of judging the distance of a shot." Actually, he was not a good judge. All the other evidence placed the shooting at no more than 200 yards from his position. But no-one was bothering too much with Yarwood The Yeoman by this stage. He had no jokes.

Charlotte Engberson, close to tears as she recalled her last conversation with Bould, said on Easter Sunday morning her husband Bernard was reading and commenting on a newspaper article about children using toy guns. Bould remarked: "They ought to be punished for selling them. There ought to be a law against carrying revolvers." This obviously struck a chord with Mr Justice Grantham. The judge wrote something down. Later he referred to the note when James Goodbody, in telling of Parrott's order for a revolver, described how Colt's marketed their .32 Pocket revolvers.

"We advertise it as particularly suitable for travellers and cyclists." Goodbody sounded so sure of himself, perhaps even boastful. If so, he had picked the wrong judge. Grantham's response was a mix of scorn and anger. "You don't mean to suggest that cyclists run such risks that they feel the need to carry revolvers – I'm sorry to hear that. They ought to be fined. Why do they carry them?"

Goodbody muttered it was for "self protection, generally from dogs. They get caught between the wheels and upset the cyclists."

Grantham by then was visibly upset, his mouth twitching:

"Therefore," he said, slamming down his pen, "cyclists are to murder dogs."

Unfortunately for Goodbody – and Colt's – the judge was not finished there. He continued to rant about the firearms industry, particularly Colt's, both in the trial and later. His comments spread far and wide, reaching Whitehall and soon licensing laws were being passed.

Near the end of the day, two Manchester tailors and former workmates of Bould, Charles Hill and Joseph Bagnall, gave the prosecution a boost by claiming that they had seen him handling a purse and coins similar to that found by Pierce in Parrott's bedroom. In fact Bagnall went a little further, as he inspected the purse: "I believe it is the same. And I saw him with a farthing and a half farthing like these. He refused to let anyone else handle them." That was backed up by a woman, Edith Brown who had known him in Ashton. She told the court: "He had coins like that and seemed quite proud of them." Abel Thomas smiled. A victory at last.

He might have enjoyed more success had he emphasised the testimony of the young Tatton Park employee John Parkes, the only witness to see John Bould alive in Mere Heath Lane, and the only one to plant an indelible question mark against Parrott's alibi that he was out of the lane, heading towards the railway station at the time of the murder. Parkes' evidence required careful thought, and to be measured along with the times, places, and distances of others like the Floods. Unfortunately, he was allowed to say his piece and to walk away, without any request for elaboration. Thomas was responsible for this crucial lapse. But Pierce had also missed the clue. Perhaps he was too focused on Mary Jane, maybe the depth of analysis necessary to make sense of it all was too much. This is not to doubt his intelligence but to highlight his lack of time and support. This aspect of the case will be detailed later in this book.

With Thomas offering no more evidence and the clock ticking towards 5pm, half the court were gathering themselves for a rush to the door but Grantham was having none of it. The defence could begin, he said. Griffith called his first witness. Tom Jackson's name brought a few smiles within the Knutsford contingent. One of the town's best known figures. Dorothy's father. She was still there, sitting quietly with her mother. A less mature child might have giggled and whispered: "Look there's Daddy." But she knew it was important to keep quiet.

Jackson informed the jury of his trip to Liverpool. The smaller of the two coins in the purse, the 'half farthing' was not a genuine one but a metal commemorative coin of the same size and design issued in the Queen's Jubilee year and sold in their thousands, but only in the North-West at Bowker's shop. Anyone could have bought one. Jackson had done so, at the cost of one penny. A penny worth its weight in gold to the defence.

Edwin Ashworth, switching from the solicitors' bench behind Griffith to the witness box, ended the day by affirming that Parrott had no great financial problems. He had already received £120 from his grandfather's legacy and, although that had quickly disappeared, he was still owed £30.

It could hardly have gone better for the defence. Mr Justice Grantham looked hard at Abel Thomas who, they all sensed, was beaten. But, to general astonishment, Griffith pulled his opponent off the floor and offered him a second chance.

"Your Honour," he advised Grantham, "it is the desire and the intention of the prisoner to go into the witness box." This was Griffith's' one major lapse, but an expensive one. While he had heard Bentley's concerns, he had not tried hard enough to change Parrott's mind about giving evidence. The judge replied: "It certainly is his right but does he understand the full implications?", adding with a little emphasis: "I expect he has been well instructed in that." There was still time for Griffith to change Parrott's mind.

The judge rose, stiffly. A long day, and the next might be even longer. The Clerk wearily cleared the court only for a tremendous clap of thunder to stop everyone in their tracks. As they cautiously left the hall, lightning seared the sky, rain fell in torrents. The weather had broken, Chester was enveloped in the gloom of a massive storm which ripped tiles off roofs and caused widespread flooding.

CHAPTER 20

'VERDICT IN BALANCE' – trial bulletin posted in window
of newsagent's in Knutsford, July 27, 1901

PARROTT had been warned good and proper. "It is dangerous," they had told him. "They could make a fool of you." Parrott was unmoved. Determined to face his accusers, he planned not simply to ward them off, but to launch a counter attack. A 21 years-old grocer's assistant he might be, but he was as good as them, if not better. His behaviour during the first day was perplexing, sometimes flexing himself bolt upright as a piece of evidence kindled his interest, sometimes appearing so laid back he might have been dozing, though the plain, wooden chair which accommodated him for over six hours offered little in the way of comfort. His own counsel had described him as 'eccentric' and those who glimpsed his antics in the dock understood why.

Overnight, he stayed in the cells at Chester. He listened to the thunder, thinking it more appropriate to a murder trial than the sunshine of recent weeks, and wondered what the family were up to. Mother and his brothers were due to give evidence on the second day. Vital evidence about the purse. Quite a family re-union. They would not let him down.

Supper at the Parrotts' home that night was a sombre affair. With them were Mary Ann's sister Annie, her husband Alf, and Henry Heywood who was courting the elder daughter Mary. Four of the ensemble were on the witness list for the following day, knowing that a mistake could cost James his life.

Jackson had planned to stay in Chester with his wife and daughter, a walk along the walls and by the river, a meal at a nice little restaurant – Bolland's had turtle soup and calves's feet jelly ('ideal for invalids') on the menu. But the storm forced a re-think. As rainwater turned the historic streets into fast flowing streams, he, Annie and Dorothy caught the train home. Knutsford was wet, too. Maybe the match at Kersal would be called off. In any event he knew he would not be batting with Leicester Caldecutt, the trial would not be settled until late on the Saturday and might even go over to the Monday. He settled down to read the cricket news. Tyldesley, Lancashire's star batsman, was on the brink of completing 2000 runs and still over a month of the season left! Dorothy, in a window seat, had her head over a piece of embroidery, her role in the case over, the long summer holiday and a possible trip to the seaside ahead.

After turning down the offer of an overnight stay at Superintendent Leah's home, Pierce was also back in Knutsford. Constable Turner welcomed him with a grimace. "Sarge, they've opened a book on it." For a moment, Pierce was fazed. What the heck was Turner talking about? "The verdict," Turner explained. "there's been a bookie at the back of the White Bear taking bets. He got a signal from someone and legged it when we went for a look-see, but he'll have to come back tomorrow and we'll nab him." Pierce's anxiety turned to anger. "Just make sure you do."

Back in Chester, Abel Thomas and his second Ralph Bankes got their heads together over dinner to draw up the order of battle for the second day. They were astounded but elated that Parrott was putting himself in the firing line. Both accepted that, on the prosecution evidence alone, he could not have been convicted but now they had a gilt-edged chance to pin him down, to show he was a liar, to turn the jury against him. Victory might yet be snatched from the jaws of defeat.

On Saturday morning the platform at Knutsford railway station again thrummed under the feet of dozens of passengers waiting for the Chester train. The Parrotts were there in force alongside Jackson, Bentley and Ashworth and a large company of supporters. "You'd have thought they were going to a football match," Turner, a soccer fan, commented. He had accompanied Pierce ready to give protection if things turned nasty but the crowd seemed good-humoured. The storm over, the weather was also set fair. Pierce, standing at the back of the platform, close to the station-master's office, told the constable to go and 'get some work done. Grab that bookie.' He noticed one of the porters John Webb pushing his way through the crowd. The previous day, Webb, a part-time barman at the Sword and Sceptre, had been in the witness box at the court, insisting he had not seen Parrott in the pub on Easter Sunday. The licensee Robert Lee, his wife and daughter had also debunked Parrott's claim that he had a drink there. But if Webb had pushed Parrott a little closer to the edge of the abyss, now he was politely steering Mrs Parrott away from the edge of the platform. "It's coming," Pierce heard him say.

The squat tank engine pulled three coaches. Mary Ann was given precedence but a mad scramble ensued once she was inside. Then they realised that Pierce was still to board. He refused to rush. Webb found him room in the rear carriage, closed the door carefully, and moved away as the guard raised his flag. With a rattle of couplings the train chugged out. The compartments, each seating a squashed 12, were soon foetid. Fresh air was demanded but when windows were opened, by means of leather straps, passengers were treated to acrid gusts from the locomotive's smokestack. In Chester a mopping-up operation was in process with dust in the air and water still creeping along the street gutters. By the time they reached the courtroom many were hot, sweaty and distinctly uncomfortable.

Parrott arrived feeling refreshed and ready for the fight after sleeping well. His big day. He brushed his suit with the palms of his hands, tightened the knot of his tie, pulled at the shirt collar and rubbed his spectacles with a handkerchief. The one he used in Mere Heath Lane that night. To mop his brow, he said. To signal someone, the conspiracy theorists said.

One of the warders went up the stairs into the dock, returned quickly and motioned to him. Up they went. He heard his younger sister Edith issue a startled: "James!" The hall had superb acoustics. He searched for the family in the direction of her voice but, even with polished lenses, his eyesight let him down. There, over there, he felt rather than saw where they sat. A few minutes later he heard another voice, the Clerk's, issuing his name. One of the warders opened the gate of the dock and he walked to the stand, fully conscious of the sudden quiet.

Much of Parrott's evidence tested common sense but he proved a redoubtable opponent for Thomas, ducking, diving, and sometimes, with his back to the ropes, hitting out with a force which surprised even those who had long recognised his inner strength. The scrap lasted for 90 minutes and left the verdict on a tightrope.

Parrott's story, as told to Ellis Griffith, took some believing.

Around the end of 1900 and the start of 1901 he received £120 of his grandfather's legacy of £150, gave his mother £30 to pay household bills, loaned some to his siblings 'and others' and opened an account at a bank in King Street, Knutsford. Eventually he would get the remaining £30 held by the family solicitors.

During the early weeks of 1901 he applied for a job with Welsh and Co as a clerk at their trading post in West Africa. In March, believing that he would be taken on, he bought the revolver, advertised as a weapon for travellers, and cartridges and, not wanting his mother to learn about it, had the gun case delivered to a 'drop shop' in the centre of Manchester, while he was spending a few days with his Uncle Alf and Auntie Annie. He collected it on Thursday March 21. That same day he left Irlams o' the Height taking the case with him, and returned to Knutsford where he found a letter from the bank waiting for him showing he had only 7s 5d in his account.

On Friday March 22, he travelled to Liverpool to spend the night with his brother Thomas Holland Parrott, taking the revolver and 50 cartridges with him. The following day he was at Haydock Park races where he lost £2-£3 in bets. That evening, temporarily hard up and with only a few shillings on him, he came to a deal with a sailor in the Old Haymarket, St John's Lane, Liverpool, selling him the revolver and cartridges for £1 plus the promise of some smuggled tobacco, worth about £2. He got rid of the remaining 50 cartridges by throwing them down 'the closet at the back' of King Street and was to receive the tobacco when he met the sailor at the Oxford Inn, Manchester some days later, and sell it, keeping 10s out of the proceeds.

"So you were to become a dealer in smuggled tobacco," asked the judge.

"Yes," Parrott admitted.

"And what would a sailor be doing in Manchester?" further inquired Grantham, possibly unaware of the existence of the Manchester Ship Canal which was transforming the city of cotton into a major port   with a proposed direct route to Chicago. Parrott replied: "I don't know." Also, he admitted, he did not know the man's name, or which ship he served on. "I had met him before in a pub in Liverpool," he asserted. "He was about 5 feet 9 inches, had a dark moustache, wore a peaked cap and a serge suit."

At that stage, Parrott appeared bright and breezy, speaking clearly, apparently eager to give details, but this was the easy part with Griffith steering a steady course through his evidence. Blatant anomalies had already surfaced which Abel Thomas would fasten on later in cross-examination but for now he had to wait his turn.

Parrott claimed that on Saturday, April 6, he visited his brother in Liverpool, leaving on Easter Sunday morning and arriving in Manchester at 10am.

While he still had enough to pay the fare from Manchester to Knutsford (1s) there was not a train until the afternoon and so he decided to walk it, a distance of about 17 miles through Stretford and Altrincham. Nearing Knutsford he turned off Manchester Road into Mere Heath Lane because it was quicker. As he got closer to the town, he stopped to rest, sitting on a gate. "I remember taking my handkerchief out to wipe my brow." Then he went into a field 'for a purpose', found that he could still be seen by passers-by, and crossed the lane, unfastened a gate and went into another field where a man emerged from a shed and ordered him to 'clear out'.

Parrott went back to the first field. A few minutes later he continued towards Knutsford. He could remember seeing various people, 'Miss Francis', the Floods and Dorothy

Jackson, a man and a woman, but not any of the Three Horsemen nor Bould. His route took him through Tatton Street and along the main road to the station where, he thought, he might see someone he knew getting off the train only to find he was too late. Not being pressed for time, he had a drink at the Sword and Sceptre, served by Florrie Lee, and then went home for supper.

As for the purse and coins, they were his, the smaller coin – the Jubilee token – coming from a shop in Liverpool.

Griffith left it there. Parrott might be a liar. But a liar was not necessarily a killer and it was still up to the prosecution to prove their case. He believed he had done enough but, under some relentless interrogation from Thomas, Parrott's defence creaked and sagged and he betrayed something of his true nature. Bentley, evermore anxious, put his head into his hands. This was not what he had wanted. He looked up to see the judge apparently sneering at one of Parrott's answers.

Thomas set off by inquiring about the revolver. Why had he bought it, saying he was going to West Africa, when, in fact, Welsh and Co had rejected his application in late January-early February? "I had several interviews with them," Parrott countered. "It is not true to say I was told my services would not be required." Thomas pointed out that this was contrary to the evidence of the firm's owner, Thomas Welsh. The barrister then referred to Parrott's decision to take the Colt and cartridges with him when he visited his brother on the Saturday.

"Why?" the prosecutor, asked, glancing round at the jury.

"I did not want my mother to find them. I might have stayed in Liverpool for a few weeks. In fact I might have gone abroad."

"But," said Thomas, "you left the other 50 cartridges in a case at Knutsford. Might she not have seen it?"

"I don't think so. It was only a small case."

Thomas paused. "Yes, a small case. Marked 'Explosives'. Was it not?"

Parrott did not reply. As had been spotted before, one of his few displays of emotion was a slight colouring of the cheeks and a rise in his voice. Both were discernible already, and

Thomas was barely under way.

"And, if you were going abroad," he said, "I suggest you might have taken some luggage with you."

Again, Parrott let that go. But he was ruffled. His replies became curt, then ill-mannered. One journalist wrote: 'He was beginning to lose his great self-control but then an argument between counsel and the judge as to one of his answers gave him a welcome minute or two of relief.' This came as Thomas was probing the amount of time which Parrott spent in Mere Heath Lane after stopping for a rest at the field gate. "You reckon it up," Parrott said abruptly.

Thomas went through the various timings of other witnesses and suggested it might have been 20 minutes. Parrott refused to answer. When Thomas inisisted that the jury had a right to know, Parrott gave a sulky sounding: "Five minutes," which was completely at odds with his own evidence, never mind anyone else's.

All this was exactly what Bentley and Jackson had feared. Defence optimism was further eroded when Parrott was invited to put on the overcoat he wore on Easter Sunday and to walk a few yards along the well of the court towards the jury box. It flapped around his calves. Though a dark brown, it appeared slightly different in colour depending on Parrott's position in relation to the light from the windows, possibly explaining Mary Jane's problems in describing it. Certainly, the length of the coat was similar to that she saw on the man running away from Bould's body. Incidentally, neither the coat, nor Parrot's clothes, were ever expertly examined for bloodstains.

Next, Thomas produced the purse. Several witnesses had testified that it was similar to Bould's. One – Bagnall – had gone further, saying he 'believed' it to be the same. Parrott had claimed it was his and had been repaired by his mother. Thomas handed it to him, saying: "Show me where she sewed it." And he admitted: "I can't."

In the absence of the revolver and any other direct evidence, this cheap piece of pigskin and its contents had always promised to be the prosecution's most potent weapon. The judge examined it under a microscope before passing it to the jury, instructing them to mark any place where they thought a 'woman might have mended it'. Each juror scanned it. It took 10 minutes. Eventually they marked a particular spot and returned it to the judge. "Yes," he said, looking at the mark, "that is what I thought but I will call a saddler to give an expert opinion." For some reason, this did not happen.

Thomas stayed on the attack, wondering why Parrott had not gone to the police immediately he heard about the murder on Easter Monday morning. Surely, an innocent, reasonable man would have done so, if only to offer help in their enquiries. Parrott, who had been in the box for well over an hour by then, appeared tired and anxious and met his accusers with an offensive of his own. "I'm wearing the same clothes now as I was then," his voice loud and edgy. " I never tried to disguise myself did I? All the time I was visible to anyone. I did not go to the police because I did not see the horsemen nor Bould and so must have been out of the lane. I could not have helped them. And there are other people who have not come forward. Where are they?"

Thomas let the flurry fade. "Never mind them. Why did you not go? Were you afraid?"

Parrott flashed back: "No. I could not help them. But I read a report of the inquest in the newspaper and felt that the facts were against me because Miss Francis had said she saw a man with spectacles."

Thomas: "So you were afraid?"

Parrott: "No. I have told you. I was out of the lane. I just did not want to get mixed up in the case."

Thomas: "I see. A man had been murdered and you, an innocent and reasonable man, did not want to get mixed up in it. Am I right?"

Silence.

"Have you ever shot a revolver?" Thomas snapped at him.

"No." Parrott retorted.

Thomas gathered his gown around him. "No further questions, your Honour."

Our Knutsford Correspondent reported: 'The prisoner stepped down from the witness box looking very relieved. He had been there for one and a half hours. There followed corroborative evidence from members of his family and the court then adjourned for luncheon.'

During the interval he nipped over to the local newspaper offices where he could use a phone. A message was conveyed to Gilliatts' newsagent's in King Street, transferred in bold capitals onto a sheet of paper, and stuck onto the inside of the front window.

PARROTT HAS GIVEN EVIDENCE. COURT AT LUNCH.
JUDGE TO SUM UP. VERDICT IN BALANCE

People were starting to gather outside the shop. Others in pubs and at street corners were laying out plans – a Volunteer like welcome party if an acquittal, some offer of support for Mary Ann if a conviction. Whatever the verdict she faced a massive legal bill.

Mary Ann had done everything possible to clear her son, giving evidence in the morning session, and stating firmly that the purse was James's, that she had repaired it once, but it had again worn through and he had left it in a box in his bedroom for her to mend a second time. The repair was impossible to distinguish because she had regulated the needle on her Singer machine so that it passed the thread through the original sewing holes in the seam. She had tied the end of the black thread in a loop but this seemed to have disappeared. While she had not seen the coins, she had heard James talk about them. On Easter Sunday evening he came home about 7 40pm – there was nothing exceptional in his behaviour.

John Parrott, the tallest person in the court, confirmed the overcoat was his. In one pocket was a 'toy' pistol which could not have fired the bullets which killed Bould and a Post Office pouch containing some stamps and a small amount of cash. When his brother came home on Easter Sunday evening he seemed his usual self. While they briefly mentioned the murder the following morning they did not go into detail. Thomas Holland Parrott said James stayed with him on the Saturday night, and on previous occasions when, he thought, he was looking for work. He had seen him with the purse.

The family's backing for Parrott was as expected, although Mary Ann's modesty and John Parrott's physique made extra impact, but Alfred Islip provided a surprise. Said to be a soap salesman, he told the jury of the days Parrott stayed with him at Irlams o' the Height leading up to the week of Easter. On March 29 Parrott left without warning. Later, Islip received a letter from him, apologising for his sudden exit and explaining that he had had to meet a sailor in Manchester to receive some 'smuggled goods'. As such, that dovetailed neatly with Parrott's story. But Islip then revealed that he had received the letter sometime *after* the murder and had since burned it. Thomas did not question him. The jury could infer what they liked from that.

Grantham made it a long lunch, the court to reconvene at 2 20 pm, partly because he wanted a few minutes to compile notes for his summing-up. One of his memos referred to: 'Guns for cyclists'.

CHAPTER 21

*'I am innocent as a child unborn' – James
Crossley Parrott, July 1901*

ELLIS Griffith poured scorn and evermore doubt on the police investigation when he addressed the jury first thing after lunch. It was, he admitted, 'a case which teemed with mystery from beginning to end'. But robbery as a motive? Rubbish. Bould had nothing worth stealing. As for the evidence of Mary Jane Francis – "Would you commit anybody on the evidence of Miss Francis's evidence which was contradicted by Rowe and Yarwood?"

Griffith then said something which turned Rowe's stomach when he read it in the paper the following Monday. "I would not suggest that George Rowe was the murderer - not at all," he stated with a touch of sarcasm. "But is it not strange and fruitful of consideration that only 100 yards from the scene of a murder, and at the very same time, another very serious offence was in process? It is for the jury to say whether or not out of this remarkable incident...a moment arrived which accounted for the murder and that the motive was not robbery but private malice and spite." The involvement of Rowe and Yarwood in the killing had been rumoured and hinted at throughout the case but this thinly veiled accusation, in front of an Assize jury and dozens of journalists, was far more serious. Neither was in court to hear it but Rowe, particularly, never lived it down. Nor did his wife and her family.

Finally, Griffith turned to the purse and coins. The defence had proved that they belonged to Parrott, so fracturing the strongest link in the prosecution's chain of circumstantial evidence. He finished: "The chain has not so much broken as shattered. The prosecution did not have to prove motive, but without one the jury has to decide whether this man, this young grocer's assistant, is such a desperado that he would shoot a stranger for no apparent reason."

While not the most fluent speech – Griffith had zig-zagged

through the issues – he had left the jury with plenty to think about and he and Lance Bentley had reason to feel pleased with themselves. Only for a few minutes, however, because Mr Justice Grantham quickly wiped the smile from the face of the defence with a summing-up which brutally exposed the crass decision for Parrott to go into the witnesss box.

Pulling his chair at an angle to better face the jury, he said: "If the case had closed and the prisoner had not been called it would have been my duty to tell you that, although there was grave suspicion against him, it is not sufficient to justify a conviction. It is one of the most extraordinary cases I have ever dealt with and the prosecution evidence was purely circumstantial.

"But now your opinion may be changed by the construction that he *(Parrott)* has put on the case. His evidence was as unsatisfactory as it could possibly be, not consistent with the truth, not consistent with the actions of a rational and reasonable man."

One or two reporters looked to the dock hoping to see a reaction from a man whom a judge, essentially, had called a liar. Parrott leaned forward as if to say something but sat back, silent.

Grantham took the opportunity to express his views about the open sale of guns saying: "I am startled and shocked that Colt's could demean themselves to such a low level that they can sell revolvers to cyclists. Just imagine someone riding along with a loaded pistol... the legislature must stop this practice." Parrott's story that he sold his Colt to a sailor was 'rubbish'. But the judge warned the jury: "You have to eliminate all doubt. Although the evidence might point to his guilt, yet if there is a loophole, it would not be safe to find him guilty. It is impossible to remedy a mistake in a case like this."

With those words ringing in their ears, the 12 good men of Cheshire retired to their room to discuss whether James Crossley Parrott should hang or walk away a free man.

Who were this dozen of Parrott's 'peers'? This random group of citizens who held his life in their hands. It would be interesting to know what type of person each was, for surely, the character of a juror might influence his judgement.

The author admits failure on this score as no available documents carry their identities, save for Mr Lindop who had to withdraw because of his diminished hearing. However, there is no reason to consider them as anything but typical, a hotch-potch of commercial, professional and merchant men, few if any being less than solidly conservative. I cannot help but wonder - were any of them anti-Irish, or prejudiced against intinerant workers (there was plenty of such bias about), or sympathetic towards young Englishmen who wanted to carry the Imperial flag into new colonies like West Africa? Were they all for capital punishment or did some of them recoil at the very thought of sending such a young man to his doom, guilty or not?

Moreover, did any of these jurors suffer long-term stress from such an experience? Little work has been done on this subject. Researchers at Leicester University carried out a project in 2020 claiming it was the first of its type and which ascertained that jury service, particularly for crimes against people, 'can cause significant anxiety, and for a vulnerable minority it can lead to severe clinical levels of stress or the symptoms of post-traumatic stress disorder.'

One case which highlighted this problem was that of the Davies brothers, mentioned earlier, where Richard and the younger George were convicted of murdering their abusive father. The foreman of that jury Thomas Farrell obviously felt tremendous strain, breaking the traditional code of silence to campaign in vain for Richard's reprieve. He had to cope with the detailed reports of Richard's execution in which the young, God-fearing, family loving 19 years-old repeated his plea of innocence and called on Christ to receive his soul. Farrell's anguish illuminated his letters to the Home Office while other jurors argued publicly about the rights and wrongs of the execution.

Parrott's jury went out at 5 40pm. Parrott disappeared below the dock. Half the court's population dispersed into corridors and rooms, but most of the public stuck to their seats in the gallery, worried that they might lose their places for the climax. The Press stayed close, too, several reporters scribbling updated reports and handing slips of copy paper to 'runners'. At the newsagent's in King Street, close to Parrott's home, an update appeared on the window. 'JURY OUT. PARROTT AWAITS HIS FATE'. The fast growing crowd outside went quiet.

"However it goes, we did well for him," Bentley told Tom Jackson, but both were grim-faced. The judge's denounciation of Parrott's story had un-nerved them. Jackson tried to lighten the mood: "Wonder how Leicester's doing?" Knutsford's game at Kersal was still under way. Life went on. Forty minutes later, an usher whispered into the Clerk's ear. "The jury are ready." The judge was informed, people hurried back into their positions, and Parrott re-appeared in the dock, oblivious apparently to the family, tightly grouped just a few yards away. Mary Ann, her face drawn and as grey as the court's stone pillars, plucked nervously at her jacket sleeve, Edith clutched her chest. The jury shuffled into their seats, settled, and the Clerk went through the procedure.

"Will the foreman please stand." And when the dark-suited man at the front corner of the jury box rose to his feet, the Clerk continued: "Foreman of the jury, have you reached a verdict?"

"We have," he answered.

"Is that a verdict on which you are all agreed?"

"It is."

"And what is that verdict? Do you find the defendant guilty or not guilty?"

A vague hesitation, a split second, in which several hearts jumped. Parrot, however, smiled.

The foreman recovered his poise. "Not guilty, your honour."

Cheering and applause broke out at the back of the court. Mary Ann was bemused. She had not heard properly. "Not guilty Mother, Not guilty!" Edith shouted. Parrott leaned over the dock rail to shake Bentley's outstretched hand. Thomas stiffly congratulated Griffith. Grantham patiently waited for calm before telling Parrott: "You are discharged." A warder opened the dock gate but Parrott seemed unsure of what to do. "You are free to go," added the judge.

The Clerk, ushers and police officers cleared the court

efficiently but outside, in the corridor, pandemonium reigned. Edith led the rush towards him as Parrott came through the door. She, Mary Ann and Aunt Annie hugged him, although his arms stayed limply by his sides – he was perhaps a little embarrassed. He shook hands with his brothers and uncle, then with Jackson and Edwin Ashworth, and started to head for the main door leading into the courtyard where a crowd had been accumulating through the afternoon. "Not there," said Ashworth, pulling Parrott with him. With Mary Ann, Jackson and the Islips, they left through a side door, where a cab was waiting. Hundreds of well wishers and the Press were to be disappointed.

Within minutes the final and shortest bulletin appeared in the King Street window. 'PARROTT ACQUITTED!' Knutsford prepared for the homecoming.

The train from Chester was noisy, boisterous, especially in those compartments where bottles were passed around. Parrott had a slurp of beer but said little, listening intently to his solicitor. Ashworth had a plan.

"I think it would be wise to stay away from Knutsford for a short while," he said. "There will be a lot of drink taken and you will be pestered beyond suffering. Tom will get out and deal with whatever needs to be dealt with but we can go onto Manchester and you and your mother can stay at your aunt's."

No-one would have criticised Pierce if he, too, had bypassed Knutsford. The wait at Chester railway station and the journey itself was a tortured hour of unbridled heckling and undisguised contempt from other passengers. At Knutsford he had to elbow his way past sullen faces and hissing mouths. Someone spat at him. It spread across his sergeant's stripes. 'Friends of Parrott, my backside', he muttered to himself. 'Never had any friends, 'til now.' Mounting the stairway off the platform, he heard a shout from behind: "Sarge. Sarge." As Pierce turned, Our Knutsford Correspondent, red-faced, caught up with him, demanding: "Does this mean that the murderer is still at large?"

Pierce's pale blue eyes glared at him. "We are not looking for anyone else," he said. "Stick that in your newspaper."

In their kitchen, his wife wiped the spittle off him. "Disgusting, You're only doing your job." A number of constables came in and went out without saying much – Pierce was not the type for consolatory words. He told three of them Davies, Smith and Turner to be on the watch for unruliness that night and to inform him immediately. "No point in worrying about it," he told Annie. "We did our best. And there's work yet to be done."

"Sooner we're out of Knutsford the better," she said.

Jackson met Caldecutt at The Angel where the cricketers quenched their thirst after a game. "What a result!" Caldecutt slapped him on the back. "Are you talking about the trial or the game?" joked Jackson, knowing Knutsford had beaten Kersal. They joined the throng around the bar.

A little later Parrott, his mother, the Islips and Ashworth reached Manchester. Ashworth paid for a cab to take the family to Irlams o' the Height. "Come and see me on Monday," he told Mary Ann, doffed his topper and strolled away towards his city office. The cab halted outside 15 Claremont Street. Not wanting to alert the neighbours, the homecoming was restrained. His Aunt Annie, eyes moist, grabbed hold of her sister, sat her down, knelt at her side. Soon both were in tears. Alf's arm was around Parrott's shoulder. They all had tea and biscuits.

"What are you going to do now?" asked Uncle Alf.

Parrott carefully placed a half-eaten digestive on the edge of his saucer. "I think I'll go for a nice walk."

Meanwhile, Our Knutsford Correspondent compiled an unshackled article of police incompetence and a young man's 'heroic and stoic' battle against injustice, worthy even of Baden-Powell's respect, only to slam it on his spike. One of his Press colleagues had argued: "He's no hero. The judge basically called him a liar. And 'not guilty' doesn't mean innocent, does it? It just means there wasn't enough evidence."

It was a point. And Pierce had rammed it home. Beaten in court but unbowed, he had no other suspect. Young and enthusiastic as he was, the reporter had a conscience. He did not want to be unfair to Pierce. He was also pragmatic, knowing he would have to work with the sergeant for a while, at least until one of them earned a promotion and moved to a bigger job in a bigger town. He typed out a toned-down re-write.

'At Chester Assizes on Saturday the young Knutsford man James Crossley Parrott was found not guilty of the murder of John Bould but later, in an exclusive interview with your correspondent, Sergeant William Pierce revealed that the police were not seeking another person for the shooting which took place in Mere Heath Lane on the evening of Easter Sunday. Sgt Pierce had been in charge of the investigation since arresting Parrott on April 20. Parrott went into hiding after the jury had acquitted him. Some family members returned to their home in King Street, Knutsford, after the trial but the freed man and his mother were not to be seen when dozens of townsfolk greeted the Chester train at the station. Their absence, however, did not pour cold water on the celebrations which marked the end of a remarkable episode.'

On the Sunday Parrott went for his walk, along the streets and through the parks of Manchester's northern outskirts. Fresh air – sort of. Although a warm mid-summer Sabbath, chimneys still spouted smoke. He flicked specks of ash from the lapels of his suit and stopped to clean his spectacles, but the trek lifted his spirits. New ideas floated towards him. If not West Africa, what about America? He might have to buy a new gun...

Next day Parrott gave an interview to a journalist who had tracked him down thanks to a tip-off from Ashworth who had spoken to Mary Ann. "Perhaps," he had advised her, "James could throw in a suggestion about compensation for the time lost at work, and it might not be a bad thing to talk about starting up a public fund to cover your legal costs. But I'll leave it with you."

It was an affable hour or two in Aunt Annie's front room where net curtains, jaundiced by smoke, were drawn tightly to defeat curious neighbours. The journalist accepted a cup of tea, tried unsuccessfully to balance the saucer on his knee, and, apologetically, set it down on the floor. In his forties, balding slightly, with fingers stained by nicotine, he seemed amiable and more than willing to let Parrott ramble, interspersing his note-taking with encouraging expressions of "Yes, I see," or "Hmm, interesting, very interesting." Occasionally a member of the family broke into the dialogue. Annie insisted he had another cup of well-brewed tea. "Well, I must say, that's very kind."

Parrott sat on a wooden chair brought in from the kitchen, his legs reaching out in front, feet crossed. He began by pointing to his spectacles. "My eyesight was badly affected by an illness I had many years ago."

"I'm sorry about that." The reporter was a sympathetic type, at least while he was conducting an interview, but he did not want Parrott to linger for too long on irrelevancies. "May I ask why you came to Irlams o' the Height rather than Knutsford?"

Parrott shifted to a more upright position. "I came here with Mother to avoid the crowds outside the court and they were waiting for us at Knutsford as well. We got out of the court building and a cab took us to the station. As far as my trial is concerned, I am innocent as a child unborn. But I confess to wondering what might have been if I had not been so well defended. Mr Ashworth has worked hard for me, going to see me several times when I was in gaol and, in court, I couldn't have been in better hands than Mr Griffith'.

"But it has been hard lines on my mother," here, a soulful glance at Mary Ann, "and myself that we have been put through this experience. I don't know what the costs of my defence will be but my aunt believes it will be over £100. I think we ought to be relieved of the cost to say nothing of the compensation I'm entitled to for my 14 weeks loss of work and incarceration."

A carefully scripted little speech, of course, decorated with all his solicitors' hints and suggestions, and fine-tuned by a collaborative reporter who had readily agreed to insert the propaganda, as long as Parrott came up with a genuine headline-worthy comment. Which he did.

"I had every confidence in the result," Parrott went on. "I am glad to say that I slept well the whole time I was in gaol. My mother sent me food every day and came to see me as often as regulations permitted. This serious charge against me has had far more effect on her than it has on me. She has borne it however because I kept telling her it would be alright."

Mary Ann sobbed. Annie comforted her. The reporter was very experienced, 20 years in the job. He paused his questioning, took a sip of by then tepid tea and waited for the right moment to continue when he asked Parrott about the trial.

"I was never anxious," he stated. "But it was embarrassing in the witness box to have questions put to you, first by one, then by another, and even the judge sometimes. I was perfectly straightforward throughout the case but I was not dealt with properly by the police. For instance I was never asked if I had worn a coat until I was at the police station and I pointed to the one on the table and said I had worn one like that. However I am here and glad of it."

And had he any plans for the future?

"Well, I have been for a long walk through Swinton with a friend and I intend to enjoy my freedom."

The introduction of a 'friend' was not questioned. Just another Parrott story. His mother's face bore resignation, his aunt's defiance, and his 10 years-old cousin Annie's, adoration. Her feelings for him led to another twist in the tale all of 40 years later.

The article appeared in that evening's editions, along with a quote from Ashworth saying that he had given his services free and the Parrotts would only have to pay his 'out of pocket expenses'. They delayed their departure from Irlams o' the Height until 10pm, catching the last train to Knutsford where they saw only a couple of other passengers and a porter, and walked quickly home. The night was warm, the town dark and peaceful.

CHAPTER 22

*'A study of bizarre murders indicates a state of extreme
and unbearable mental and emotional tension and turmoil
preceding the act. A majority of them are characterized by
unnecessary ferocity. With few exceptions the murderers in
such cases seem strikingly calm after the act, and quite free of
remorse. The violence served as a means of releasing them from
tension' – Edward Podolsky (Mind Of The Murderer, 1954)*

AND so who killed John Bould?

Teresa Neagle had no complaint about the verdict – she never believed that Parrott was the murderer. In a public statement after the trial she re-affirmed that, in her view, the killer was someone with experience of handling a gun, possibly with combat experience, ie: a soldier. More specifically, a Volunteer. That struck a chord with a lot of people. Yet the police remained unshaken in their belief that it was Parrott. They just had not been able to accumulate enough evidence. As Sergeant Pierce asserted, they were not looking for anyone else – and no-one, other than Parrott was ever charged with the crime. The case was put into cold storage.

Does it matter? Is a mystery best left unsolved?

The Manchester Courier, in its leader of August 3 1901, commented: 'Everyone expected that James Parrott would be acquitted as the evidence against him, though pointing to his being the hand that committed the crime, was not strong enough for the jury to convict him – there being no remedy for capital punishment. Want of motive has been the stumbling block.

'There is evidence that the criminal was a person whose conduct could not be measured by a common standard, indicating that the murder was the unreasoned act of a lunatic who, if there had been 12 shots in his revolver, would have emptied them all into the body of his victim. At any rate, in Knutsford, Parrott's innocence is believed in. What is to be regretted is that the murderer is still at large.'

One issue which the Press failed to address was whether its own power had influenced the case. Throughout, newspapers offered a sympathetic (and mis-cued) image of Parrott while constantly undermining what was already questionable evidence. The jury knew what to expect when Parrott entered the court. A 'harmless', 'innocent looking', 'no more than a boy' defendant against whom the police had concocted a possibly malicious case. The law restrained, and still does, prejudicial information such as the defendant's criminal record, but allowed the Press Box scribes to comment freely on his youthful charm and looks, ignoring, for example, visible scars on his neck and wrist. How those marks had come about is not known, but if they had creased his face, the general portrayal of Parrott might have been a lot darker.

Three types of suspect had been considered. A robber, favoured by the prosecution; a ruthless killer who wanted to silence Bould for personal or political reasons as suggested by Neagle (and, eventually, by Ellis Griffith); a madman as described in the Courier.

One - the robbery theory was gossamer thin and easily ripped apart by the defence team.

Two - Neagle's veiled accusation made to reporters was, in effect, a shot over the bows of Rowe and Yarwood but targeting them means a slow and rather unsteady walk through the gloom with the inconsistent Mary Jane Francis. If either was the assassin, she must have known or have been party to a cover-up.

As an extra spanner in the prosecution's spokes, Griffith hinted that Bould was shot because he saw the indecent assault. A murder 'of personal malice' in which Captain Blackadder (Rowe), and his sidekick with a cunning plan (Yarwood) kill Bould because he has seen something untoward, then order Mary Jane not to 'grass' them up - or else! - before riding off into the night. Why then, if so violently threatened, did she continue to accuse Rowe of a sex attack which, if not serious enough to hang him, certainly ended life as he had known it? And how did Bould's body finish up on the other side of the bend, 100 yards away from where the indecency took place? And how did Rowe or Yarwood happen to have on them a revolver capable of discharging a .32 bullet? Of all the equations which failed to add up in this case, this was the two plus two equals zilch.

Griffith used the Rowe/Yarwood link as a red herring. The blackguard and the maverick acted despicably, but neither was the murderer.

Three: - the Courier's 'lunatic' who popped up out of nowhere to end the life of a stranger. It happens. But who of all the people in the vicinity that evening could possibly have been mad enough to commit such an atrocity and to have the means, a .32 revolver and ammunition.

Before reviewing Parrott's state of mind, it is necessary to re-assess some of the evidence against him and the manner in which it was presented. A river of doubt ran through it and, eventually, the prosecution's strongest chance of a conviction was Parrott's decision to go into the witness box and tell some ridiculous lies.

While Pierce suffered the open criticism, the responsibility for a leaky case went right to the top. Chief Constable Hammersley, Superintendents Leah and Okell were all heavily involved at the early stages. Hammersley even took it upon himself to visit Mary Jane Francis at the Speakmans' several times. But then, suddenly, he left it all in the hands of a station sergeant who, though doggedly painstaking, had little expertise to organise a complex investigation. Why? Pierce's subsequent rise in the Cheshire police force offers an insight. In 1901 he had ambitions to become a detective, a role which was still in its infancy in some county forces although the 'Met' had used plain clothes officers for over 50 years and Manchester's Jerome Caminada was a household name.

Whether real or fictional, detectives had a certain status, over and above their nominal rank. They were trendy. Charles Dickens had written about them in newspaper serials, Arthur Conan Doyle was paid big money to bring Sherlock Holmes out of 'retirement' and, with the development of forensic science such as fingerprinting, Pierce could envisage a brilliant career. Hammersley gave him his head in this case – a chance to make his mark and add a touch of glitter to the prestige of the Cheshire Constabulary.

Generally, Pierce responded well, working hard, keeping problems in-house, and refusing to buckle under pressure. Whether he had a real detective's 'nose' or not, he was of the right type for a county police force steeped in conservatism. But, like the purse, the seam of the prosecution case was fragile, and the defence was able to poke a hole here, another there, which Abel Thomas was unable to sew together again. (One report of the trial stated: 'Thomas submitted Parrott to a searching cross-examination but in the main failed completely to shake his story in any vital particular..').

Pierce slipped up badly with his one-man band approach. He needed more back-up (and, no doubt, more advice). Faith in your own ability is a virtue until it grows into conceit and then arrogance.

Take his interview style. Pierce's methods left massive potential for mistakes and misunderstanding. Conducting most of the interviews by himself, he failed to wring out vital details, and left himself open to allegations of mis-representaton. His 'I'm in charge' outlook also came to the fore when searching Parrott's bedroom. Finding the purse he opened it and palmed the coins for a few seconds before replacing them 'hurriedly'. That was how Mary Ann described it, the inference being that Pierce might have planted them, and there was no other officer present to countermand it.

Other criticism could be levelled at the careless way Parrott's clothing was treated, particularly the overcoat which might have carried bloodstains. Microscopic examination was available – in fact one of the Flatters' family, Henry's brother Abraham who manufactured high quality microscopes in Manchester, was an expert in the field. And the hunt for the murder gun was mainly restricted to the Mere Heath Lane/ Tatton Park vicinity. Parrott claimed he despatched half his cartridges down the closet, but the police did not bother to mount a detailed search either in or around his home for the Colt.

One of Pierce's problems was to Beat The Clocks. One which ticked between 6 and 7pm on April 7 – a more diligent study of it might have wrecked Parrott's claim that he 'was out of the lane' before the murder occurred - and one which told him constantly that the investigation had to be wrapped up in a very brief period. One way and another he did not have the time.

The figurative Easter Sunday clock was important in checking the events of that evening but some of the timings were obscured. Apparently none of the witnesses had a pocket watch, or, if they had, bothered to look at it. However, if more carefully scrutinised, Pierce and, later, Thomas, could have minced Parrott's alibi by arching a

time-line over his own evidence, starting with his trek from Manchester. The author benefits from such a time-line created from the evidence by Christopher Wetherell MA.

Parrott claimed he got into Manchester from Liverpool at 10am and chose to walk home rather than wait until the afternoon for a train to Knutsford. The journey, through Stretford, Sale and Altrincham, was 16-17 miles and, as a fit, young man, who enjoyed long walks, he could have done it in a maximum of six hours of continuous effort, even though wearing a long, heavy coat. But he did not reach Mere Heath Lane until well after 6pm, leaving a gap of more than two hours unaccounted for. Perhaps he had rests, or stopped for a drink. A minor matter, maybe, but one of many which the police did not fully probe.

Parrott was generally evasive, and particularly so about times, but, at least on one occasion, he insisted that he got to Knutsford railway station by 6 45pm, that he was drinking in the Sword and Sceptre at 7pm and was home between 7 30pm and 7 40pm, a time corroborated by Mary Ann and John Parrott.

Disregarding times, he stuck to his alibi throughout that a: he did not see John Bould in Mere Heath Lane; b: he was out of the lane when the murder occurred. The evidence, when analysed, suggests otherwise.

The distance from the field gate where he stopped and the station was less than a mile. For the lightweight, quick striding Parrott, a march of around 12-15 minutes.

To get there for 6 45pm meant starting at around 6 30pm and, despite his denials, he was seen by several people including Mary Jane Francis, either in the field or coming out of it through a gate, when it was at least 6 40pm and probably closer to 6 45pm. These timings could easily be disputed but it was here that the evidence of John Parkes became significant – or should have done.

Parkes and Jessie Groucott first spotted Parrott sitting on the fence gate, messing about with his handkerchief between 6 15pm and 6 20pm. This accorded with the statements of Thompson and Mary Flood. Parkes and Groucott, at that stage, were standing by the hedge, enjoying the evening air and remained there for some time. When the weather worsened they hurried to Groucott's home, Tatton Lodge at the Knutsford entrance to the park. They arrived at 7pm – he knew by the chiming of a clock – which meant they reached the end of the lane at about 6 55pm, the lodge being a few minutes away.

Taken in isolation, all this meant very little. But Parkes also stated that as they headed home they were passed, going the other way, by, in order; the Floods, Mary Jane Francis, Pritchard, Rowe and Yarwood, and, finally, *John Bould*. Crucially, they were not overtaken by anyone going in their direction, that is towards Knutsford. And so, if Parrott were to be believed, he must have gone well ahead of them. However, Mary Jane met Parrott, the man with 'rambling eyes', by the field gate *after* she had passed Parkes and Groucott.

The truth was that he was still in the lane as Bould strolled up it. Accepting that this does not prove he killed Bould, it does show that he either lied or was completely mistaken or confused about his movements, and that while, curtly, he refused to give a proper reply to Thomas, he was in the lane for a lot longer than he thought or cared to admit.

During that period he either went straight past Bould or stopped to shoot him.

Could Parkes be trusted? Why not? Here was a young man, out with his girlfriend, with no axe to grind, merely reporting what he saw and did, and everything he put forward linked neatly with that of other witnesses. Yet he was treated as peripheral, not mentioned either in Thomas's address to the jury or the judge's summing-up. Insufficient attention was given to this issue.

One last point about Pierce's investigation. As stated earlier, the author must remind both the reader and himself that police work in 1901 was on the brink of major modernisation, it was still a world away from that of today. No modern officer would dream of arresting a murder suspect, and one possibly armed with a revolver, in the smooth, almost friendly manner in which Pierce met Parrott off the train and walked him up to the police station for a chat and a cuppa. In fact, Pierce displayed courage and a surprising humanity throughout. One ploy to persuade Parrott to confess was to get him into a cell and kick him black and blue while threatening to tell his mother what he was really like (actually, she already knew). But the sergeant had earned a reputation for the sympathetic way he treated juveniles, and there was more than a touch of kindliness for the young-looking Parrott. Maybe he went out of his way to be fair. Too far out of his way. It might be asked – was this case properly prosecuted? Did people pull back, perhaps sub-consciously from their invidious role of trying to get a young bloke hanged? A young, local bloke.

Cheshire Police after a medal ceremony in 1912. Former Chief Constable, Colonel Hammersley is seated, front left; ex- Superintendent William Leah, by then the Deputy Chief Constable, is standing, front row, centre, wearing a cap. © Museum of Policing in Cheshire

While Parrott and Mary Ann evaded the great homecoming, Knutsford rejoiced. This was not just a victory for Parrott, it was a triumph for the town. But rolling out the red carpet was difficult because too many things had been swept under it.

Parrott's criminal record, for example. While kept secret from the jury, the author has to consider it, as it might help to glean an insight into his psychological make-up.

People in Knutsford knew he had been 'in trouble', a euphemistic phrase used in one report. In fact, he was a thief and a shopbreaker who had done time with hard labour at Strangeways (Manchester) and Knutsford prisons and, although his last known offence was in 1897, his criminality had been on an upward curve from lifting some ties, to stealing a large amount of cash, to burglary, establishing a platform for a life of crime – but for the intervention of his mother.

Mary Ann rescued him twice, at the murder trial and in 1897, telling the Cheshire Quarter Sessions that her son was 'not responsible for his actions – to an extent.' And, for the next three years or so, she and the rest of the family, particularly her sister Annie and brother-in-law Alf, tried to wrap him in cotton wool. But what did she mean exactly by 'not responsible for his actions'? What was Ellis Griffith referring to when he asked Pierce if he thought Parrott was 'eccentric'? And why did the judge query Parrott's behaviour after the murder as 'not consistent with the actions of a rational and reasonable man'?

Other aspects of his atypical character have cropped up in this book. A loner who would hardly speak a word to workmates, unable or unwilling to make friends, 'a bit queer', enjoyed long walks by himself etc. And, intriguingly, on the Calendar of Prisoners 1868-1929, he was listed as 'Degree of Instruction – Imperfect', a category in which many uneducated convicts fell, attributing them with only basic reading and writing skills and, generally, a below average education. Yet Parrott's letter to Colt's was immaculate, grammatically precise, and he had applied for a job as a clerk with Welsh and Co.

Psychological analysis was little known in 1901. A shame because Parrott would have been a suitable subject.

Psychopath. The word conjures up a bleak landscape. Sadly, that is where Parrott lived. A psychopath may be witty, charming, intelligent with the skill to negotiate a path through everyday society but he/she can also kill without pity, indeed without any particular show of emotion either before or after the event, and forever without any glint of sorrow.

One standard method for identifying psychopathic tendencies is Hare's which, in its simplest form, offers 20 check boxes covering character, lifestyle, and anti-social behaviour. These are: glib and superficial charm; grandiose self-worth; need for stimulation; pathological lying; cunning and manipulation; lack of remorse; shallowness; callousness and lack of empathy; parasitic lifestyle; poor behaviour controls; social promiscuity; early behaviour problems; lack of realisation of long term goals; impulsiveness; irresponsibility; failure to take responsibility for actions;

short term relationships; juvenile delinquency; revocation of conditional release; criminal activity.

Even on a quick read through, Parrott scores heavily – more so when considering the factors which mould psychopathic disorder.

'Many psychopaths suffer the consequence of separation caused by the death of a beloved person,' says one research paper. 'They believe that the whole world is against them and become convinced that they deserve special privileges and rights to satisfy their desires. There is hidden suffering. Outwardly they may be arrogant, but they can be lonely and lack self esteem.They feel a need for excessive stimulation leading to foolhardy adventures which end in disillusionment because of unrealistic expectations and there are risks of violent criminal behaviour.'

Parrott was a photo fit.

He suffered a ruptured childhood. In the mid-1880s when aged between five and eight, he lost his maternal grandmother, father and paternal grandfather. All died after illness at the King Street home. Physically slight, with blighted vision, reserved, unable to strike up long-term friendships, he found life a struggle and, as a youngster, desperately needed the comfort of a family bubble. Instead, when the Parrotts' fortunes nose-dived, he was sacrificed. Unable to cope, Mary Ann and influential friends arranged a place for him at the orphanage, while his four siblings stayed at home. What a traumatic experience that must have been for the 10 years-old James, a stand-out candidate for Boarding School Syndrome.

After his return he flitted around, sometimes staying and working in Knutsford, sometimes in Manchester and nearby towns. In need of stimulation and cash, he began to commit offences. Despite the family's efforts, and his mother's in particular, to rehabilitate him his whole life became unstable.

The Hare's categories of 'foolhardy adventures' and 'unrealistic expectations' clothed him as neatly as his grey suit and winged collar. For six years he worked as a shop assistant or labourer, yet in late 1900 he suddenly took a fancy to becoming a colonial clerk amid the mines of Nigeria. And he found it difficult to accept that Welsh and Co rated him as unsuitable.

Approaching Easter 1901 things began to go haywire. He was between jobs, disillusionment over his future was niggling at him, he had whistled away most of his sizeable inheritance within a few months and, although he was owed a further £30, he was fast running out of the readies having lost heavily on the horses. What he did have was a gun and ammunition and abnormal levels of neuro chemicals all set to be triggered.

Parrott was a dreamer but also an accident, or a tragedy, waiting to happen.

CHAPTER 23

'There is nothing more deceptive than the obvious fact' –
Sherlock Holmes (The Boscombe Valley Mystery, 1892)

T HE 'obvious fact' is that James Crossley Parrott got
away with murder. He had psychopathic traits and
shot John Bould, pumping the action of his Colt five
times in a 2-3 seconds burst. If, in the words of the journalist
quoted earlier, there had been 12 cartridges he might have
used them all. Parrott needed to release a spout of venom, but
also to test himself against an unfair world. A reject, hitting
out.

In coming to a 'conviction' of Parrott the author frees
himself of the legal chains binding the jury, who had to
give him the benefit of any doubt. I can consider far more
information than they received, such as his criminal record
and psychological dysfunction, and I am not constrained by
the fear of sending a young man to the gallows - a propect
which must have weighed heavily with them.

However, I have to be as 'right' as is possible. I believe I am,
but it was not an easy decision and, as well as the evidence,
I have had to search my conscience. All the characters in this
book are long gone, but, no doubt, there are descendants still
around. Is it necessary to dig up all this bad stuff, simply
to satisfy curiosity? To put a noose around the reputation
of this man 122 years after it all happened? What moral
grounds am I stamping on? I have thought long and hard on
this.

There were periods when my view, I admit, was as blurred as
Parrott's eyesight. Initially I believed his guilt to be blatant
and went hell for leather to nail him. The scaffold was
under construction. As time wore on and I worked harder at
unpicking the fabric of Parrott's life, and of life in Knutsford,
I found memories of my own childhood wandering in
and clouding things. Some of them were disconcerting. I
suppose I came, not to liking Parrott better, but maybe to
understanding him a little more, an empathy with him that

he did not have with others. For a long while I wanted the villain to be someone else.

I have also to admit that, while as overtly chauvinist as any in my youth and early adulthood, I have long despaired at man's inhumanity to woman which, surely, has swayed my approach to the story of Mary Jane Fancis. (I also felt a tremendous regard for Mary Ann Parrott although she profited by belonging to the 'respectable traders' division of the Victorian working-class whereas Mary Jane was a lowly domestic, someone to be disparaged and abused).

Eventually my thoughts went full circle. Parrott did the deed and his guilt-ridden mother, who had sent him away to an orphanage, redeemed herself by giving him sanctuary. I do not criticise Mary Ann. If I had been in her shoes I would have done the same. In fact I admire her. She did what she had to do.

All that considered, a man was killed, a poor journeyman tailor, enjoying a quiet evening stroll along a country lane, gunned down and, if nothing else, his life and death deserve some respect.

The question returns. Why John Bould?

It will never be answered with certainty. 'Now Sherlock Holmes is back,' said the Manchester Courier leader writer, referring to the new detective serial The Hound of the Baskervilles, 'this strange deed may supply Dr Conan Doyle with a theme'.

There are several possibilities, all pure guesswork. The author's version is perhaps more out of the box than others and features the incongruous packet of pepper discovered near the body and, though clearly visible, was only spotted *after* the murder.

Pierce felt it had significance, which is why the Manchester police were asked to make enquiries, but eventually, when no solid evidence was forthcoming, he, like the original owner, abandoned it. But how did it get there?

It came from Fay's the grocer's in Butler Street, Ancoats, Manchester , and was purchased close to Easter. This was confirmed by the shop manager Fred Greenhalgh, although the 35 years-old grocer was not called as a witness in the case, another alarming omission. Greenhalgh talked of a man who was not a regular customer but had come into the store on two previous occasions over a period of six weeks. The third time, 'during Good Friday week', the man bought two ounces of pepper wrapped in the shop's paper. "When the police showed me the packet *(the one found in Mere Heath Lane)* I handled it and I did not hesitate in identifying it as coming from this shop. I could tell by smelling that it had contained pepper *until it was found*." This suggested that the packet was empty, when it was recovered from the side of the lane. Who bought the packet, how did it travel from Manchester to the murder scene, and what happened to its contents?

Greenhalgh said the customer 'answers very much the description that the detectives gave me of the supposed murderer. He had an overcoat over his arm.' But going into more detail, he thought the man was about 30 and had the look of 'genteel poverty' although his clothes were well brushed. Obviously, that put a doubt against it being Parrott, but, just as obviously, Greenhalgh should have attended the identity parade following Parrott's arrest – and he was not invited.

One possible scenario is that Parrott, a regular visitor to Manchester,

bought the pepper, or someone purchased it for him, close to Easter, and it was in his pocket when he walked from Manchester to Knutsford on Easter Sunday. His intention was to use it criminally, not immediately, but possibly in a copy-cat heist following a recent series of well-publicised mailbag robberies in the North-West where pepper was hurled into postmen's faces, temporarily blinding them. But the plan went wrong. Bould came along and, as they approached each other in the lane, an altercation took place. It should be remembered that both men would stand their ground in an argument. Bould was naturally stubborn, Parrott had learned to fend for himself in the tough environments of an orphanage and prison and, whatever the cause of the confrontation, it tipped him over the brink. Angry, he pulled out the pepper and threw it towards Bould, but, due to the wind and heavy rain, only specks hit the target. Bould whipped off his hat and disdainfully wafted the packet out of Parrott's hand. Suddenly the Colt appeared. Parrott had not planned to kill and produced the gun, perhaps merely to frighten, but Bould was of sterner stuff. Only that morning he had complained about the lack of legal protection from firearms and here was a young brat, who would fall over if he breathed on him, threatening him with a tiny revolver. Bould laughed, and made as if to swat the gun away in the same manner as the pepper, only for it to explode.

As he died, the folded hat stayed in Bould's hand.

Another possible factor is that Parrott had an itchy trigger finger. Research indicates that the mere possession of a gun makes some people more aggressive and while the finger pulls the trigger, maybe also the trigger pulls the finger. There is a magnetism about it, like being tempted to jump into a river from a high bridge.

After killing Bould, Parrott, ever the opportunist, rifled his pockets, grabbing the purse and Teresa Neagle's letter before suddenly noticing someone coming around the bend. In the gloom and with his poor vision, he might not have recognised it as a woman, Mary Jane. Luckily, no-one else was in sight. Parkes and Groucott were ahead of him, close to the Tatton Park Lodge, Daniels and Toft had still to appear, and everyone else had disappeared in the opposite direction. He sprinted away – he was quick despite being hampered by the extra long coat – shoving the purse and his Colt into pockets. Suddenly spotting two figures ahead (Parkes and Groucott), he swerved off into the nursery, discarding the letter, exited into Garden Lane and then angled left and right into Tatton Street, flying past the Flatters' home where the author's grandmother to be Daisy was reading her Easter card. Further on he slowed to a walk. He reached the station and then the Sword and Sceptre but hung around, not going into either, because he was known in both places and witnesses might have recalled the exact times he was there. Eventually he found his way home.

Parrott did not throw the gun away for fear of it being found.

A simple call to Colt's would have then established him as the owner. Possibly on his way home, he hid it and the rest of the cartridges he had with him and, as he admitted, threw the other 50 bullets down the closet.

There is one outstanding issue about the Colt .32. It had six chambers but there were only five shots. Did Parrott retain one bullet? If so, why - if, as contended, he was unleashing a storm of pent-up emotion which demanded that he pulled the trigger until the chamber was empty? Two options are submitted. One: there were six shots. Yarwood heard only five, and Dr Smith's post-mortem backed that up with five entrance wounds. But, one shot might well have missed Bould and in the wind and rain of that evening might have also escaped Yarwood's hearing. Two: Parrott had already used one cartridge in a test firing, not necessarily with murder in mind, but purely to see how the gun worked, how it felt to shoot.

Where he secreted the Colt and whether he ever recovered it are mysteries. But eight years after the murder, a six-chambered pocket revolver turned up in Knutsford when another brave police sergeant named Radcliffe calmly walked into the Cross Keys in King Street and disarmed a local man who had threatened to kill his ex-girlfriend, the sister of the 1901 May Queen. The revolver was loaded with only four bullets. The gunman, whose family had lived close to the Parrotts in Knutsford, claimed he had bought it from a man in Sale called Donnelly who had advised him to try it out by shooting out of a train window, the noise of the locomotive drowning the report. The make of revolver was never made public. 'Donnelly' was never fully identified. Parrott was living in Sale at that time but no positive connection can be made.

Parrott kept Bould's purse and coins as trophies. They were stashed away and, after discovery by Pierce, a cover story made up. Parrott said he had obtained the purse some months earlier, but could not remember when and from whom it came. A nonsense. A young man with money to burn, he bought a new suit, and the most expensive small revolver on the market. He flashed cash at the races. And yet he treated a commonplace pigskin purse, old and worn, and which had suddenly appeared from out of the blue, as though it were a crown jewel, locking it away in a box.

Mary Ann might well have mended it, but only in the fortnight between the murder and her son's arrest. Of course, any repair could have been the work of Bould himself, a fully trained tailor. As for the commemorative coin, widely available at the time of its minting, Bould had owned it for several years. Parrott's claim that he had bought it in Liverpool came midway through the investigation when it was realised how important it might be, and Edward Bowker's statement that his was the only shop in the North-West to stock it was, at best, extravagant.

The row which led to the murder must have been brief and fierce. What caused it? According to the prosecution, they did not know each other, a dubious assertion. While Parrott spent periods in other places, he always returned to the King Street home which was within arm's reach of the Engbersons' cottage in Swinton Square where Bould had lived for almost four months. They were also distinctive figures - Parrott, wiry and bespectacled; Bould, tall and solid. Did they have 'history'? Had Bould seen Parrott with the Colt, or his brother John with the replica pistol kept in his overcoat? Could it be that Bould mistook the Colt for that replica and so teased Parrott: "Go on then – pull the trigger," sneering, thinking he was in no danger?

And, as he lay dying on the wet verge of Mere Heath Lane, his head crowned by hawthorn, did the journeyman tailor feel Parrott's breath as he leaned over him, whispering: "And that's done for you John Bould."

CHAPTER 24

'I'll put them all in a story by and by' – Dylan
Thomas (Old Garbo, Collected Stories, 1984)

I F, after the trial, life returned to normal, that is only because normality encompasses the extremes of human experience. The cast of The Knutsford Murder Mystery were to enjoy and to endure all that is commonplace, but the mundane greyness of their general existence was coloured at the edges by unusual scandal and tragedy. As the author followed their diverse trails through the 20th century, the words of Dylan Thomas (above) came to mind.

Pierce steeled himself against the harsh criticism, pained glances and the spittle which came his way after the trial. Knutsford was hardly the best place for an officer who had accused one of the locals of a dastardly murder. Tom Jackson and others offered commiseration, there was encouragement from Chester HQ and Pierce knew that Parrott had been lucky, but his wife Annie was right – the sooner they were away the better. Occasionally he bumped into one of the Parrotts and offered a polite greeting, although James appeared to be keeping low.

The following year he won his hard-earned promotion to Inspector, transferred to the larger beat of Altrincham where John Okell was the Superintendent and soon was being referred to as 'Detective Inspector Pierce' although he was not officially awarded this title until August 1909, when he switched to Chester HQ where Superintendent William Leah had also climbed the ladder to the rank of Deputy Chief Constable. Pierce, as Cheshire's top detective, led investigations all over the county, attracting widespread acclaim and earning commendations for capturing a team of poachers. Of course, he was no Holmes, nor a second Jerome Caminada, the audacious Manchester detective chief, although he displayed unbridled enthusiasm and eagerness to learn, to the extent that he used holidays to study police methods in Paris and Dublin.

Soon he became embroiled in another murder drama which

had disturbing echoes of the Parrott case. George Henry Storrs was a wealthy but rough-edged building contractor who lived with his family at Gorse Hall in Stalybridge, a mill town in the east of Cheshire. He had made enemies and in November 1909 was stabbed to death after tackling an intruder armed with a revolver and a knife. Pierce arrested a cousin of Storrs, Cornelius Howard, ignoring his claims that he had been playing dominoes in a pub in nearby Huddersfield on the relevant night. At the trial in Chester, March 1910, the defence produced witnesses, including the pub landlord, to back up Howard's alibi which had not been properly checked and he was cleared.

Embarrassed, Pierce renewed his efforts and a few months later he picked up a 23 years-old ex-soldier Mark Wilde as he left Knutsford Prison having finished a short sentence for a knife attack on a courting couple in Stalybridge. Wilde lived close to Gorse Hall and on the night of the murder had returned home with blood on his face and clothes. He faced a mass of circumstantial evidence but denied it from the off, supported by his family who gave evidence on his behalf, while his barrister politely pointed out that Wilde looked nothing like Howard, originally identified as the culprit. The jury returned another Not Guilty verdict and, as in The Knutsford Murder, no-one was really surprised. As the jubilant Wilde walked from court, he was greeted by Howard and, arms around each other's shoulders, they joined a crowd of cheering onlookers and went to celebrate. Again the police were forced to put the case on ice.

Two murders, three trials, three acquittals – the last two in the space of six months - and each time Pierce's methods came under the microscope. Late in June 1911, seven months after Wilde's acquittal and having just completed 25 years service, he walked into the office of the Chief Constable and announced: "I am retiring." He was only 47, and many admirers believed he would achieve higher rank. Efforts to persuade him to stay failed. "We cannot afford to lose men of this calibre," said the coroner H C Yates. His departure 'for personal reasons' was a mystery but his failures to win convictions in major cases might have played a part. The death of his mentor Superintendent Okell might also have been a factor. Okell was buried at Hale cemetery, near Altrincham, in June 1911, mourned by hundreds, his helmet, lamp, staff and handcuffs on top of his coffin.

Pierce left the police with an exemplary disciplinary record on an annual pension of a little over £80. He said at his last appearance at the Altrincham Petty Sessions: "I did my duty and I did my best." The remainder of his life was uneventful. His son had emigrated to Canada to farm, his two daughters married, and his wife Annie died in 1916. Pierce lived in North Wales and died in 1955.

Little Dot, the star of the opening act in the Parrott drama, remained in the limelight for a while. In 1904 she fulfilled her ambition of becoming Knutsford's Royal May Queen and, again, featured in glowing newspaper reports all over Britain. Dressed in flowing silk, riding in a carriage drawn by four greys, and applauded by huge crowds 'she acted her part in becoming dignity and gracefully acknowledged the salutations.' But that was it. Dorothy slipped back into everyday life. She died a widow in 1972 at the age of 82. Dorothy's last home overlooked the spot on the Heath where she was crowned.

Mary Jane Francis returned to her roots, the village of Llansantffraid in Montgomeryshire. Many times during the case she had been referred to as a 'girl', once as a 'comely young woman'. While, because of census anomalies, her age cannot be precisely ascertained, it was at least 30 and by 1904 she was a married woman, having wed a roadworker. She had four children in the space of seven years. She never returned to Knutsford and she never received justice for the way she had been abused.

Neither did Teresa Neagle who, apart from one brief comment, maintained a dignified silence after Parrott's acquittal. A devout Roman Catholic, she left Burnley to become housekeeper for a priest in Glanford Brigg, Lincolnshire, and died in the area in 1929.

Murray Speakman, a trustee of the Manchester Stock Exchange, and his wife Emily were among society's elite. Her father was a wealthy merchant and her brother a clergyman. Little wonder they were scandalised by the events of 1901. In 1921 the family name was again plastered all over the newspapers when their son Edward, a marine engineer, was involved in a truly bizarre divorce. The Speakmans ended up in Bournemouth although Emily sometimes spent her Christmases at spa hotels in Bath.

Tom Jackson was Knutsfordian to his boots and remained a prominent figure in the town. In 1904 he watched proudly as his daughter was crowned May Queen and in 1910 he was one of two central officials at the annual installation meeting of the de Tabley Lodge of Freemasons, held in the Assembly Rooms of Knutsford's Royal George Hotel, a glittering occasion. Jackson, who had strived so hard on Parrott's defence, handed over his position as Worshipful Master to a certain 'Bro W T Pierce', otherwise known as Detective Inspector, formerly Sergeant, William Pierce, who had strived equally hard on Parrott's prosecution. Pierce sat in the 'chair of King Solomon' and was invested according to ancient rites and customs'. Never had there been such a meeting of the Lodge. It attracted record numbers, and 68 members, including 27 Masters, tucked into a sumptuous banquet.

Leicester Caldecutt's name lived on in Knutsford in the title of a firm of solicitors. Clerk to the Justices for 23 years, he was a highly successful lawyer who specialised in agriculture law, and was also well known for his work in freemasonry and for his love of cricket. After ill-health he retired in 1923 and died two years later while on holiday in his favourite resort of Ramsey, Isle of Man, instructing that there should be no flowers nor mourning at his funeral. In his will he left £13000, including £50 to his housekeeper and £10 to his cleaner.

Lance Bentley was elected as the chairman of the recently formed Urban District Council in 1902 and continued his energetic activity as Mr Knutsford. Bentley was into everything, one of the figures who drove the town forward at the start of the 20th century, looking after the interests of several bodies. But his life had seen tragedy with the deaths of two young sons. The family grave at Knutsford Parish Church is marked by a modest headstone, giving the names of Lance and Harry Lance, brothers who never knew each other - each died 'in their fifth year' in 1875 and 1887 - along with Bentley himself who died in 1910, his wife Mary and their daughter Gertrude.

Of the other legal experts who featured in the case, Hercules Campbell Yates was a coroner for 50 years, dealing with over 15000 inquests and a Cheshire Quarter Sessions chairman for 32 years before his retirement in 1929; Mr Justice

Grantham died at his home, 100 Eaton Square, London, in 1912 after a bout of pneumonia and following a rebuke in the House of Commons from Prime Minister Asquith for 'indiscreet comments to the Grand Jury at Liverpool'; Abel Thomas's only impact as an MP was to stand up in the House of Commons to make a joke about coal owners only then to accidentally sit on his silk topper crushing it; while Ellis Griffith became Asquith's Under Secretary of State for the Home Department.

Several of the Mere Heath Lane witnesses suffered terribly in later life.

Thompson and Mary Flood's son Noel – who was in the pram they were pushing on the murder night - became a bank clerk before serving in WW1 as a gunner-signaller in the Royal Artillery. Within days of the end of the war, on November 1 1918 having survived over two years of active duty, he was wounded by a shell explosion and also gassed. He lived but with a 40 per cent disability and died in 1934 while being cared for at a special orthopaedic hospital in Shropshire. Noel left £401 to his father. Mary died in 1937 and Thompson in 1947. He had progressed in Knutsford society under the auspices of Freemasonry and the Volunteers, being made a junior steward of de Tabley Lodge in 1910 under the watchful eye of the new Worshipful Master Bro W T Pierce, and, that same week, receiving cheers and applause at a Volunteers' party in the Red Cow. The Floods were all buried in the peaceful graveyard of St Mary's Church, Rostherne, on the edge of Tatton Park. Close to them are John and Jessie Parkes (nee Groucott) who married in 1905.

The Pritchard family were also badly hit, both in peacetime and in WW1. Three of the brothers William Bridgett (Lt Col), Harry Washington (Major), and Sydney (Captain) were medical officers with the East Lancashire Field Unit in the Gallipoli campaign. In June 1915 William and Harry were at each other's side, treating wounded troops in a field dressing station when a shell burst nearby. William was seriously injured. Harry, unscathed, tended him and got him evacuated on a ship bound for Malta only for William to die during the voyage. Buried at sea, he was honoured on war memorials in Helles and Manchester. After the war Harry took up general practice in the Welsh seaside town of Abergele naming his house Brooklands after the district where he had lived with the Rowes in 1901.

And what of his sister, Gertrude, and her husband George William Rowe? Their story is perhaps the saddest.

Inevitably, their marriage hit the rocks. Mary Jane's allegations put it under terrific strain and, to all intents and purposes it ended when George transferred his boot polish business from Altrincham to much bigger premises in Watford – not far from Parrott's orphanage. He took a flat in Bedford Court Mansions, London, while Gertrude remained in Brooklands with their son Walter. In December 1905 she launched divorce proceedings, swearing a deposition which stated: 'On the 22nd of November I wrote to my husband demanding him to return home and reside with me or to provide a home for me elsewhere.' The letter was signed 'affectionately yours, Gertrude'.

Rowe's reply complained bitterly of financial problems, claiming that he had bought a suit for their son Walter and that Gertrude had wasted money on silver ornaments.

'My firm has lost money so far,' he continued, 'and if it cannot show a dividend at the end of the year Walter's remarks will indeed be too true – 'We are so poor'. You promised to ruin me and I think you have succeeded. My furniture and other things are gone now. I have nothing but my weekly allowance and that is only too tentative.' He signed it 'G W Rowe'.

Gertrude did not have to wait for the divorce to be finalised. Just over two months after this acidic exchange of letters, George went to see his solicitor in Manchester, collapsed in agony from a perforated gastric ulcer and died of peritonitis after an operation at Manchester Royal Infirmary. Apart from a terse one paragraph notice of the funeral arrangements, there was no newspaper coverage of his death. From a journalistic stance, this is scarcely believable. Rowe was an inventor, some said a 'genius', a member by marriage of one of Manchester's most distinguished families, had been involved in a sex scandal linked to a sensational murder case, and had died suddenly in the middle of a divorce. But editors refused to touch it.

Only two years later in 1908, Gertrude, aged 42, also collapsed and died suddenly from a stroke at the Pritchards' family home in Upper Brook Street, Manchester. This, too, was recorded in the briefest possible death notice which read 'Rowe – Gertrude, eldest daughter of Councillor W B Pritchard, suddenly, 296 Upper Brook St. Crematorium, one o'clock on Saturday. No flowers by request'. Neither was she worthy of a mention in the news sections. They lie in separate graves in Manchester's Southern Cemetery. It seems their deaths were hushed up. Walter was taken on by the Pritchard family and became a surveyor with the city's corporation while Rowe's firm of Blyth and Platt was carried on by his brother Frank, and became a global success, particularly in Australia where it made Cobra shoe polish.

Rowe's pal, Harry Yarwood also went into the 'blacking' trade, describing himself as a 'boot polish manufacturer' and in 1911 was in contact with the Blyth and Platt operation in Watford. He died in 1938.

The fortunes of the Parrott family waxed and waned over the years.

John Parrott married Madge Dalton, who hailed from Manchester but had moved to Knutsford to work in the new steam laundry. They lived in Knutsford for several years. John became a telegraphist at the King Street Post Office, later moving to Liverpool.

The rest of the family remained closely linked, geographically and in spirit, throughout the first half of the century. Except for a brief early spell when James, who had been living with his aunt in Irlams o' the Height, boarded a ship in Liverpool bound for North America where he solved the murder of John Bould. At least that is what he said! It is not clear when he left Britain and when he returned but in May 1905, while still in America, he wrote to a 'Knutsford gentleman' – possibly his brother John or Tom Jackson – claiming he had met a man (un-named) who had confessed to the murder. 'I intend to return to England very shortly and produce evidence which will help to show who really was the murderer of John Bould.' Informed of this, Pierce merely raised his eyebrows and said: "We (the police) have nothing to say on the matter." Nothing ever came of it. Neither, when Parrott did return, would he clarify where exactly he had been in America, nor what he had done there, nor what his 'evidence' was.

In the years leading up to WW1, Parrott stayed in the arms of his family. His sister Edith gave birth to a girl in 1910, and she, the baby, Parrott and Mary Ann lived together in a property in Longsight, Manchester, where they looked after a boot repairing shop. While Edwin Ashworth had kept his costs to the minimum, the legal bill had crippled their finances, forcing them out of Knutsford. Midway through the war Parrott was conscripted into the Cheshire Regiment at the age of 35, based at their reserve depot in Chester. Later he transferred to the Labour Corps and then to the Royal Inniskilling Fusiliers at a massive army camp in Oswestry. On discharge Parrott received a small disability pension and, again, he went back to his mother who had moved with Edith and grand-daughter to a house in Sale, then in Cheshire, now part of Trafford.

Through the first 20 years of the century his sister Mary and her husband Henry Goodwin had made a decent life for themselves. The Goodwins had a large house, several children and a maid, Susan Rutter who served them for over 20 years and became Parrott's wife in 1920. He was then 40, she 44. They lived in terraced cottages in nearby areas, and he worked at an RAF stores depot, but his 'dearly beloved wife', as he described her in an obituary, died in 1939. It seems as though married life had suited him because in 1941, while Manchester was being bombed by the Luftwaffe and at the age of 61, he proposed again – to his widowed first cousin and life-long friend, Annie Lancaster, his aunt Annie's daughter who, as a 10 years-old, had been present when he gave his Press interview after the trial. Parrott liked to keep things in the family.

Some murderers with psychopathic traits go on to become serial killers. But some 'burn out' and are no longer a threat. There is no evidence that Parrott committed any other crime whatsoever. He outlived his siblings and died in 1964 in Manchester's Withington hospital aged 84 after a stroke at his home, a flat in Upper Brook Street, Manchester as shown in the death certificate here, the document witnessed by his widow, Annie.

James Parrott's death certificate,
witnessed by his widow Annie

EPILOGUE

'Peace to Cranford' – Elizabeth Gaskell (Cranford)

'IT is every man's business to see justice done', said Sherlock Holmes (The Adventure Of The Crooked Man) but apart from the so-called confession, nothing else about the murder ever returned to the public arena.

Parrott had been acquitted but the police, by abandoning the case, had made their opinion clear. They could do nothing more. There was no other suspect.

The consensus seemed to be, let sleeping dogs lie. Nowadays the victim's family and friends would launch a campaign to revive the case,but Teresa Neagle, Bould's only surviving relative, let it go and he did not have close friends, at least none influential enough to make an impact.

Generally Knutsford folk were embedded in the notion that the good name of the town had been disturbed enough already, and that the principles of justice had been properly served. That left the Press but they had other fish to fry. A new era, the Edwardian, had begun and great events were in the offing. As the years passed the journeyman tailor's demise was quietly put out to grass, like his untended grave.

It lies on the periphery of the parish church graveyard but there is no visible headstone. Burials stopped during WW2 and in a controversial redevelopment in the 1970s, many headstones were removed and relaid as walkways or lined up in a long soul-less row against a wall. Some still stand in their original plots, but others lie on the ground, either fallen or pulled down for safety reasons to be completely or partly masked by earth, leaf mould, and moss. The church's own records indicate that Bould never had a memorial but he was certainly laid there, somewhere near the perimeter wall. Very close by lie together Parrott's father Thomas and his grandfather James snr but also in a plot now unmarked.

Perhaps because it is so worn and tired, this part of the graveyard offers a tranquil space amid the bustle of such a thriving, affluent town. It is possible to sit for a while contemplating life and death with the occasional glance towards the Sessions House just across the road. Behind it is the site of the old prison where Parrott would have been hanged, now it is a supermarket car park.

Towards the west door of the church, headstones have been used to form the path and there is a very unusual one, describing two burials over 200 years apart. One of the inscriptions reads: 'In Loving Memory of Mary Ann Parrott, beloved wife of Thomas Parrott, died May 24, 1937, aged 82 years. Thy Will Be Done'. Mary Ann died in Sale, 11 miles away, but, obviously, the family arranged for her burial in Knutsford.

Knutsford Parish Church. On the left-hand side of the path is the grave of Lance Bentley and family; Mary Ann Parrott's headstone forms part of the path, midway along; the graves of her husband, father-in-law and John Bould are close by to the right

And what of Parrott's final resting place? Those who died in Manchester's Withington Hospital, as he did, invariably finished up at the nearby Southern Cemetery. As there is no burial record of him there, nor at any other municipal cemetery in the UK, it can be assumed he was cremated. Whether he left his widow with any money is not known, but the author has been unable to locate a death notice in the Press or any sign of a will.

It is possible he had a pauper's funeral paid for by the local authority with no mourners or flowers. A cold, dispassionate finale.

So maybe Bould had the last laugh. At least he got a decent send-off. His coffin was taken to the Engbersons' cottage in Swinton Square. Six former workmates acted as bearers, lifting him onto their shoulders and carrying him up the steep incline into King Street, up Church Hill and through the main gate of the parish church. People stood reverently outside their homes and shops. The procession of mourners was led by Teresa Neagle with Bernard and Charlotte Engberson just behind followed by members of St Vincent's R.C. Church. Among those waiting at the church were the church warden Lance Bentley, Sergeant Pierce and other police officers, representatives of the council and the Board of Guardians and a fair number of respectful spectators. Several floral crosses were on display, one sent by his former landlady Mrs Rhodes of Glossop, whom he had referred to as 'Mother'. Tears were shed. And as Teresa looked down at the lowered coffin, she clutched something precious, a simple but thoughtful gift John had sent in his last letter to her to mark St Patrick's Day. She wondered whether to toss it into the grave, so that he could take a piece of Ireland with him, but instead she carefully returned the sprig of shamrock to her purse, a keepsake, like it was a piece of him.

END

ACKNOWLEDGEMENTS

A S a former journalist I duly honour all my colleagues of yesteryear who wrote copiously, and in some style, about the murder which shocked Britain in 1901. Their reports have informed and entertained. For those interested in our history, I cannot recommend the British Newspaper Archive too highly. Find My Past, Ancestry UK, the National Archives, the British Library, Cheshire Archives, Manchester Libraries and the register offices of Manchester and East Cheshire have also provided invaluable help.

Will Brown, a retired detective superintendent who now runs the superb Museum Of Policing In Cheshire explained some aspects of early 20th century police work and, under the auspices of the museum, he also gave me career details of some officers and certain images. His book 'A Bobby's Job' is a richly illustrated history of policing. I am also indebted to Simon Dell whose book The Victorian Policeman also provided valuable insights.

However, if there are any errors in my understanding of Victorian/Edwardian policing they are wholly mine, and neither Will nor Simon had any input into the fictional dramatisation with which I have decorated some characters and events.

Phil Robinson helped me to a better understanding of the work of his ancestor, the public executioner James Berry, and Bob Findlay provided insights into Freemasonry although any reference to Freemasonry's influence within the life of a small town, the police and the justice system are mine alone. Ange Findlay recalled her days as a court shorthand writer, reminding me of the value of such a role.

Christopher Wetherell M.A. offered images and worked out a detailed time-line of events immediately leading up to the crime, spent a pleasant morning with me in a graveyard searching unsuccessfully for headstones and encouraged me generally. Chris Hogg, administrator of St John's, the parish church of Knutsford, Cheshire, was extremely co-operative, as were Sue and Bob Marshall who allowed me to visit their home to take images. Jane Lewis at Surrey History Centre and the archive department of Reed's School, Cobham, diligently researched 19th century life at the London Orphan Asylum.

My wife, Fi, supported me throughout two years of research and writing and became avidly involved in this project.

Lastly, I am indebted to Knutsford, the model for Mrs Gaskell's novel 'Cranford'. A unique town where I was born and raised, where my family has held a continuous presence of over 150 years and where, in 1901, the peace of Easter Sunday evening was shattered by a brutal murder.

BIBLIOGRAPHY

A Bobby's Job, Images Of Policing in Cheshire (Will Brown, 2014)

The Victorian Policeman (Simon Dell, 2010)

Twenty-Five Years Of Detective Life (Jerome Caminada, 1895)

The Great British Bobby, A History Of British Policing From The 18th Century To The Present (Clive Emsley, 2009)

Crime And Society In England 1750-1900 (Clive Emsley, 1987)

The Age Of Decadence, Britain 1880-1914 (Simon Heffer, 2017)

The Age Of Empire 1875-1915 (Eric Hobsbawm, 1987)

Hey Day, The 1850s And The Dawn Of The Global Age (Ben Wilson, 2016)

The Edwardians (Roy Hattersley, 2004)

Murder As Entertainment (article, Judith Flanders, British Library)

Listening To Killers (James Garbarino, 2015)

The Mile End Murder (Sinclair McKay, 2017)

Tracked And Taken (Dick Donovan, 1890)

My Experiences As An Executioner (James Berry, reproduced 2020)

A Radical History of Britain (Edward Vallance, 2009)

A Brief History Of Life in Victorian Britain, A Social History Of Queen Victoria's Reign (Michael Paterson, 2008)

Boarding School Syndrome (Joy Schaverien, 2015)

Perpetration-induced Traumatic Stress (Rachel M McNair, 2006)

Cranford (Elizabeth Gaskell, 1853)

Knutsford, A History (Joan Leach, 2007)

Knutsford Prison, The Inside Story (David Woodley, 2002)

The Story Of Knutsford (Charles R Bennett, 1975)

Mrs Gaskell And Knutsford (Rev George A Payne, 1900)

Knutsford, Its Traditions & History (Henry Green, 1859)

Cheshire Women's Institute's Book Of Recipes (1946)

Mrs Beeton's Cookery Book (Isabella Beeton, 1861)

victorianweb.org
victoriansociety.org
victorianera.org
workhouses.org.uk
gmpmuseum.co.uk *(Greater Manchester Police Museum)*
museumofpolicingincheshire.org.uk
manchester.gov.uk/libraries
bl.uk *(British Library)*
cheshirearchives.org.uk
socialsciences.exeter.ac.uk
britishnewspaperarchive.co.uk
livesofthefirstworldwar.iwm.org.uk
SamLister'sColtAutos.com
cyclehistory.wordpress.com
psychologytoday.com
google.com/site/thestoryofjamesberry/executioner
1900s.org.uk

Images of James Parrott, Dorothy Jackson, the Floods and Mary Jane Francis are copyright of Reach PLC and are reproduced with their permission and courtesy of the British Library.

Images of Cheshire police officers are copyright of The Museum of Policing in Cheshire and reproduced courtesy of Will Brown.

ABOUT THE AUTHOR

Colin Evans

A journalist (1964-2006), he launched his career at the age of 16 at his home-  town newspaper and was soon covering Cheshire Quarter Sessions cases at the Knutsford Sessions House. Later he worked for a busy Press agency based in Manchester's Courts of Justice, reporting on crime and sport - 'strange sounding bedfellows but which dovetailed neatly. A murder trial during the week might be followed by a soccer or cricket match at the weekend.' As such he came into contact with top detectives, lawyers, criminals and sportsmen. Eventually he became the cricket correspondent of the Manchester Evening News. In retirement, he has written a number of books, enjoys gardening and strumming a guitar, and remains passionate about life.

BOOKS BY THIS AUTHOR

Mods & Blockers

Summer of 1965 - Mods and Rockers, Vietnam, the Civil Rights struggle, and cricket, lovely cricket, viewed through the eyes of a pseudo teenage rebel. MAX Books.

Farokh - The Cricketing Cavalier

Authorised biography of the flamboyant Lancashire and India cricket star, Farokh Engineer. MAX Books.

Red Traitor - A Football Odyssey

A passionate fan and a cynical reporter - Colin Evans was both as he watched the rise and fall of Manchester's big two soccer clubs, United and City, during the 1950s, '60s, and '70s. 'A chaotic, wonderful time to be a fan and a sports journalist'. Etive Independent Publishing.

Printed in Great Britain
by Amazon